THE COLLECTED WORKS
OF W. B. YEATS
VOLUME VIII

THE COLLECTED WORKS OF W. B. YEATS

Richard J. Finneran and George Mills Harper, General Editors

W. B. YEATS

The Irish
Dramatic Movement

EDITED BY
Mary FitzGerald AND Richard J. Finneran

Scribner
NEW YORK   LONDON   TORONTO   SYDNEY   SINGAPORE

SCRIBNER
1230 Avenue of the Americas
New York, NY 10020

For information about special discounts for bulk purchases,
please contact Simon & Schuster Special Sales:
1-800-456-6798 or business@simonandschuster.com

Text set in Sabon

Manufactured in the United States of America

1   3   5   7   9   10   8   6   4   2

Library of Congress Cataloging-in-Publication Data
Yeats, W. B. (William Butler), 1865–1939.
The Irish dramatic movement / W. B. Yeats ;
edited by Mary FitzGerald and Richard J. Finneran.
p.   cm.—(The collected works of W. B. Yeats ; v. 8)
Includes index.
1. English drama—Irish authors—History and criticism.
2. Theater—Ireland—History. 3. Ireland—Intellectual life.
4. Ireland—In literature.
I. FitzGerald, Mary, 1946–2000. II. Finneran, Richard J. III. Title.
PR5900.A2 F56 1989 vol. 8 [PR5900.A5]
821'.8 s—dc21 [792'.09415]   2002044669

ISBN 0-684-80706-8

To George Bornstein,
friend of us both

PREFACE AND ACKNOWLEDGMENTS

As early as 1919, Yeats hoped to see his early dramatic criticism, first published in a series of pamphlets and collected only as part of one of the volumes in an expensive collected edition in 1908, available in a separate, regular edition. Although more often than not successful in his dealings with publishers, in this instance Yeats eventually had to be content with *The Irish Dramatic Movement* as a section of the 1923 *Plays and Controversies*. If either of the two expensive collected editions planned in the 1930s had come to fruition, *The Irish Dramatic Movement* would have still been denied a volume of its own, sharing space with the early prose fiction. After Yeats's death the work was finally published in a rather miscellaneous collection of prose, *Explorations* (1962). The present edition is thus a belated fulfillment of Yeats's wish. To *The Irish Dramatic Movement* as Yeats last approved it has been added the uncollected material from the original pamphlets.

As with any editorial endeavor, this volume would not have been possible without the assistance of many others. We are especially indebted to Joseph Black; George Bornstein; D. Allen Carroll; Kathleen Clune; Morris Eaves; Robert Essick; Nora FitzGerald; Ed Folsom; Roy Foster; John Frayne; Stan Garner; Nancy Moore Goslee; John E. Grant; George Mills Harper; Margaret Mills Harper; Thomas Heffernan; George Hutchinson; K. P. S. Jochum; Mary Lynn Johnson; Declan Kiely; J. C. C. Mays; Jerome McGann; William H. O'Donnell; Morton Paley; Alan Raitt; Peter Robinson; Ann Saddlemyer; Ronald Schuchard; Colin Smythe; Mary Speer; Wayne Storey; Jeff Tamaroff; Joseph Trahern; Anne Yeats; and Michael B. Yeats. We are also grateful to the staffs of the Berg Collection, New York Public Library; the British Library; the National Library of Ireland; the University of North Carolina Library; and the University of Tennessee Library. A special thanks goes to my graduate students Stephen Holcombe and Lauren Todd Taylor for their tireless efforts in tracking down some of Yeats's obscure allusions.

We are also grateful to Sarah McGrath at Scribner for her support of this edition and to John McGhee for his care in seeing the manuscript through the press.

Mary FitzGerald died from metastatic breast cancer on 8 August 2000, before this edition could be finished. It has been my privilege to bring it to completion. To her many students, friends, and colleagues, Mary was known as a superb teacher, a generous and loving companion, and a fine scholar. Only Richard Edmond, Catherine Anne, and I also knew her as the very model of a mother and a wife. As Yeats once wrote,

> time may bring
> Approved patterns of women or of men
> But not that selfsame excellence again.

R.J.F.
Wildwood, Missouri
15 March 2002

CONTENTS

The Irish
Dramatic Movement

Prefaces and Note

Uncollected Contributions to Beltaine, Samhain, and The Arrow

Textual Matters and Notes

ABBREVIATIONS

Au   *Autobiographies*. Edited by William H. O'Donnell
            and Douglas N. Archibald. New York: Scribner,
            1999.
BL   British Library Additional Manuscript
CL2   *The Collected Letters of W. B. Yeats: Volume Two,
            1896–1900*. Edited by Warwick Gould, John Kelly,
            and Deirdre Toomey. Oxford: Clarendon, 1997.
CL3   *The Collected Letters of W. B. Yeats: Volume Three,
            1901–1904*. Edited by John Kelly and Ronald
            Schuchard. Oxford: Clarendon, 1994.
Foster   Roy Foster, *W. B. Yeats: A Life—I: The Apprentice
            Mage, 1865–1914*. Oxford and New York: Oxford
            University Press, 1997.
L   *The Letters of W. B. Yeats*. Edited by Allan Wade.
            London: Rupert Hart-Davis, 1954.
LAR   *Later Articles and Reviews*. Edited by Colton John-
            son. New York: Scribner, 2000.
LE   *Later Essays*. Edited by William H. O'Donnell. New
            York: Scribner, 1994.
Mem   *Memoirs*. Edited by Denis Donoghue. London:
            Macmillan, 1972.
NLI   National Library of Ireland
P   *The Poems*. 2nd edition. Edited by Richard J.
            Finneran. New York: Scribner, 1997.
Pl   *The Plays*. Edited by David R. Clark and Rosalind
            E. Clark. New York: Scribner, 2001.
Princeton   Princeton University Library
SR   *The Secret Rose, Stories by W. B. Yeats: A Variorum
            Edition*. 2nd ed. Edited by Warwick Gould, Phillip
            L. Marcus, and Michael J. Sidnell. London: Macmil-
            lan, 1992.

UP1   *Uncollected Prose by W. B. Yeats—1: First Reviews
           and Articles, 1886–1896.* Edited by John P. Frayne.
           New York: Columbia University Press, 1970.

UP2   *Uncollected Prose by W. B. Yeats—2: Reviews, Arti-
           cles, and Other Miscellaneous Prose, 1897–1939.*
           Edited by John P. Frayne and Colton Johnson. New
           York: Columbia University Press, 1976.

VPl   *The Variorum Edition of the Plays of W. B. Yeats.*
           Edited by Russell K. Alspach. New York: Macmil-
           lan, 1966.

INTRODUCTION

I. Theatrical Pamphlets, 1899–1909

"Great hatred, little room": thus W. B. Yeats once described his native Ireland (*P* 259). By the time that the Irish Literary Theatre was ready to offer its first production, Yeats was no stranger to controversy. An occasional publication in which he could present his views on the drama and respond to the inevitable attacks must have seemed altogether in order. The germ of the idea may be found in a letter to Lady Gregory on 16 December 1898:

> We have arranged with Gill [editor of the Dublin *Daily Express*] that he is to bring out a series of articles on the literary theatre in various countries of which yours will be one. The articles are to be published afterwards in a pamphlet.[1]

This project did not come to fruition, but the opening of the Irish Literary Theatre on 8–9 May 1899 was indeed accompanied by the first issue of *Beltaine* (May 1899), published by E. J. Oldmeadow in "London: At the Sign of the Unicorn" and in "Dublin: at the 'Daily Express' Office." Described as "The Organ of the Irish Literary Theatre," the title—meaning "The Irish May Festival, the month of May," or "May Day" as Yeats told a correspondent—would stress the Irishness of the venture as well as confound his English critics, who would be able neither to translate nor to pronounce it (*CL3* 250). Although as of 21 April 1899 Yeats planned to distribute it "free in the theatre" (*CL2* 398), the pamphlet is headed "Threepence—Including Programme." A substantial publication of twenty-four pages, the first *Beltaine* included contributions not only by Yeats but also by C. H. Herford, Lionel Johnson, and George Moore.

The second performances of the Irish Literary Theatre on

19–20 February 1900 were accompanied by the next number of *Beltaine* (February 1900). The program was not included, the size had increased to thirty-two pages, and the price had doubled to six-pence. The contributors in addition to Yeats were Lady Gregory, Alice Milligan, Edward Martyn, and George Moore. The third and what turned out to be the last number of *Beltaine* was published in April 1900. A mere six-page shadow of the earlier incarnations and priced at a halfpence, a single essay by Yeats was its sole contents. A month earlier Yeats had told Lady Gregory that the publisher wants "to issue both numbers of 'Beltaine' together, in stiff boards" and that the "little book should be useful to us in many ways" (*CL2* 497, 498). All three numbers were so published, probably in the third week of May 1900.

On 21 May 1901, Yeats suggested to Lady Gregory that "'Beltaine' ought to come out quite early this year" and that it "should be a Gaelic propaganda paper this time & might really sell very well" (*CL3* 72). On 24 May 1901, Lady Gregory wrote in reply that *Beltaine* "should be printed and published in Ireland," as "the home industry people would be put in good humour" and that "we want all the aids to popularity we can get for the theatre"; she also recommended that any profits should go to the Gaelic League (*CL3* 74n1). Yeats at once agreed on both counts, suggesting that if the Dublin publishers refused, a note to that effect could be published in the next issue: "I don't know which would do most good, publication in Dublin or the note on publishers" (*CL3* 74). The search for an Irish publisher undercut Yeats's hopes for an early publication, but he wrote Lady Gregory on 1 June 1901 that "It will be very pleasant putting Beltaine together at Coole . . ." (*CL3* 77). On 3 August 1901, he informed Cornelius Weygandt that "'Beltaine' has not come to an end. A substantial number . . . will be issued in September but whether by its old publishers or not I cannot say" (*CL3* 100).

With the assistance of George Moore, who was no doubt ignorant of Yeats's comment on 17 November 1900 that he might "write a whole number of 'Beltaine' about Moore" and the controversy over *Diarmuid and Grania* (*CL2* 589), it was agreed that the volume would be printed and published by Sealy Bryers & Walker in Dublin, with T. Fisher Unwin in London as co-publisher (*CL3*

115n1). The first number under this arrangement appeared in October 1901, but the title was no longer *Beltaine* but rather *Samhain*—Irish for "All-Hallowtide, the feast of the dead in pagan and Christian times, signaling the close of harvest and the initiation of the winter season lasting till May," or as Yeats more cogently explained, "Hallow-Eve" (*CL3* 250). Yeats noted that "I have called this little collection of writing *Samhain,* the old name for the beginning of winter, because our plays this year are in October, and because our Theatre is coming to an end in its present shape." One might also suspect that the new publishers did not object to the new name.

Priced at sixpence (as were the next three issues) and published in conjunction with the 21 October 1901 production of the Irish Literary Theatre, the inaugural *Samhain* (October 1901) at thirty-eight pages was a more substantial volume than even the second issue of *Beltaine*. In addition to essays by Yeats as well as by Edward Martyn and George Moore, it included both the Irish text and the English translation by Lady Gregory of Douglas Hyde's *The Twisting of the Rope* (one of the two plays produced). The inclusion of both primary texts and criticism would continue in later issues of *Samhain*.

The volume enjoyed considerable success, as Yeats wrote to Lady Gregory on 19–20 January 1902.

I have just received through A P Watt an account of the sales of 'Samhain'. They printed 2000 & have sold 1628 & sent about 100 out to review so they have only about 300 (rather less) unsold. Royalties amount to £5.14.3. which I shall ask A P Watt to send (minus his 10 percent) to the Sec of Gaelic League Dublin. (*CL3* 147)

On 12 April 1902, Yeats told F. J. Fay that "In the autumn I had better write a new Samhain" (*CL3* 173). Yeats corrected the proofs of the second number in late September and early October 1902 (*CL3* 234–35), and it was published in conjunction with the 29–31 October 1902 performances of the Irish National Dramatic Company. In addition to a reprint of part of an essay by AE, the October 1902 *Samhain*, now called "An occasional review," included the text of Yeats's *Cathleen ni Hoolihan* and another play in Irish by Douglas Hyde with translation by Lady Gregory, *The Lost Saint.*

By 13 September 1903, Yeats was correcting the proofs of the third number of *Samhain,* published later that month in conjunction with the 8 October 1903 production of the Irish National Theatre Society.² In addition to essays by Yeats and A. B. Walkley, this number included the text of John Millington Synge's *Riders to the Sea* as well as yet another play by Douglas Hyde with translation by Lady Gregory, *The Poorhouse.*³

The 1904 *Samhain,* published in December, was an expanded number—fifty-six pages and priced at a shilling—to celebrate the opening of the Abbey Theatre on 27 December 1904. In addition to three important essays by Yeats, the issue included the text of Synge's *In the Shadow of the Glen* and Lady Gregory's *The Rising of the Moon* as well as the letter from Annie Horniman offering "my assistance in your endeavours to establish a permanent Theatre in Dublin." Promising on Christmas Day 1904 (in a letter dictated to Horniman) to send a copy to George P. Brett, Yeats described *Samhain* as "a publication I issue here in connection with my theatrical work" (*CL*3 690).

On 3 August 1905, Yeats told A. H. Bullen that he had "Samhain notes ahead of me." (*L* 457). Published in November 1905, this *Samhain* reverted to its more typical size, thirty-six pages, and its traditional price, sixpence.⁴ A series of comments by Yeats was followed by the text of Lady Gregory's *Spreading the News* and then of *An Fear Siubhail,* an Irish translation of Lady Gregory's *The Travelling Man* by Tadg Ó Donnchadha under the pseudonym "Tórna"—the first and only time that an Irish text would appear in *Samhain* without an accompanying translation.

Before the next issue of *Samhain* was published, Yeats began a new publication, at last with a title than everyone could understand and pronounce: *The Arrow.* These were shorter pamphlets, eight pages except for one issue of twelve, and they allowed Yeats to comment quickly on developments in the theatre. Promising that the new publication was "not meant as a substitute" for *Samhain,* Yeats explained its purpose in the inaugural issue of 20 October 1906:

It will interpret or comment on particular plays, make announcements, wrap up the programme and keep it from being lost, and
leave general principles to *Samhain*.

The first number included three short essays by Yeats, as did the
second number, published on 24 November 1906. Of this material, only part of "The Season's Work" from the 20 October 1906
issue would be republished.[5]

Yeats then returned to the more elaborate format of *Samhain*
with a volume published in December 1906.[6] The contents would
have come as no surprise to regular readers of *Samhain*: critical
commentary by Yeats and the text of Lady Gregory's *Hyacinth
Halvey*. A new addition, however, was the list of "Dates and
Places of the First Performance of Plays produced by the National
Theatre Society and its Predecessors," Yeats's attempt to ensure that
the history of the theatre movement would be written correctly.

Samhain was not published in 1907. Instead, Yeats reverted to
The Arrow, publishing the third number on 23 February 1907 and
the fourth on 1 June 1907. Sections of two of his three contributions to the earlier issue—"The Controversy Over 'The Playboy'"
and "Mr. Yeats' Opening Speech at the Debate of February 4th, at
the Abbey Theatre"—would be combined and reprinted, as was
most of his only contribution to the later issue, "On Taking 'The
Playboy' to London."

Yeats's vacillation between *The Arrow* and *Samhain* continued.
The seventh and last regular issue of *Samhain* appeared in
November 1908, the editor explaining that "There has been no
SAMHAIN for a couple of years, principally because an occasional
publication, called *The Arrow*, took its place for a time."[7] Along
with two essays by Yeats as well as his "Alterations in 'Deirdre,'"
this volume offered the text of Lady Gregory's *Dervorgilla* and a
revised list of performances. Three portraits were also included, portraits having been a regular feature of *Samhain* since the third number in 1903.

Yeats's career as a writer of theatrical pamphlets came to an end
with the fifth and final number of *The Arrow*, published on 25
August 1909. Neither his joint statement with Lady Gregory

about George Bernard Shaw's *The Shewing-Up of Blanco Posnet* nor his "The Religion of Blanco Posnet" would be reprinted. As of 27 August 1909, Yeats was planning a new issue of *Samhain*, much of which doubtless would have been devoted to the controversy over the production of Shaw's play on 25 August 1909. It was to offer "extracts from patent and show that Shaw's play came within it"; it would also "insist on freedom from censor and quote basis in [W. J.] Lawrence's article on censorship in Ireland." More importantly, it would include "something . . . on the union of love of ideas with love of country. Easy to have one without the other, easy to hate one in service of the other, but if they are combined one gets a great epoch" (*Mem* 228–29). Unfortunately, for reasons not entirely clear, no regular issue of *Samhain* was published in 1909. Yeats would use the name in a series of fund-raising pamphlets, but for all intents and purposes what he once called "a little annual published in the interest of the [theatre] movement" had come to an end (*Au* 330).[8]

II. *Friends and Enemies* and *The Collected Works in Verse and Prose* (1908)

Yeats's dramatic criticism would not remain only in pamphlet form for long. As early as 30 May 1905, he seems to have discussed a comprehensive edition of his canon with the publisher A. H. Bullen, telling Lady Gregory that he had agreed "to put off the expensive collected edition until next year" (*L* 449). The project began to move forward in 1907, helped by a surety from Annie Horniman.[9] As of 12 July 1907, a five-volume Edition was projected, with the last to be *Discoveries*, "a book of essays, very largely theatrical" (*L* 488). Bullen was to have an active role in selecting the contents for that volume, as on 26 August 1907 Yeats asked him, "Would you mind looking through the *Samhains* that you have, and noting as you suggested what seems to you most suitable for the book of essays, and sending them to me?" (*L* 491). By 26 September 1907, the project had grown to seven volumes, but Yeats had yet to submit final copy for *Discoveries* (*L* 494). On 4 October 1907, Yeats attempted to spur Bullen to action:

By the by don't forget that you have all my *Samhains*; you offered
to look through them and make suggestions as to what extracts I
should put into the book of essays. I wish you would do so as there
is no reason why you should not, if there is enough material, which
I am pretty confident there is, print the volume of criticism immediately after the volume of stories. . . . the sooner you send me these
Samhains again with your suggestions the better. (*L* 497)

Bullen eventually complied, and Yeats wrote him in March 1908
that "I have looked through the *Samhains* and sent them but
could you print in galley, as I think I shall interpolate a couple of
controversial letters" (*L* 505). As it turned out, the production
process was not without problems, as Yeats explained to Bullen's
assistant on 27 March 1908:

There has been a mix up in the *Samhain* proofs. First of all Mr.
Bullen writes to me for the preface, which I sent you when I sent the
copy. Secondly, an article of George Moore's has been printed as part
of the text. I don't understand this, for I believe that I tore out from
the *Samhains* my part of them, and sent that to you. Mr. Bullen may
have copied my corrections into some other text, in which case
please look up my original copy, and see if you can find the preface, which I don't now remember. I think something must have gone
astray for I suggested for this section the title *Friends and Enemies*.
If Mr. Bullen prefers, he can call it *The Irish Dramatic Movement*,
or *Samhain*, however. The preface was quite short, and can go at
the back of the page which contains the title, as Mr. Bullen suggests.
(*L* 506–7)

By 27 April 1908, however, Yeats could write John Quinn that the
"collected edition is going to be a beautiful thing. I have seen the
first specimen volume and am well content with my share of it and
with Bullen's" (*L* 509). The Edition was eventually published in eight
volumes from September to December 1908. *The Irish Dramatic
Movement* (the title apparently selected by Bullen) was the final item
in volume four; published in October, it was the third of three volumes devoted to the plays.[10]

Yeats did not include any of the material from *Beltaine* in *The Irish Dramatic Movement*. "The Theatre" (May 1899) and part of "The Irish Literary Theatre, 1900" (February 1900) had been combined and printed as "The Theatre" in *Ideas of Good and Evil* (1903) and would therefore be found in volume six of the *Collected Edition;* and the essay *"Maeve,* and certain Irish Beliefs" (February 1900) had at best a tangential relationship to the drama. The remaining material was apparently considered too topical for inclusion. What Yeats did include were his major contributions to the *Samhain*s of 1901–6 and to three of the five numbers of *The Arrow* (1906–7). The "couple of controversial letters" which Yeats had promised or threatened to include turned out to be two pieces from the 1903 *United Irishman:* "An Irish National Theatre" (10 October) and "The Theatre, the Pulpit and the Newspapers" (17 October).[11] As we have noted, there was no *Samhain* in 1907, and the 1908 installment was not available until November, a month after volume four of the *Collected Edition* had been published. This omission of material from the 1908 *Samhain* was not to be rectified in Yeats's lifetime.[12]

III. *The Marble Quarry*
and *Plays and Controversies*

As early as 1912, Yeats was pressing Bullen for a revision of the *Collected Edition*.[13] On 5 March 1913, he was delighted to inform Lady Gregory that "There is to be a refurbished edition of my collected edition, all pages I have re-written replaced, with illustrations. . . . The books will be rearranged, all the *Samhains* and theatre essays in general making up one volume . . ." (*L* 578). On 16 March 1913, he wrote the publisher as follows:

> I have come to the conclusion that you had better start a new issue of the Collected Works with the volume of dramatic criticism . . . The reason why I suggest it coming first is that it contains matter which has never been reviewed and never been accessible in a volume by itself. . . . It would contain the only serious criticism of the new craft of the Theatre. It is the exact moment for it. (*L* 578–79)

In the event, however, Bullen declined to proceed with a revised *Collected Edition.*

A few years later, Yeats renewed his campaign to have his dramatic criticism available in a single volume. On 30 October 1919, Yeats's agent, H. Watt, wrote to Macmillan (by then his primary English publisher) about a letter he had received from Yeats concerning three new books. The last of them had been described as follows:

> 'The Marble Quarry' (or it might be called 'Irish Essays') a volume of the dramatic criticisms in the Bullen collected edition with a longish introduction which is new and also some new criticisms. I think this book good and also likely to get well reviewed as it is topical both in relation to Ireland and to the stage. (BL 54898/44)[14]

Apparently the "longish introduction" was never written; the "new criticisms" presumably refer at least in part to "A People's Theatre," soon to be published in two installments in *The Irish Statesman* (29 November–6 December 1919).

Macmillan was slow to take up the matter of the projected volume. On 16 November 1919, Yeats wrote again to Watt, indicating that he was "most anxious" about both *Four Plays for Dancers* and *The Marble Quarry:*

> If these two books could be printed at once and proof sheets sent to Macmillan Company New York they might come out while I was in America and be helped by my lecturing tour!!! especially as I am lecturing on subjects connected with both.

He added that "In case of the 'Marble Quarry' (or 'Irish Essays' if preferred) I would have to revise two new essays myself, Macmillan's reader could revise the rest" (BL 54898/49–50). However, two days before Yeats's letter, Macmillan had in fact replied to Watt's of 30 October 1919, apologizing for the delay and suggesting a meeting to discuss the matter on 17 or 19 November 1919. Whenever they met, Macmillan must have declined to proceed with any of the suggested volumes. Yeats apparently did not take this rejection lightly, as witnessed by a letter from Macmillan to his agent on 14 January 1920:

> I have had your letter of the 8th inst. and Mr. Yeats's 'copy' lying before me for some time. It seems to me that the things as they stand are so slight that they could hardly be published as two separate books; but before settling anything I should like to see you on the subject. Could you conveniently call here, say, on Friday afternoon next between 3 and 4 o'clock. (BL 55559/531)

It is uncertain (though quite likely) that *The Marble Quarry* was one of the items submitted, but it is clear that the meeting on 16 January 1920 did not result in Macmillan's agreeing to undertake any of the three volumes Yeats had proposed the previous October.

The publication by Macmillan of *The Irish Dramatic Movement* therefore had to await the appearance of a new collected edition. Yeats had been anxious for some time about such a project, which had been a part of his agreement with Macmillan on 27 June 1916 (BL 54898/138). Early in January 1922, Yeats sent to Watt a plan for a six-volume Uniform Edition. One of them was to be called *Plays written in prose for an Irish Theatre; and The Irish Dramatic Movement*, Yeats explaining that

> I have included in the third volume what I call the 'Irish Dramatic Movement', extracts from my defense of our Irish Theatre from year to year. I am particularly anxious at the moment to get them published in some marketable form. Hitherto they have only been published, apart from their publication in pamphlets when first written, in Bullen's edition the volumes of which were not sold separately. (BL 54848/55)

Watt forwarded Yeats's letter to Macmillan on 10 January 1922; Macmillan replied to Watt on 12 January 1922, suggesting a meeting the following day (BL 55576/106).

In the event, Watt was again not especially successful in convincing Macmillan of the wisdom of Yeats's proposal. On 18 January 1922, Macmillan wrote to Watt offering to publish only three volumes of poems and plays:

We cannot however undertake at this point to publish any further volumes, and it must be distinctly understood that we are not to announce or bind ourselves in any way to issue more than the poetical and dramatic works. There is of course nothing to prevent the publication of three or four more volumes of prose in time to come if it seems reasonable. (BL 55576/243)

Watt replied on 20 January 1922, reminding Macmillan of the 1916 agreement (BL 54898/138). But the publishers were adamant: responding on 23 January 1922, two reasons were offered for the refusal to undertake a larger edition:

In the first place, if we were to announce an edition containing the prose works it would at once put out of action all the separate editions of the prose works which are now on sale and of which, as you know, we have a very considerable stock. Secondly, it would be impossible for us to publish as a complete work, and ask payment for it, the Large Paper Edition of the Poetical and Dramatic Works if, as you suggest, the publication of the prose works was announced but not immediately carried out.[15]

Further, Macmillan argued that "Unless I am very much mistaken Mr. Yeats himself suggested in a letter which he wrote about a year ago that the present publication should consist of the Poetical and Dramatic Works, so our proposal is not in any way new" (BL 55576/381).[16]

Watt apparently replied on 6 February 1922 with a further suggestion from Yeats. Macmillan wrote to Watt on 10 February 1922 that

I think that we had better fall in with Mr. Yeats's latest suggestion, which I take to be (1.) that we should publish a volume of poems to contain all the poems hitherto published by Mr. Yeats which are not included in Fisher Unwin's volume; and (2) a volume of plays to contain what originally appeared under the title of 'Plays for an Irish Theatre' and such others of his plays as are at our disposal, which I take to be 'The Golden Helmet', 'Unicorn from the Stars' and 'Pot of Broth' (BL 55576/875).

Thus both *Later Poems* and *Plays in Prose and Verse* were published by Macmillan on 3 November 1922.

Yeats persisted about additional volumes. On 4 January 1923, he asked Watt to propose to Macmillan "that they bring out two new volumes of their Collected Edition of my work," describing the first as follows:

> The Irish Dramatic Movement, this volume to contain all the dramatic criticism which I have published in pamphlet form during the fight for The Abbey Theatre and some criticism made later; it will also contain The Countess Cathleen and The Land of Heart's Desire. (BL 54898/217).

More than three years after he had first proposed the collection, Macmillan at last agreed to it in a letter of 9 January 1923 (55585/13).[17]

By 19 March 1923, Yeats had completed preparing copy for the volume—which by then also included *Four Plays for Dancers* (1921) and was to be called *Plays and Controversies*. But this material did not reach the publishers for over two months.[18] Forwarding the copy to Macmillan on 25 June 1923, Watt quoted from a letter "just received" which Yeats "wrote to me on 19 March but did not post": "I send you the materials for the next volume in my collected edition" (BL 54898/243-44). Macmillan acknowledged receipt of the copy on 27 June 1923 (BL 55589/344) and did not delay long in putting the work into production. A problem with some errant proofs on 8 September 1923 (55590/770) was quickly solved.[19] Macmillan was able to inform Yeats on 29 November 1923 that "your book 'Plays and Controversies' was published on Tuesday last, November 27th, and we have sent you six copies, which we hope you safely received" (BL 55594/271). Finally, *The Irish Dramatic Movement* was available to a wide audience.[20]

IV. The Edition de Luxe and the Scribner Edition

By February 1930, Macmillan had become interested in publishing a limited edition of Yeats's major works. The project was discussed during the year, Yeats writing Olivia Shakespear on 27 December 1930 that "Macmillan are going to bring out an Edition de Luxe of all my work published and unpublished. . . . I am to be ready next autumn at latest. Months of re-writing. What happiness!" (*L* 780). The formal contract, dated 17 April 1931, was sent by Macmillan to Watt on 20 April 1931 (BL 55715/241) and returned signed by Yeats on 4 May 1931 (BL 54901/160).[21] Macmillan undertook to publish the Edition no "later than the 30th day of September 1932"; as it turned out, the marginal addenda "unless prevented by circumstances over which they had no control" was to prove prophetic.

The second volume of the Edition de Luxe to be set in proof (*Poems* being the first) was a collection which other evidence indicates was called *Mythologies and The Irish Dramatic Movement*. The proofs were printed from 30 September to 26 October 1931 but were not sent to Yeats until 22 June 1932 (BL 55729/605). Yeats returned the proofs of the first two volumes of the Edition de Luxe to Macmillan on 5 July 1932, indicating that "The volume called 'Mythologies' I need not see again. Your reader can complete the revision better than I could" (BL 55003/129). Thomas Mark (Macmillan's "reader") had a new set of proofs prepared, but there is no evidence that these were sent to Yeats for additional checking (*SR* xxxviii and n44).

Over the next few years, Macmillan continued to postpone publication of the Edition de Luxe. In November 1935, Yeats received an offer from Charles Scribner's Sons in New York to publish a similar edition in America. By May 1936, Yeats was "favorably inclined" towards the proposal.[22] By early October 1936, the arrangements had been completed.

Yeats thus met with Watt on 23 October 1936 and asked him to obtain from Macmillan "a note of the contents of the De Luxe edition of his works which you are proposing to publish when the proper time comes" (BL 54903/133), doubtless so that Yeats could ensure that the contents of the two Editions were essentially identical. Macmillan prepared two copies of a nine-page typed document headed "W. B. YEATS / DE LUXE EDITION" and forwarded them to Watt on 27 October 1936 (BL 55786/497), asking Yeats to annotate and return one copy and retain the other. Watt was able to send the copy with Yeats's comments to Macmillan on 10 November 1936 (BL 54903/148), Macmillan receiving it on 12 November 1936 (BL 55787/362).

On this list, volume two is called "MYTHOLOGIES AND THE IRISH DRAMATIC MOVEMENT," the contents being "The Celtic Twilight," "The Secret Rose," "Stories of Red Hanrahan," "Rosa Alchemica, The Tables of the Law, and The Adoration of the Magi," and "The Irish Dramatic Movement."²³ Probably at some time after 14 November 1936, when Macmillan refused to let Scribner's have their proofs for the Edition de Luxe (55787/444–45), Yeats added a note indicating that they should take the text of *The Irish Dramatic Movement* from *Plays and Controversies*.

In January 1937, Yeats prepared tables of contents for the Scribner Edition and sent them to Watt, who forwarded them to New York on 28 January 1937. The list for volume two is typed "MYTHOLOGIES AND THE IRISH DRAMATIC MOVE-MENT," but the first part of the title is revised in Yeats's hand to "Mythical Stories" (Princeton). Scribner's was unable to proceed with the project because they had not received copy, and a series of letters and cables ensued to both Watt and their agent in London, Charles Kingsley. Yeats may well have been at last spurred to action by a letter from Macmillan which he would have received on 7 June 1937 asking about additional poems for the Edition de Luxe (BL 55795/298) as well as by his scheduled departure for London the next day. He thus took out his copy of the November 1936 Edition de Luxe list and made further annotations. After his departure, his wife prepared new tables of contents for the Scribner Edition, which she sent in segments to Watt, along with copy, from 11–22 June 1937.²⁴

The list for volume two was forwarded to Yeats's agent on 14 June 1937. It is headed "MYTHOLOGIES AND THE IRISH DRAMATIC MOVEMENT": either Yeats had changed his mind about "Mythical Stories," or he had forgotten about the revision. However, the table of contents for the volume prepared by Scribner's after they received copy from Watt in July 1937 is untitled, perhaps indicating their confusion about the intended title.

In the event, neither the Edition de Luxe nor the Scribner Edition was ever published.

V. The Coole Edition

After Yeats's death there occurred a flurry of activity on the Edition de Luxe, renamed The Coole Edition by Mrs. Yeats on 15 April 1939.[25] A printed Prospectus was prepared and probably sent to Mrs. Yeats on 28 February 1939 (BL 55820/203–05). The Edition had now grown to eleven volumes. *The Irish Dramatic Movement* was placed in volume ten, after *Ideas of Good and Evil;* the volume was the first of two called *Essays and Reviews,* but the titles of both were changed by Mrs. Yeats to, respectively, *Essays* and *Essays and Introductions. Mythologies* was now volume eight, with *Per Amica Silentia Lunae* replacing *The Irish Dramatic Movement* (BL 55890). The authority for this expansion and rearrangement is open to question. The editors of *The Secret Rose* have breezily indicated that the changes "had been instigated by Thomas Mark at the time of drawing up the 'Preliminary Notice'" for the Edition: this is somewhat imprecise in detail and rather too categorical in assertion. It is at least possible that some of the revisions were agreed to during a meeting between Yeats and his publisher in London in late October or November 1938.[26]

Mark was able to send the proofs of the first volume of *Essays* to Mrs. Yeats on 26 June 1939, along with the 1931–32 Edition de Luxe proofs of *Mythologies* (BL 55826/50).[27] Apparently Allan Wade, who had published his first bibliography of Yeats in the 1908 *Collected Works,* was assisting Macmillan in the project, as on 5 July 1939 Mark forwarded to Mrs. Yeats a letter from him, "suggesting the addition of some further notes to the Irish Dramatic Movement in Volume X of the Coole Edition. Perhaps you will kindly let me know what you think of this idea, and perhaps send the material" (BL 55826/298). What Wade had pointed out was the omission of any material from the 1908 *Samhain* in *The Irish Dramatic Movement*. Mrs. Yeats replied in a letter of 9 July 1939:

> Mr Wade is quite right: that last *Samhain* essay was not included in the *Irish Dramatic Movement* when WBY re-published with Macmillan. I shall send you a typed copy tomorrow (I have only one printed copy available which does not belong to me, so cannot send it). . . .

The new section will be about nine pages of Coole Ed, and should come after the section dated 1907 (*On taking the Playboy to London*) present p. 475–6, and before "*A People's Theatre*["].
As all the pages in this vol will have to be re-numbered this will not upset things very much?

It would be a pity to put it in the last volume XI, with the rather miscellaneous collection that is there.[28]

Mark replied on 11 July 1939: "I note that you think the last *Samhain* essay should be included in the *Irish Dramatic Movement* and that you will be sending me the typescript. It will not greatly upset the volume" (BL 55826/436). Two copies of Mrs. Yeats's type-script survive, one in the British Library (BL 55897) and the other in the collection of Anne Yeats.[29] On the same day Mark acknowl-edged receipt of the proofs (BL 55826/436).[30]

It seems clear that there was no immediate attention given to the expanded version of *The Irish Dramatic Movement*. Mrs. Yeats had told Mark in a letter of 22 June 1939 that she would "be moving about July 23rd, and that will take a week"; in turn, Mark had informed her on 11 July 1939 that since he would be "starting my holiday on Saturday next [15 July 1939], you will not be troubled with any more proofs until the end of month." True to his word, on 4 August 1939 he forwarded the proofs of *Last Poems & Plays*, "accompanied by the 'copy' supplied for *Purgatory* and *The Death of Cuchulain*" (BL 55828/13). As that edition was his pri-mary concern at the moment, it was not until 24–29 August 1939 that new proofs of *The Irish Dramatic Movement*, marked "Fourth Proof," were prepared. Two sets are extant (BL 55897). There is no evidence that these proofs were sent to Mrs. Yeats at this time. Mark would have been unlikely to burden her with additional proofs while he awaited the return of the proofs for the new volume. When he finally received the corrected proofs of *Last Poems & Plays* on 19 October 1939, Mark had to inform her that the Coole Edition "has to wait for better times" (BL 55830/334).[31] Mark did not immediately abandon his work on the Edition, but it clearly became less and less of a priority.

VI. *Explorations* (1962)

No further activity about *The Irish Dramatic Movement* can be documented until late 1959 or early 1960, when Macmillan drafted a letter proposing a volume to be called *Explorations,* to follow *Essays and Introductions* (1961), then in page proof.[32] Although the suggested contents differ considerably from what was finally included, *The Irish Dramatic Movement* was always planned as part of the collection. On 11 August 1960, Lovat Dickson sent Mrs. Yeats some of the materials for the projected volume, including the 24–29 August 1939 proofs of *The Irish Dramatic Movement,* and asked for a final list of the contents (NLI Ms. 30,755). Sometime after 19 April 1961, when Dickson wrote to spur her on, Mrs. Yeats provided the list and presumably returned the proofs. *Explorations* was eventually published in London on 23 July 1962.

There are two extant sets of the 24–29 August 1939 proofs of *The Irish Dramatic Movement* (BL 55897). These were corrected by Thomas Mark, most likely in 1939. Although there are no markings by Mrs. Yeats, she presumably did review the proofs in 1960–61. On the set she apparently was sent Mark had circled the second "m" in "M. Trebulet Bonhommie" and queried "correct? don't know allusion." Mrs. Yeats is the most likely person to have provided the correction to "M. Tribulat Bonhomet," the reading on the 24 November–8 December 1961 galley proofs of *Explorations* (BL 55986).

Mrs. Yeats must have been sent a set of those galley proofs as well, but again there are no markings by her on the single extant set. The text was subject to further correction, but the extent of Mrs. Yeats's involvement is unknown. One of the most significant changes occurs in the 1905 *Samhain.* Next to Yeats's reference to "a nigger newspaper" is a query in red ink "? correct" and a note in pencil, "it was used in 1905." Nevertheless, in *Explorations* the text is silently emended to "a negro newspaper." Doubtless Macmillan would not have revised the text without seeking Mrs. Yeats's approval, and thus one may assume that they received it.

It is quite clear, then, that Yeats last corrected the text of *The Irish Dramatic Movement* in late June/early July 1932 for the Edition de

Luxe, and those proofs have thus been used as the base-text for this edition.³³ Other materials have been taken from the original publications. Further information is provided in "History of the Text" and "Textual Emendations and Corrections."

Notes to Introduction

1. *CL2* 321. The policy of *The Collected Letters* to attempt to reproduce Yeats's erratic spelling has not been followed in the case of obvious and distracting errors, such as "to geather" for "together."

2. Allan Wade, *A Bibliography of the Writings of W. B. Yeats*, 3rd ed., rev. Russell K. Alspach (London: Rupert Hart-Davis, 1968), 248, records a second issue of this *Samhain* in October 1903.

3. In *The Irish Dramatic Movement,* Yeats included two letters from *The United Irishman*—"An Irish National Theatre" (10 October 1903) and "The Theatre, the Pulpit and the Newspapers" (17 October)—both headed after the 1908 edition "*Samhain: 1903.*" However, neither piece had been included in that volume. *CL3* 439n1 incorrectly states that the earlier letter was included in *Samhain*.

4. For this issue, the Dublin imprint was that of Maunsel & Co. and the English imprint that of A. H. Bullen, though the printing continued to be done in Dublin by Sealy, Bryers & Walker.

5. The Berg Collection at the New York Public Library also has a one-page "Supplement to 'The Arrow,'" dated 8 December 1906, which offers an engraving of Queen Elizabeth by William Rogers and "Captain Headley's Song" from Lady Gregory's *The Canavans*.

6. For this issue, the only imprint is that of Maunsel & Co.; the printing was again by Sealy, Bryers & Walker. A variant cover for this number is reproduced as the last item in the facsimile edition of *Samhain* with an Introductory Note by B. C. Bloomfield (London: Frank Cass, 1970). A parallel facsimile edition of *Beltaine* by the same publisher was also issued in 1970.

7. For this issue, the Dublin imprint is that of Maunsel & Co., the London imprint that of T. Fisher Unwin. The printing again was the work of Sealy, Bryers & Walker. If and when *The Collected Letters* reaches 1906–8, the reason for these annual shifts in publisher may become known.

8. Yeats issued a series of fund-raising pamphlets in 1909–10 in an attempt to recover the anticipated loss of Annie Horniman's subsidy of the Abbey Theatre: *Paragraphs from the Forthcoming Number of 'Samhain'* ([September?] 1909); *Paragraphs from 'Samhain' 1909* ([December 1909?]); *Supplement to Paragraphs from 'Samhain,' 1909 / February 21st, 1910* ([March?] 1910); and *Paragraphs Written in Nov., 1909, with Supplement and Financial Statement*

([March?] 1910). The Wade *Bibliography* records only the first and last of these; I am grateful to Colin Smythe for further details.

9. See Foster, 371. Bullen requested a surety of £1,500 (599n64). Foster's statement that "Since January 1907 discussion had been under way" about the Collected Edition (371) apparently overlooks the 1905 letter to Lady Gregory.

10. Yeats's earliest choice for the title, *Discoveries,* had been used for a 1907 Cuala Press edition of essays, included under that title in volume eight of the Collected Edition.

11. Yeats may have had second thoughts about including this material. Foster quotes a letter of 8 May 1908 in which Yeats "complained about 'fragments of letters reprinted from the United Irishman (just where mistakes are most likely & mistakes that might be very injurious to me for I have quarreled with the paper & its party)'" (372).

12. For Yeats's contributions to *Beltaine* and the uncollected material from *Samhain* and *The Arrow,* see pp. 141 ff.

13. ". . . he plagued his publisher with demands for addenda or—better still—revision of the sheets which were not yet bound" (Foster, 457).

14. The other volumes were *Four Plays for Dancers,* eventually published by Macmillan on 28 October 1921, and *The Player Queen,* eventually published by Macmillan in *Plays in Prose and Verse* on 3 November 1922 as well as in a separate volume on 21 November 1922.

15. In a letter of 18 January 1922, Macmillan had indicated that they were "prepared to publish a Definitive Edition of the Poems and Plays in three volumes" and that "we should also propose to issue an edition limited to 250 copies on large paper to be sold only in sets at a higher price" (BL 55576/243–44).

16. Macmillan is referring to an alternative proposal which Yeats had made in a letter of 23 December [1920]: "Another scheme would be to bring out 'Collected Poetical Works of W B Yeats' in 3 vols (1 of lyrical & narrative work & 2 vols of plays) and to leave the prose works till later. The objection to this is you will hardly want to include contents of 'Four Plays for Dancers' (this however might be added in a fourth volume some years later or as a new section at end of vol 3 when the present edition is ex[h]austed" (BL 55003/65).

17. Macmillan was no doubt motivated by the fact that "We have sold over 1,200 copies of *Later Poems* and over 900 of *Plays in Prose and Verse*" (BL 55585/13).

18. Ann Saddlemyer has suggested to me that the delay was probably due to Mrs. Yeats's being in isolation with scarlet fever, as it was she who usually looked after such matters as the posting of materials. It is also possible that Mrs. Yeats delivered the copy to Watt herself, as she was in London until at least 23 June 1923.

19. See BL 54898/249–50 and 252.

20. The American edition of *Plays and Controversies* did not appear

until 16 September 1924, the delay perhaps caused both by the new printing and by the simultaneous publication of a signed limited edition of 250 copies.

21. I am grateful to Linda Shaughnessy of A P Watt Ltd for a copy of the contract.

22. Letter from John Hall Wheelock of Scribner's to Yeats, 26 May 1936 (Princeton). Wheelock is quoting what he heard from "my friends, the Colums" (the Irish writer Padraic Colum and his wife).

23. Further evidence that the title of the volume had never been simply *Mythologies* is found in a letter from Macmillan to Yeats on 15 April 1932, citing the various volumes in the Edition de Luxe: volume two is called "Mythologies, etc." (BL 55727/271). Although the first page of the 1931–32 proofs is headed "MYTHOLOGIES" and has "Vol II" in the lower left-hand corner, that does not indicate that *Mythologies* was the title for the entire volume. The proofs begin with gathering B and do not include a title page or a table of contents, and this was the standard practice with the Edition de Luxe proofs. For example, the 21 December 1936 proofs of the first volume of *Plays* starts with gathering B with the title *The Countess Cathleen* and with "vol. III" in the lower left-hand corner. Yet the volume as a whole was of course not called *The Countess Cathleen*.

Finally, one should observe that rather than writing a new Note for a supposedly unified volume of *Mythologies,* Yeats simply reprinted his note on the fiction from *Early Poems and Stories* (1925) and supplied a new comment on *The Irish Dramatic Movement*, separating the two notes by a considerable degree of white space. The cross-reference in the second note to the fiction is doubtless an attempt to explain why two different kinds of work were published together. Yeats was well aware of the necessity of making the seven volumes of the Edition de Luxe approximately equal in size—on 7 May 1931 he had asked Macmillan to let him know the number of pages in the Uniform Edition of 1922–26 so that he could arrange the contents for the new Edition (BL 55003/121)—and it is clear that anyone attempting to apportion the canon as of 1931 would inevitably face the same predicament that Yeats did, with the fiction too short to stand by itself and an orphaned *Irish Dramatic Movement*.

24. Two copies of this list are in National Library of Ireland MS 30,202. A copy of the list sent to Watt, made by Kingsley, is in the Princeton University Library. The materials sent to Scribner's are in the Humanities Research Center, University of Texas. The copy submitted for *The Irish Dramatic Movement* consisted of uncorrected pages from the London edition of *Plays and Controversies*. Had the Scribner Edition gone forward in his lifetime, Yeats would of course have corrected proofs, and the resultant text of *The Irish Dramatic Movement* would surely have differed from that found on the corrected

page proofs of *Mythologies*. But since that process did not occur, the *Mythologies* proofs embody Yeats's last known corrections to the text.

25. Letters from Mrs. Yeats to Macmillan are in the archives of Macmillan, London (now Palgrave).

26. *SR* xxxviii. The rearrangement and expansion were first made not on the printed Prospectus with the indication of "Preliminary Notice," which is headed "The Collected Edition of the Works of W. B. Yeats" (Princeton), but rather on an earlier state of same headed "The [blank space] Edition of the works of W. B. Yeats" (BL 55890). The "Preliminary Notice" version was in print no later than 25 March 1939, when a copy was sent to Scribner's; it was doubtless approved at the meeting between Mrs. Yeats and Macmillan in London on 17 March 1939. The earlier version, which has "Mrs Yeats" in orange crayon on the top, was almost surely sent to her on 28 February 1939, although Macmillan's letter refers only to a "list" and a "second list" (BL 55820/203–05). It is clear, however, that an expanded Edition was projected as of that date, Macmillan writing that "We have now planned it as eleven volumes, provisionally arranged as shown on the list I enclose."

It is not impossible that Macmillan may have undertaken the expansion of the Edition de Luxe on their own authority. But to disassemble a volume which Yeats had carefully read and corrected—and especially to add to what remained a new work, subsuming it under Yeats's title *Mythologies*—without the approval of Yeats would have been a rather atypical occurrence. In accord with their usual practice, they would have first consulted with Mrs. Yeats, which would have been unlikely in the weeks immediately after Yeats's death and for which there is no evidence; or they would have called her particular attention to the rearrangement in their letter of 28 February 1939, which they did not. One must therefore consider the possibility that the rearrangement had been approved by Yeats.

A comment on BL 55896 (the 24 November–8 December 1961 galley proofs of *Explorations*) indicates that Yeats met with his publishers when he "was passing through London 1938 before his last visit to France." Yeats was in England from 26 October 1938 until 26 November 1938. Ann Saddlemyer, who has graciously supplied those dates, has suggested that the meeting with Macmillan would have occurred on either 26 October, 15 November, or 25 November 1938, with the last most likely. Whatever the precise date, by the time of the meeting it would have been self-evident that the materials which Macmillan recently had published or were aware of had made a seven-volume Edition de Luxe all but impossible, and at least a general discussion of how to proceed would have been an important item on the publisher's agenda. They would have been delighted to get Yeats's agreement in principle for a revised and expanded project, as this would have greatly increased the "divergence" between their Edition and the Scribner Edition that they had always desired. As far as they knew, the Scribner Edition (still in seven volumes) was in active preparation, so their more expansive project would quite trump the Americans when the time came. Indeed, when Charles Kingsley discovered a notice of an eleven-volume Edition in *The Bookseller* (30 March 1939), he wrote John Hall Wheelock on 4 April 1939 that "It rather looks to me as if they [Macmillan] had put a fast one over on us" (Princeton). To their rather belated credit, Macmillan—of course aware of the forthcoming printed announcement—had in fact informed Scribner's of the extent of their Edition a few days previously, in a letter of 27 March 1939 (Princeton).

Unfortunately, there appears to be no record of what transpired at the 1938 meeting, so the possibility that Yeats approved any or all of the revisions to the Edition remains no more than that, as does the assertion that all was done solely by Macmillan.

27. Mark sent proofs of three volumes, the others being *Mythologies* and *Discoveries* (i.e., volumes 8, 9, and 10 of the Edition de Luxe as then constituted). Of *Mythologies,* it has been argued that "The new proof must have been a marked set of the 'revise' of the 1931–32 proofs prepared at Mark's request after Yeats had returned them" (*SR* xxxviii), but this is quite unlikely. Since the contents had changed so drastically, Mark surely would have had a new set of proofs produced, with *Per Amica Silentia Lunae* in place of *The Irish Dramatic Movement*. Since it is improbable that any further revisions had been accomplished on the 1932 revised proofs, Mark would have considered them irrelevant, which would explain why they apparently were not preserved. The proofs of *The Irish Dramatic Movement* included in *Essays*, likewise not known to be extant, thus would have been a "Third Proof," which explains why the extant 24–29 August 1939 proofs of the section are marked "Fourth Proof."

28. Mrs. Yeats's comment is somewhat misleading. As we have noted, since it had not been in print at the appropriate moment, nothing from the 1908 *Samhain* had been included in volume four of the *Collected Works in Verse and Prose*. Yeats apparently overlooked the omission when both *Plays and Controversies* (1923) and the Edition de Luxe proofs of *Mythologies* (1931–32) were produced. Wade's suggestion of the addition of further "notes" may indicate that he recommended the inclusion of both "Events" and "First Principles" from the 1908 *Samhain,* though obviously Mrs. Yeats authorized the incorporation of only the latter.

29. In *A Descriptive Catalog of W. B. Yeats's Library* (New York & London: Garland, 1985), 236 (item #1827), Edward O'Shea mistakenly describes this posthumous typescript as corrected by Yeats.

In the process of checking for material from the 1908 *Samhain,* Mrs. Yeats would have come across the revisions to *The Irish Dramatic Movement* in Yeats's copy of the *Collected Works in Verse and Prose.* She must have supplied these to Mark, as they are incorporated in the 24–29 August 1939 proofs, even though the revisions had been superseded by Yeats's later corrections. Probably at the same time, she drew on the 1908 changes in preparing a corrected text of the 1924 New York edition of *Plays and Controversies,* no doubt as revised copy for the Scribner Edition. If that volume was sent to Scribner's, it must have been returned, as it is preserved in Yeats's library.

30. The fact that neither set of the third proof of *The Irish Dramatic Movement* apparently survives suggests that they were subject to little if any correction. Once both Mark and Mrs. Yeats were aware of the omission of material from the 1908 *Samhain,* it was clear that the proofs would have to be superseded by a new set.

31. There is no record in the Macmillan Letter Books of the period of the dispatch or receipt of the 24–29 August 1939 proofs of *The Irish Dramatic Movement.* Moreover, had Mark received corrected proofs from Mrs. Yeats, his usual practice would have called for the production of a revised set, which is not known to exist.

It is also clear that around this time Mrs. Yeats began to be less responsive to Mark's letters. On 31 August 1939, for instance, he sent a set of page proofs of *Last Poems & Plays* to Yeats's agent, complaining that "The press proofs were sent to Mrs. Yeats for approval on August 4th, and we have not had any reply from her" (BL 55828/511). When he finally received the proofs from Mrs. Yeats on 19 October 1939, he informed her rather curtly that they "were just in time, as the book was about to go to press" (BL 55830/334). On 12 February 1940 Mark again complained to Yeats's agent about Mrs. Yeats: not only had she failed to return the signed contract for the American edition of *Last Poems and Plays,* but also "I have written to her several times about some outstanding proofs of the big edition of her husband's works, but have had no reply" (BL 55834/522–23). The state of things during the rest of the decade can be reconstructed from a letter to Yeats's agent from Macmillan on 12 May 1949: "Mrs. Yeats has written from time to time about certain details to Mr. Mark, who has been preparing the book [*Poems* (1949)]. It is so satisfactory for her to write and answer letters that I have rather encouraged her without bothering you; you will remember how difficult we found it to get a reply from her." Ann Saddlemyer's *Becoming George: The Life of Mrs. W. B. Yeats* (Oxford and New York: Oxford University Press, 2002) details her myriad responsibilities during these years.

32. The draft letter, probably composed by Lovat Dickson of Macmillan, is now found in BL 55986, the 24 November 1961–8 December 1961 galley proofs of *Explorations*.

33. Mrs. Yeats apparently retained these proofs in 1939. In "Yeats Digitally Remastered," *Yeats Annual No. 14* (2001), Warwick Gould has recently congratulated himself and the other co-editors of *The Secret Rose* for "the discovery of the 1931–32 page proofs of *Mythologies and the Irish Dramatic Movement* and the subsequent establishment of the copy-text of *The Secret Rose*" (346). Leaving aside the fact that the proofs had never been lost—having been in the care of, in order, Macmillan, London; Mrs. W. B. Yeats; and Senator Michael B. Yeats, until Senator Yeats donated them to the National Library of Ireland—this statement rather overlooks the citation of the proofs and an indication of their relevance to the text of Yeats's work in *The Prose Fiction of W. B. Yeats: The Search for 'Those Simple Forms'* (Dublin: Dolmen Press, 1973), 40.

THE COLLECTED WORKS
OF W. B. YEATS

VOLUME VIII

The Irish
Dramatic Movement

1901 to 1919†

SAMHAIN: 1901

When Lady Gregory, Mr. Edward Martyn, and myself planned the Irish Literary Theatre, we decided that it should be carried on in the form we had projected for three years.[1] We thought that three years would show whether the country desired to take up the project, and make it a part of the national life, and that we, at any rate, could return to our proper work, in which we did not include theatrical management, at the end of that time. A little later, Mr. George Moore* joined us; and, looking back now upon our work, I doubt if it could have been done at all without his knowledge of the stage; and certainly if the performances of this present year bring our adventure to a successful close, a chief part of the credit will be his.[2] Many, however, have helped us in various degrees, for in Ireland just now one has only to discover an idea that seems of service to the country for friends and helpers to start up on every hand. While we needed guarantors we had them in plenty, and though Mr. Edward Martyn's public spirit made it unnecessary to call upon them, we thank them none the less.

Whether the Irish Literary Theatre has a successor made on its own model or not, we can claim that a dramatic movement which will not die has been started. When we began our work, we tried in vain to get a play in Gaelic. We could not even get a condensed version of the dialogue of Oisin and Patrick.[3] We wrote to Gaelic enthusiasts in vain, for their imagination had not yet turned

*Both Mr. Moore and Mr. Martyn dropped out of the movement after the third performance at the Irish Literary Theatre in 1901. —March 1908.

3

towards the stage, and now there are excellent Gaelic plays by Dr.
Douglas Hyde, by Father O'Leary, by Father Dinneen, and by Mr.
MacGinley; and the Gaelic League has had a competition for a one-
act play in Gaelic, with what results I do not know.[4] There have been
successful performances of plays in Gaelic at Dublin and at Macroom, and at Letterkenny, and I think at other places; and Mr. Fay
has got together an excellent little company which plays both in
Gaelic and in English.[5] I may say, for I am perhaps writing an epitaph, and epitaphs should be written in a genial spirit, that we have
turned a great deal of Irish imagination towards the stage. We could
not have done this if our movement had not opened a way of expression for an impulse that was in the people themselves. The truth is
that the Irish people are at that precise stage of their history when
imagination, shaped by many stirring events, desires dramatic
expression. One has only to listen to a recitation of Raftery's
'Argument with Death' at some country Feis to understand this.[6]
When Death makes a good point, or Raftery a good point, the audience applaud delightedly, and applaud, not, as a London audience
would, some verbal dexterity, some piece of smartness, but the
movements of a simple and fundamental comedy. One sees it too
in the reciters themselves, whose acting is at times all but perfect
in its vivid simplicity. I heard a little Claddagh girl tell a folk-story
at Galway Feis with a restraint and a delightful energy that could
hardly have been bettered by the most careful training.[7]

The organisation of this movement is of immediate importance. Some of our friends propose that somebody begin at once
to get a small stock company together, and that he invite, let us say,
Mr. Benson, to find us certain well-trained actors, Irish if possible,
but well trained of a certainty, who will train our actors, and take
the more difficult parts at the beginning.[8] These friends contend that
it is necessary to import our experts at the beginning, for our company must be able to compete with travelling English companies,
but that a few years will be enough to make many competent Irish
actors. The Corporation of Dublin should be asked, they say, to give
a small annual sum of money, such as they give to the Academy of
Music; and the Corporations of Cork and Limerick and Waterford,
and other provincial towns, to give small endowments in the

shape of a hall and attendants and lighting for a week or two out of every year; and the Technical Board to give a small annual sum of money to a school of acting which would teach fencing and declamation, and gesture and the like. The stock company would perform in Dublin perhaps three weeks in spring, and three weeks in autumn, and go on tour the rest of the time through Ireland, and through the English towns where there is a large Irish population. It would perform plays in Irish and English, and also, it is proposed, the masterpieces of the world, making a point of performing Spanish, and Scandinavian, and French, and perhaps Greek masterpieces rather more than Shakespeare, for Shakespeare is seen, not well done indeed, but not unendurably ill done, in the Theatre of Commerce. It would do its best to give Ireland a hardy and shapely national character by opening the doors to the four winds of the world, instead of leaving the door that is towards the east wind open alone. Certainly, the national character, which is so essentially different from the English that Spanish and French influences may well be most healthy, is at present like one of those miserable thorn-bushes by the sea that are all twisted to one side by some prevailing wind.

It is contended that there is no reason why the company should not be as successful as similar companies in Germany and Scandinavia, and that it would be even of commercial advantage to Dublin by making it a pleasanter place to live in, besides doing incalculable good to the whole intellect of the country. One, at any rate, of those who press the project on us has much practical knowledge of the stage and of theatrical management, and knows what is possible and what is not possible.

Others among our friends, and among these are some who have had more than their share of the hard work which has built up the intellectual movement in Ireland, argue that a theatre of this kind would require too much money to be free, that it could not touch on politics, the most vital passion and vital interest of the country, as they say, and that the attitude of continual compromise between conviction and interest, which it would necessitate, would become demoralising to everybody concerned, especially at moments of political excitement. They tell us that the war between an Irish Ireland and an English Ireland is about to become much fiercer, to divide families and friends, it may be, and that the organisations that will lead in the war must be able to say everything the people are thinking. They would have Irishmen give their plays to a company like Mr. Fay's, when they are within its power, and if not, to Mr. Benson or to any other travelling company which will play them in Ireland without committees, where everybody compromises a little. In this way, they contend, we would soon build up an Irish theatre from the ground, escaping to some extent the conventions of the ordinary theatre, and those English voices which give a foreign air to our words. And though we might have to wait some years, we would get even the masterpieces of the world in good time. Let us, they think, be poor enough to whistle at the thief who would take away some of our thoughts, and after Mr. Fay has taken his company, as he plans, through the villages and the country towns, he will get the little endowment that is necessary, or if he does not, some other will.

I do not know what Lady Gregory or Mr. Moore thinks of these projects. I am not going to say what I think. I have spent much of my time and more of my thought these last ten years on Irish organisation, and now that the Irish Literary Theatre has completed the plan I had in my head ten years ago, I want to go down again to primary ideas. I want to put old stories into verse, and if I put them into dramatic verse it will matter less to me henceforward who plays them than what they play, and how they play. I hope to get our heroic age into verse, and to solve some problems of the speaking of verse to musical notes.

There is only one question which is raised by the two projects I have described on which I will give an opinion. It is of the first importance that those among us who want to write for the stage should study the dramatic masterpieces of the world. If they can get them on the stage, so much the better, but study them they must if Irish drama is to mean anything to Irish intellect. At the present moment, Shakespeare being the only great dramatist known to Irish writers has made them cast their work too much on the English model. Miss Milligan's *Red Hugh,* which was successfully acted in Dublin the other day, had no business to be in two scenes; and Father O'Leary's *Tadgh Saor,* despite its most vivid and picturesque, though far too rambling dialogue, shows in its half-dozen changes of scene the influence of the same English convention, which arose when there was no scene-painting, and is often a difficulty where there is, and is always an absurdity in a farce of thirty minutes, breaking up the emotion and sending our thoughts here and there.⁹ Mr. MacGinley's *Eilis agus an Bhean Déirce* has not this defect, and though I had not Irish enough to follow it when I saw it played, and excellently played, by Mr. Fay's company, I could see from the continual laughter of the audience that it held them with an unbroken emotion. The best Gaelic play after Dr. Hyde's is, I think, Father Dinneen's *Creideamh agus Gorta,* and though it changes the scene a little oftener than is desirable under modern conditions, it does not remind me of an English model. It reminds me of Calderón by its treatment of a religious subject, and by something in Father Dinneen's sympathy with the people that is like his. But I think if Father Dinneen had studied that great Catholic dramatist he would not have failed, as he has done once or twice, to remember some necessary detail of a situation. In the first scene he makes a servant ask his fellow-servants about things he must have known as well as they; and he loses a dramatic moment in his third scene by forgetting that Seagan Gorm has a pocketful of money which he would certainly, being the man he was, have offered to the woman he was urging into temptation. The play towards the end changes from prose to verse, and the reverence and simplicity of the verse makes one think of a mediaeval miracle play. The subject has been so much a part of Irish life that it was bound to be used by an Irish dramatist, though certainly I shall always prefer plays which attack a more eternal devil than the proselytiser. He has been defeated, and the arts are at their best when they are busy with battles that can never be won. It is possible, however, that we may have to deal with passing issues until we have re-created the imaginative tradition of Ireland, and filled the popular imagination again with saints and heroes. These short plays (though they would be better if their writers knew the masters of their craft) are very dramatic as they are, but there is no chance of our writers of

Gaelic, or our writers of English, doing good plays of any length if
they do not study the masters. If Irish dramatists had studied the
romantic plays of Ibsen, the one great master the modern stage has
produced, they would not have sent the Irish Literary Theatre imitations of Boucicault, who had no relation to literature, and
Father O'Leary would have put his gift for dialogue, a gift certainly
greater than, let us say, Mr. Jones' or Mr. Grundy's, to better use
than the writing of that long, rambling dramatisation of the *Táin
Bó Cuailgne,* in which I hear in the midst of the exuberant Gaelic
dialogue the worn-out conventions of English poetic drama.[10] The
moment we leave even a little the folk-tradition of the peasant, as
we must in drama, if we do not know the best that has been said
and written in the world, we do not even know ourselves. It is no
great labour to know the best dramatic literature, for there is very
little of it. We Irish must know it all, for we have, I think, far greater
need of the severe discipline of French and Scandinavian drama than
of Shakespeare's luxuriance.

If the *Diarmuid and Grania* and the *Casadh an tSúgáin* are not
well constructed, it is not because Mr. Moore and Dr. Hyde and
myself do not understand the importance of construction, and
Mr. Martyn has shown by the triumphant construction of *The
Heather Field* how much thought he has given to the matter; but
for the most part our Irish plays read as if they were made without a plan, without a 'scenario', as it is called. European drama
began so, but the European drama had centuries for its growth,
while our art must grow to perfection in a generation or two if it
is not to be smothered before it is well above the earth by what is
merely commercial in the art of England.[11]

Let us learn construction from the masters, and dialogue from
ourselves. A relation of mine has just written me a letter, in which
he says, 'It is natural to an Irishman to write plays; he has an inborn
love of dialogue and sound about him, of a dialogue as lively, gallant, and passionate as in the times of great Eliza. In these days an
Englishman's dialogue is that of an amateur—that is to say, it is never
spontaneous. I mean in *real life.* Compare it with an Irishman's,
above all a poor Irishman's, reckless abandonment and naturalness,

or compare it with the only fragment that has come down to us of
Shakespeare's own conversation'. (He is remembering a passage in,
I think, Ben Jonson's *Underwoods*). 'Petty commerce and puritanism
have brought to the front the wrong type of Englishman; the
lively, joyous, yet tenacious man has transferred himself to Ireland.
We have him and we will keep him unless the combined nonsense
of . . . and . . . and . . . succeed in suffocating him'.[12]

In Dublin the other day I saw a poster advertising a play by a
Miss . . . under the patronage of certain titled people.[13] I had little
hope of finding any reality in it, but I sat out two acts. Its dialogue
was above the average, though the characters were the old rattle-
traps of the stage, the wild Irish girl, and the Irish servant, and the
bowing Frenchman, and the situations had all been squeezed dry
generations ago. One saw everywhere the shadowy mind of a
woman of the Irish upper classes as they have become to-day, but
under it all there was a kind of life, though it was but the life of a
string and a wire. I do not know who Miss . . . is, but I know that
she is young, for I saw her portrait in a weekly paper, and I think
that she is clever enough to make her work of some importance.[14]
If she goes on doing bad work she will make money, perhaps a great
deal of money, but she will do a little harm to her country. If, on
the other hand, she gets into an original relation with life, she will,
perhaps, make no money, and she will certainly have her class
against her.

The Irish upper classes put everything into a money measure.
When any one among them begins to write or paint they ask him,
'How much money have you made?' 'Will it pay?' Or they say, 'If
you do this or that you will make more money'. The poor Irish clerk
or shopboy,* who writes verses or articles in his brief leisure,
writes for the glory of God and of his country; and because his
motive is high, there is not one vulgar thought in the countless little ballad books that have been written from Callanan's day to this.[16]

---

*The mood has gone, with Fenianism and its wild hopes.[15] The National
movement has been commercialised in the last few years. How much real
ideality is but hidden for a time one cannot say. —March 1908.

They are often clumsily written, for they are in English, and if you have not read a great deal, it is difficult to write well in a language which has been long separated from the 'folk-speech'; but they have not a thought a proud and simple man would not have written. The writers were poor men, but they left that money measure to the Irish upper classes. All Irish writers have to choose whether they will write as the upper classes have done, not to express but to exploit this country; or join the intellectual movement which has raised the cry that was heard in Russia in the seventies, the cry, 'To the people'.[17]

Moses was little good to his people until he had killed an Egyptian; and for the most part a writer or public man of the upper classes is useless to this country till he has done something that separates him from his class.[18] We wish to grow peaceful crops, but we must dig our furrows with the sword.

Our plays this year will be produced by Mr. Benson at the Gaiety Theatre on October the 21st, and on some of the succeeding days. They are Dr. Douglas Hyde's *Casadh an tSúgáin,* which is founded on a well-known Irish story of a wandering poet; and *Diarmuid and Grania,* a play in three acts and in prose by Mr. George Moore and myself, which is founded on the most famous of all Irish stories, the story of the lovers whose beds were the cromlechs.[19] The first act of *Diarmuid and Grania* is in the great banqueting hall of Tara, and the second and third are on the slopes of Ben Bulben in Sligo.[20] We do not think there is anything in either play to offend anybody, but we make no promises. We thought our plays inoffensive last year and the year before, but we were accused the one year of sedition, and the other of heresy.[21]

I have called this little collection of writings *Samhain,* the old name for the beginning of winter, because our plays this year are in October, and because our Theatre is coming to an end in its present shape.

SAMHAIN: 1902

The Irish Literary Theatre wound up its three years of experiment last October with *Diarmuid and Grania,* which was played by Mr. Benson's company, Mr. Benson himself playing Diarmuid with poetry and fervour, and *Casadh an tSúgáin,* played by Dr. Hyde and some members of the Gaelic League. *Diarmuid and Grania* drew large audiences, but its version of the legend was a good deal blamed by critics, who knew only the modern text of the story. There are two versions, and the play was fully justified by Irish and Scottish folk-lore, and by certain early Irish texts, which do not see Grania through very friendly eyes. Any critic who is interested in so dead a controversy can look at the folk-tales quoted by Campbell in, I think, *West Highland Superstitions,* and at the fragments translated by Kuno Meyer, at page 458 of Vol. I[†] of *Zeitschrift für Keltische Philologie.*[1] Dr. Hyde's play, on the other hand, pleased everybody, and has been played a good many times in a good many places since. It was the first play in Irish played in a theatre, and did much towards making plays a necessary part in Irish propaganda.[2]

The Irish Literary Theatre has given place to a company of Irish actors. Its committee saw them take up the work all the more gladly because it had not formed them or influenced them. A dramatic society with guarantors and patrons can never have more than a passing use, because it can never be quite free; and it is not successful until it is able to say it is no longer wanted. Amateur actors will perform for *Cumann na nGaedheal*[3] plays chosen by themselves, and written by A. E., by Mr. Cousins, by Mr. Ryan, by Mr. MacGinley, and by myself.[4] These plays will be given at the Antient Concert Rooms at the end of October, but the National Theatrical Company

will repeat their successes with new work in a very little hall they
have hired in Camden Street. If they could afford it they would have
hired some bigger house, but, after all, M. Antoine founded his
Théâtre Libre with a company of amateurs in a hall that only held
three hundred people.[5]

The first work of theirs to get much attention was their performance, last spring, at the invitation of *Inghinidhe na hÉireann,* of
A. E.'s *Deirdre,* and my *Cathleen ni Houlihan.*[6] They had Miss Maud
Gonne's help, and it was a fine thing for so beautiful a woman to
consent to play my poor old Cathleen, and she played with nobility and tragic power. She showed herself as good in tragedy as Dr.
Hyde is in comedy, and stirred a large audience very greatly.[7] The
whole company played well, too, but it was in *Deirdre* that they
interested me most. They showed plenty of inexperience, especially
in the minor characters, but it was the first performance I had seen
since I understood these things in which the actors kept still
enough to give poetical writing its full effect upon the stage. I had
imagined such acting, though I had not seen it, and had once
asked a dramatic company to let me rehearse them in barrels that
they might forget gesture and have their minds free to think of speech
for a while. The barrels, I thought, might be on castors, so that I
could shove them about with a pole when the action required it.
The other day I saw Sarah Bernhardt and De Max in *Phèdre,* and
understood where Mr. Fay, who stage-manages the National Theatrical Company, had gone for his model.*[8] For long periods the
performers would merely stand and pose, and I once counted
twenty-seven quite slowly before anybody on a fairly well-filled stage
moved, as it seemed, so much as an eyelash. The periods of stillness were generally shorter, but I frequently counted seventeen, eigh-
teen, or twenty before there was a movement. I noticed, too, that
the gestures had a rhythmic progression. Sarah Bernhardt would
keep her hands clasped over, let us say, her right breast for some
time, and then move them to the other side, perhaps, lowering her

---

*An illusion, as he himself explained to me. He had never seen *Phèdre.*
The players were quiet and natural, because they did not know what else
to do. They had not learned to go wrong. —March 1908.

chin till it touched her hands, and then, after another long stillness, she would unclasp them and hold one out, and so on, not lowering them till she had exhausted all the gestures of uplifted hands. Through one long scene De Max, who was quite as fine, never lifted his hand above his elbow, and it was only when the emotion came to its climax that he raised it to his breast. Beyond them stood a crowd of white-robed men who never moved at all, and the whole scene had the nobility of Greek sculpture, and an extraordinary reality and intensity. It was the most beautiful thing I had ever seen upon the stage, and made me understand, in a new way, that saying of Goethe's which is understood everywhere but in England, 'Art is art because it is not nature'.[9] Of course, our amateurs were poor and crude beside those great actors, perhaps the greatest in Europe, but they followed them as well as they could, and got an audience of artisans, for the most part, to admire them for doing it. I heard somebody who sat behind me say, 'They have got rid of all the nonsense'.

I thought the costumes and scenery, which were designed by A. E. himself, good, too, though I did not think them simple enough. They were more simple than ordinary stage costumes and scenery, but I would like to see poetical drama, which tries to keep at a distance from daily life that it may keep its emotion untroubled, staged with but two or three colours. The background, especially in small theatres, where its form is broken up and lost when the stage is at all crowded, should, I think, be thought out as one thinks out the background of a portrait. One often needs nothing more than a single colour, with perhaps a few shadowy forms to suggest wood or mountain. Even on a large stage one should leave the description of the poet free to call up the martlet's procreant cradle or what he will.[10] But I have written enough about decorative scenery elsewhere, and will probably lecture on that and like matters before we begin the winter's work.[11]

The performances of *Deirdre* and *Cathleen ni Houlihan*, which will be repeated in the Antient Concert Rooms, drew so many to hear them that great numbers were turned away from the doors of St. Teresa's Hall. Like the plays of the Irish Literary Theatre, they started unexpected discussion. Mr. Standish O'Grady, who had done more than any other to make us know the old legends, wrote in his *All Ireland Review* that old legends could not be staged without danger of 'banishing the soul of the land.' The old Irish had many wives, for instance, and we had best leave their histories to the vagueness of legend. How could uneducated people understand heroes who lived amid such different circumstances? And so we were to 'leave heroic cycles alone, and not to bring them down to the crowd'.[12] A. E. replied in *The United Irishman* with an impassioned letter. 'The old, forgotten music' he writes about in his letter is, I think, that regulated music of speech at which both he and I have been working, though on somewhat different principles.[13] I have been working with Miss Farr and Mr. Arnold Dolmetsch, who has made a psaltery for the purpose, to perfect a music of speech which can be recorded in something like ordinary musical notes; while A. E. has got a musician to record little chants with intervals much smaller than those of modern music.[14]

After the production of these plays the most important Irish dramatic event was, no doubt, the acting of Dr. Hyde's *An Pósadh,* in Galway.[15] Through an accident it had been very badly rehearsed, but his own acting made amends. One could hardly have had a play that grew more out of the life of the people who saw it. There may have been old men in that audience who remembered its hero the poet Raftery, and there was nobody there who had not come from hearing his poems repeated at the Galway Feis. I think from its effect upon the audience that this play, in which the chief Gaelic poet of our time celebrates his forerunner in simplicity, will be better liked in Connacht at any rate than even *Casadh an tSúgáin. His An Tincéir agus an tSidheóg,* acted in Mr. Moore's garden, at the time of the Oireachtas, is a very good play, but is, I think, the least interesting of his plays as literature.[16] His imagination, which is essentially the folk-imagination, needs a looser construction, and probably a more crowded stage. A play that gets its effect by keeping close to one idea reminds us, when it comes from the hands of a folk-poet, of Blake's saying, that 'Improvement makes straight roads, but the crooked roads are the roads of genius'.[17] The idea loses the richness of its own life, while it destroys the wayward life of his mind by bringing it under too stern a law. Nor could charming verses make amends for that second kiss in which there was profanation, and for that abounding black bottle.[18] Did not M. Tribulat Bonhomet discover that one spot of ink would kill a swan?[19]

Among the other plays in Irish acted during the year, Father Dinneen's *Tobar Draoidheachta* is probably the best. He has given up the many scenes of his *Creideamh agus Gorta,* and has written a play in one scene, which, as it can be staged without much trouble, has already been played in several places.[20] One admires its *naïveté* as much as anything else. Father Dinneen, who, no doubt, remembers how Finn mac Cumhal when a child was put in a field to catch hares and keep him out of mischief, has sent the rival lovers of his play, when he wanted them off the scene for a moment, to catch a hare that has crossed the stage.[21] When they return the good lover is carrying it by the heels, and modestly compares it to a lame jackass. One rather likes this bit of nonsense when one comes to it, for in that world of folk-imagination one thing seems as possible as another. On the other hand, there is a moment of beautiful dramatic tact. The lover gets a letter telling of the death of a relative in America, for whom he has no particular affection, and who has left him a fortune. He cannot lament, for that would be insincere, and his first words must not be rejoicing. Father Dinneen has found for him the one beautiful thing he could say, 'It's a lonesome thing death is'. With, perhaps, less beauty than there is in the closing scene of *Creideamh agus Gorta,* the play has more fancy and a more sustained energy.

Father Peter O'Leary has written a play in his usual number of scenes which has not been published, but has been acted amid much Munster enthusiasm. But neither that nor *La an Amadán,* which has also been acted, is likely to have any long life on our country stages.[22] A short play, with many changes of scene, is a nuisance in any theatre, and often an impossibility on our poor little stages. Some kind of play, in English, by Mr. Standish O'Grady, has been acted in the open air in Kilkenny. I have not seen it, and I cannot understand anything by the accounts of it, except that there were magic-lantern slides and actors on horseback, and Mr. Standish

O'Grady as an Elizabethan night-watchman, speaking prologues, and a contented audience of two or three thousand people.[23]

As we do not think that a play can be worth acting and not worth reading, all our plays will be published in time. Some have been printed in *The United Irishman* and *The All Ireland Review*. I have put my *Cathleen ni Houlihan* and a little play by Dr. Hyde into this *Samhain*.[24] Once already this year I have had what somebody has called the noble pleasure of praising, and I can praise this *Lost Saint* with as good a conscience as I had when I wrote of *Cuchulain of Muirthemne*.[25] I would always admire it, but just now, when I have been thinking that literature should return to its old habit of describing desirable things, I am in the mood to be stirred by that old man gathering up food for fowl with his heart full of love, and by those children who are so full of the light-hearted curiosity of childhood, and by that schoolmaster who has mixed prayer with his gentle punishments. It seems natural that so beautiful a prayer as that of the old saint should have come out of a life so full of innocence and peace. One could hardly have thought out the play in English, for those phrases of a traditional simplicity and of a too deliberate prettiness which become part of an old language would have arisen between the mind and the story. We might even have made something as unreal as the sentimental schoolmaster of the Scottish novelist, and how many children who are but literary images would we have had to hunt out of our minds before meeting with those little children?[26] Even if one could have thought it out in English one could not have written it in English, unless perhaps in that dialect which Dr. Hyde had already used in the prose narrative that flows about his *Love Songs of Connacht*.[27]

Dr. Hyde has written a little play about the birth of Christ which has the same beauty and simplicity.[28] These plays remind me of my first reading of *The Love Songs of Connacht*. The prose parts of that book were to me, as they were to many others, the coming of a new power into literature. I find myself now, as I found myself then, grudging to propaganda, to scholarship, to oratory, however necessary, a genius which might in modern Irish or in that idiom of the English-speaking country-people discover a new region for the mind to wander in. In Ireland, where we have so much to prove and to disprove, we are ready to forget that the creation of an emotion of beauty is the only kind of literature that justifies itself. Books of literary propaganda and literary history are merely preparations for the creation or understanding of such an emotion. It is necessary to put so much in order, to clear away so much, to explain so much, that somebody may be moved by a thought or an image that is inexplicable as a wild creature.

I cannot judge the language of his Irish poetry, but it is so rich in poetical thought, when at its best, that it seems to me that if he were to write more he might become to modern Irish what Mistral was to modern Provençal.[29] I wish, too, that he could put away from himself some of the interruptions of that ceaseless propaganda, and find time for the making of translations, loving and leisurely, like those in *Beside the Fire* and *The Love Songs of Connacht*.[30] He has begun to get a little careless lately. Above all I would have him keep to that English idiom of the Irish-thinking people of the west which he has begun to use less often. It is the only good English spoken by any large number of Irish people to-day, and we must found good literature on a living speech. English men of letters found themselves upon the English Bible, where religious thought gets its living speech. Blake, if I remember rightly, copied it out twice, and I remember once finding a few illuminated pages of a new decorated copy that he began in his old age.[31] Byron read it for the sake of style, though I think it did him little good; and Ruskin founded himself in great part upon it. Indeed, we find everywhere signs of a book which is the chief influence in the lives of English children. The translation used in Ireland has not the same literary beauty, and if we are to find anything to take its place we must find it in that idiom of the poor, which mingles so much of the same vocabulary with turns of phrase that have come out of Gaelic.[32] Even Irish writers of considerable powers of thought seem to have no better standard of English than a schoolmaster's ideal of correctness. If their grammar is correct they will write in all the lightness of their hearts about 'keeping in touch', and 'object-lessons', and 'shining examples', and 'running in grooves', and 'flagrant violations' of various things. Yet, as Sainte-Beuve has said, there is nothing immor-

tal except style.³³ One can write well in that country idiom without much thought about one's words; the emotion will bring the
right word itself, for there everything is old and everything alive and
nothing common or threadbare. I recommend to the Intermediate
Board—a body that seems to benefit by advice—a better plan than
any they know for teaching children to write good English. Let every
child in Ireland be set to turn a leading article or a piece of what is
called excellent English, written perhaps by some distinguished
member of the Board, into the idiom of his own countryside. He
will find at once the difference between dead and living words,
between words that meant something years ago and words that have
the only thing that gives literary quality—personality, the breath
of men's mouths. Zola, who is sometimes an admirable critic, has
said that some of the greatest pages in French literature are not even
right in their grammar: 'They are great because they have personality'.³⁴

The habit of writing for the stage, even when it is not country-
people who are the speakers, and of considering what good dialogue
is, will help to increase our feeling for style. Let us get back in everything to the spoken word, even though we have to speak our lyrics
to the psaltery or the harp, for, as A. E. says, we have begun to forget that literature is but recorded speech, and even when we write
with care we have begun 'to write with elaboration what could never
be spoken'.³⁵ But when we go back to speech let us see that it is the
idiom either of those who have rejected, or of those who have never
learned, the base idioms of the newspapers.

Mr. Martyn argued in *The United Irishman* some months ago
that our actors should try to train themselves for the modern
drama of society.³⁶ The acting of plays of heroic life or plays like
Cathleen ni Houlihan, with its speech of the country-people, did
not seem to him a preparation. It is not; but that is as it should be.
Our movement is a return to the people, like the Russian movement
of the early seventies, and the drama of society would but magnify
a condition of life which the country-man and the artisan could but
copy to their hurt.³⁷ The play that is to give them a quite natural
pleasure should tell them either of their own life, or of that life of

poetry where every man can see his own image, because there alone does human nature escape from arbitrary conditions. Plays about drawing-rooms are written for the middle classes of great cities, for the classes who live in drawing-rooms; but if you would ennoble the man of the roads you must write about the roads, or about the people of romance, or about great historical people. We should, of course, play every kind of good play about Ireland that we can get, but romantic and historical plays, and plays about the life of artisans and country-people, are the best worth getting. In time, I think, we can make the poetical play a living dramatic form again, and the training our actors will get from plays of country life, with its unchanging outline, its abundant speech, its extravagance of thought, will help to establish a school of imaginative acting. The play of society, on the other hand, could but train up realistic actors who would do badly, for the most part, what English actors do well, and would, when at all good, drift away to wealthy English theatres. If, on the other hand, we busy ourselves with poetry and the country-man, two things which have always mixed with one another in life as on the stage, we may recover, in the course of years, a lost art which, being an imitation of nothing English, may bring our actors a secure fame and a sufficient livelihood.

SAMHAIN: 1903

I cannot describe the various dramatic adventures of the year with as much detail as I did last year, mainly because the movement has got beyond me. The most important event of the Gaelic Theatre has been the two series of plays produced in the Round Room of the Rotunda by the Gaelic League. Father Dinneen's *Tobar Draoidheachta,* and Dr. Hyde's *An Pósadh,* and a chronicle play about Hugh O'Neill, and, I think, some other plays, were seen by immense audiences.[1] I was not in Ireland for these plays, but a friend tells me that he could only get standing-room one night, and the Round Room must hold about 3000 people. A performance of *Tobar Draoidheachta* I saw there some months before was bad, but I believe there was great improvement, and that the players who came up from somewhere in County Cork to play it at this second series of plays were admirable. The players, too, that brought Dr. Hyde's *An Pósadh* from Ballaghadereen, in County Mayo, where they had been showing it to their neighbours, were also, I am told, careful and natural. The play-writing, always good in dialogue, is still very poor in construction, and I still hear of plays in many scenes, with no scene lasting longer than four or six minutes, and few intervals shorter than nine or ten minutes, which have to be filled up with songs. The Rotunda chronicle play seems to have been rather of this sort, and I suspect that when I get Father Peter O'Leary's *Meadhbh,* a play in five acts produced at Cork, I shall find the masterful old man, in spite of his hatred of English thought, sticking to the Elizabethan form.[2] I wish I could have seen it played last week, for the spread of the Gaelic Theatre in the country is more important than its spread in Dublin, and of all the performances of Gaelic plays in the country during the year I have seen but one—Dr. Hyde's new play, *Cleamhnas,* at Galway Feis. I got there a day late for a play by the Master of Galway Workhouse, but heard that it was well played, and that his dialogue was as good as his construction was bad.³ There is no question, however, about the performance of *Cleamhnas* being the worst I ever saw. I do not blame the acting, which was pleasant and natural, in spite of insufficient rehearsal, but the stage-management. The subject of the play was a match-making. The terms were in debate between two old men in an inner room. An old woman, according to the stage directions, should have listened at the door and reported what she heard to her daughter's suitor, who is outside the window, and to her daughter. There was no window on the stage, and the young man stood close enough to the door to have listened for himself. The door, where she listened, opened now on the inner room, and now on the street, according to the necessities of the play, and the young men who acted the fathers of grown-up children, when they came through the door, were seen to have done nothing to disguise their twenty-five or twenty-six birthdays. There had been only two rehearsals, and the little boy who should have come in laughing at the end came in shouting, 'Ho ho, ha ha', evidently believing that these were Gaelic words he had never heard before.

The only Gaelic performances I have seen during the year have been ill done,† but I have seen them sufficiently well done in other years to believe my friends when they tell me that there have been good performances. *Inghinidhe na hÉireann* is always thorough, and one cannot doubt that the performance of Dr. Hyde's *An Naomh ar Iarraidh,* by the children from its classes, was at least careful. A powerful little play in English against enlisting, by Mr. Colum, was played with it, and afterwards revived, and played with a play about the Royal Visit, also in English.⁴ I have no doubt that we shall see a good many of these political plays during the next two or three years, and it may be even the rise of a more or less permanent company of political players, for the revolutionary clubs will begin to think plays as necessary as the Gaelic League is already thinking them. Nobody can find the same patriotic songs and recitations sung and spoken by the same people, year in year out, anything but mouldy bread. It is possible that the players

who are to produce plays in October for the Samhain festival of
Cumann na nGaedheal may grow into such a company.

Though one welcomes every kind of vigorous life, I am, myself,
most interested in 'The Irish National Theatre Society', which has
no propaganda but that of good art. The little Camden Street Hall
it had taken has been useful for rehearsal alone, for it proved to be
too far away, and too lacking in dressing-rooms for our short
plays, which involve so many changes. Successful performances were
given, however, at Rathmines, and in one or two country places.

Deirdre, by A. E., *The Racing Lug,* by Mr. Cousins, *The Foundations,*[5] by Mr. Ryan, and my *Pot of Broth*[†] and *Cathleen ni
Houlihan* were repeated, but no new plays were produced until
March 14, when Lady Gregory's *Twenty-five* and my *Hour-Glass*
drew a good audience. On May 2 *The Hour-Glass, Twenty-five,
Cathleen ni Houlihan, Pot of Broth,* and *Foundations* were performed before the Irish Literary Society in London, at the Queen's
Gate Hall, and plays and players were generously commended by
the Press—very eloquently by the critic of *The Times.*[6] It is natural
that we should be pleased with this praise, and that we should wish
others to know of it, for is it not a chief pleasure of the artist to
be commended in subtle and eloquent words? The critic of *The
Times* has seen many theatres and he is, perhaps, a little weary of
them, but here in Ireland there are one or two critics who are so
much in love, or pretend to be so much in love, with the theatre as
it is, that they complain when we perform on a stage two feet wider
than Molière's that it is scarce possible to be interested in anything
that is played on so little a stage.[7] We are to them foolish sectaries
who have revolted against that orthodoxy of the commercial theatre which is so much less pliant than the orthodoxy of the
Church, for there is nothing so passionate as a vested interest dis-
guised as an intellectual conviction. If you inquire into its truth it
becomes as angry as a begging-letter writer when you find some
hole in that beautiful story about the five children and the broken
mangle. In Ireland, wherever the enthusiasts are shaping life, the
critic who does the will of the commercial theatre can but stand
against his lonely pillar defending his articles of belief among a wild

people, and thinking mournfully of distant cities, where nobody puts a raw potato into his pocket when he is going to hear a musical comedy.

The Irish Literary Society of New York, which has been founded this year, produced *The Land of Heart's Desire, The Pot of Broth,* and *Cathleen ni Houlihan,* on June 3 and 4, very successfully, and propose to give Dr. Hyde's Nativity Play, *Dráma Breite Críosta,* and his *Casadh an tSúgáin, An Pósadh,* and *An Naomh ar Iarraidh* next year, at the same time of year, playing them both in Irish and English. I heard too that his Nativity Play will be performed in New York, but I know no particulars except that it will be done in connection with some religious societies. The National Theatre Society will, I hope, produce some new plays of his this winter, as well as new plays by Mr. Synge, Mr. Colum, Lady Gregory, myself, and others.[8] They have taken the Molesworth Hall for three days in every month, beginning with the 8th, 9th, and 10th of October, when they will perform Mr. Synge's *Shadow of the Glen,* a little country comedy, full of a humour that is at once harsh and beautiful, *Cathleen ni Houlihan,* and a longish one-act play in verse of my own, called *The King's Threshold.* This play is founded on the old story of Seanchan the poet, and King Guaire of Gort, but I have seen the story from the poet's point of view, and not, like the old story-tellers, from the king's.[9] Our repertory of plays is increasing steadily, and when the winter's work is finished, a play* Mr. Bernard Shaw has promised us may be ready to open the summer session. His play will, I imagine, unlike the plays we write for ourselves, be long enough to fill an evening, and it will, I know, deal with Irish public life and character. Mr. Shaw, more than anybody else, has the love of mischief that is so near the core of Irish intellect, and should have an immense popularity among us. I have seen a crowd of many thousands in possession of his spirit, and keeping the possession to the small hours.

---

*This play was *John Bull's Other Island.* When it came out in the spring of 1905 we felt ourselves unable to cast it without wronging Mr. Shaw. We had no 'Broadbent' or money to get one. —March 1908.[10]

This movement should be important even to those who are not especially interested in the Theatre, for it may be a morning cockcrow to that impartial meditation about character and destiny we call the artistic life in a country where everybody, if we leave out the peasant who has his folk-songs and his music, has thought the arts useless unless they have helped some kind of political action, and has, therefore, lacked the pure joy that only comes out of things that have never been indentured to any cause. The play which is mere propaganda shows its leanness more obviously than a propagandist poem or essay, for dramatic writing is so full of the stuff of daily life that a little falsehood, put in that the moral may come right in the end, contradicts our experience. If Father Dinneen or Dr. Hyde were asked why they write their plays, they would say they write them to help their propaganda; and yet when they begin to write the form constrains them, and they become artists—one of them a very considerable artist, indeed. Dr. Hyde's early poems have even in translation a *naïveté* and wildness that sets them, as I think, among the finest poetry of our time; but he had ceased to write any verses but those Oireachtas odes that are but ingenious rhetoric.[11] It is hard to write without the sympathy of one's friends, and though the country-people sang his verses the readers of Irish read them but little, partly it may be because he had broken with that elaborate structure of later Irish poetry which seemed a necessary part of their propaganda. They read plenty of pamphlets and grammars, but they disliked—as do other people in Ireland—serious reading, reading that is an end and not a means, that gives us nothing but a beauty indifferent to our profuse purposes. But now Dr. Hyde with his cursing Hanrahan, his old saint at his prayers, is a poet again; and the Leaguers go to his plays in thousands—and applaud in the right places, too—and the League puts many sixpences into its pocket.[12]

We who write in English have a more difficult work, for English has been the language in which the Irish cause has been debated; and we have to struggle with traditional phrases and traditional points of view. Many would give us limitless freedom as to the choice of subject, understanding that it is precisely those subjects on which people feel most passionately, and, therefore, most dramatically, we would be forbidden to handle if we made any compromise with powers. But fewer know that we must encourage every

writer to see life afresh, even though he sees it with strange eyes.
Our National Theatre must be so tolerant, and, if this is not too
wild a hope, find an audience so tolerant, that the half-dozen
minds who are likely to be the dramatic imagination of Ireland for
this generation may put their own thoughts and their own characters into their work; and for that reason no one who loves the arts,
whether among Unionists or among the Patriotic Societies, should
take offence if we refuse all but every kind of patronage. I do not
say every kind, for if a mad king, a king so mad that he loved the
arts and their freedom, should offer us unconditioned millions, I,
at any rate, would give my voice for accepting them.

We will be able to find conscientious playwrights and players,
for our young men have a power of work, when they are interested
in their work, one does not look for outside a Latin nation, and if
we are certain of being granted this freedom we would be certain
that the work would grow to great importance. It is a supreme
moment in the life of a nation when it is able to turn now and again
from its preoccupations, to delight in the capricious power of the
artist as one delights in the movement of some wild creature, but
nobody can tell with certainty when that moment is at hand.

The two plays in this year's *Samhain* represent the two sides
of the movement very well, and are both written out of a deep
knowledge of the life of the people. It should be unnecessary to
praise Dr. Hyde's comedy,* that comes up out of the foundation
of human life, but Mr. Synge is a new writer and a creation of our
movement. He has gone every summer for some years past to the
Aran Islands, and lived there in the houses of the fishers, speaking
their language and living their lives, and his play** seems to me
the finest piece of tragic work done in Ireland of late years. One
finds in it, from first to last, the presence of the sea, and a sorrow
that has majesty as in the work of some ancient poet.[13]

The Poorhouse, written in Irish by Dr. Hyde on a scenario by Lady Gregory. —March 1908.
**Riders to the Sea.* This play made its way very slowly with our audi-
ences, but is now very popular. —March 1908.

THE REFORM OF THE THEATRE

I think the theatre must be reformed in its plays, its speaking, its acting, and its scenery. That is to say, I think there is nothing good about it at present.[1]

First. We have to write or find plays that will make the theatre a place of intellectual excitement—a place where the mind goes to be liberated as it was liberated by the theatres of Greece and England and France at certain great moments of their history, and as it is liberated in Scandinavia to-day. If we are to do this we must learn that beauty and truth are always justified of themselves, and that their creation is a greater service to our country than writing that compromises either in the seeming service of a cause. We will, doubtless, come more easily to truth and beauty because we love some cause with all but all our heart; but we must remember when truth and beauty open their mouths to speak, that all other mouths should be as silent as Finn bade the Son of Lugaid be in the houses of the great.[2] Truth and beauty judge and are above judgment. They justify and have no need of justification.

Such plays will require, both in writers and audiences, a stronger feeling for beautiful and appropriate language than one finds in the ordinary theatre. Sainte-Beuve has said that there is nothing immortal in literature except style, and it is precisely this sense of style, once common among us, that is hardest for us to recover.[3] I do not mean by style words with an air of literature about them, what is ordinarily called eloquent writing. The speeches of Falstaff are as perfect in their style as the soliloquies of Hamlet.[4] One must be able to make a king of Faery† or an old country-man or a modern lover speak that language which is his and nobody else's, and

26

speak it with so much of emotional subtlety that the hearer may find it hard to know whether it is the thought or the word that has moved him, or whether these could be separated at all.

If we do not know how to construct, if we cannot arrange much complicated life into a single action, our work will not hold the attention or linger in the memory, but if we are not in love with words it will lack the delicate movement of living speech that is the chief garment of life; and because of this lack the great realists seem to the lovers of beautiful art to be wise in this generation, and for the next generation, perhaps, but not for all generations that are to come.

Second. But if we are to restore words to their sovereignty we must make speech even more important than gesture upon the stage.

I have been told that I desire a monotonous chant, but that is not true, for though a monotonous chant may be a safer beginning for an actor than the broken and prosaic speech of ordinary recitation, it puts me to sleep none the less. The sing-song in which a child says a verse is a right beginning, though the child grows out of it. An actor should understand how so to discriminate cadence from cadence, and so to cherish the musical lineaments of verse or prose that he delights the ear with a continually varied music. Certain passages of lyrical feeling, or where one wishes, as in the Angel's part in *The Hour-Glass,* to make a voice sound like the voice of an immortal, may be spoken upon pure notes which are carefully recorded and learned as if they were the notes of a song. Whatever method one adopts, one must always be certain that the work of art, as a whole, is masculine and intellectual, in its sound as in its form.

Third. We must simplify acting, especially in poetical drama, and in prose drama that is remote from real life like my *Hour-Glass.* We must get rid of everything that is restless, everything that draws the attention away from the sound of the voice, or from the few moments of intense expression, whether that expression is through the voice or through the hands; we must from time to time substitute for the movements that the eye sees the nobler movements that the heart sees, the rhythmical movements that seem to flow up into the imagination from some deeper life than that of the individual soul.

Fourth. Just as it is necessary to simplify gesture that it may accompany speech without being its rival, it is necessary to simplify both the form and colour of scenery and costume. As a rule the background should be but a single colour, so that the persons in the play, wherever they stand, may harmonise with it and preoccupy our attention. In other words, it should be thought out not as one thinks out a landscape, but as if it were the background of a portrait, and this is especially necessary on a small stage where the moment the stage is filled the painted forms of the background are broken up and lost. Even when one has to represent trees or hills they should be treated in most cases decoratively, they should be little more than an unobtrusive pattern. There must be nothing unnecessary, nothing that will distract the attention from speech and movement. An art is always at its greatest when it is most human. Greek acting was great because it did all but everything with the voice, and modern acting may be great when it does everything with voice and movement. But an art which smothers these things with bad painting, with innumerable garish colours, with continual restless mimicries of the surface of life, is an art of fading humanity, a decaying art.

SAMHAIN: 1903—
MORAL AND IMMORAL PLAYS

A writer in *The Leader* has said that I told my audience after the performance of *The Hour-Glass* that I did not care whether a play was moral or immoral.[1] He said this without discourtesy, and as I have noticed that people are generally discourteous when they write about morals, I think that I owe him upon my part the courtesy of an explanation. I did not say that I did not care whether a play was moral or immoral, for I have always been of Verhaeren's opinion that a masterpiece is a portion of the conscience of mankind.[2] My objection was to the rough-and-ready conscience of the newspaper and the pulpit in a matter so delicate and so difficult as literature. Every generation of men of letters has been called immoral by the pulpit or the newspaper, and it has been precisely when that generation has been illuminating some obscure corner of the conscience that the cry against it has been more confident.

The plays of Shakespeare had to be performed on the south side of the Thames because the Corporation of London considered all plays immoral. Goethe was thought dangerous to faith and morals for two or three generations. Every educated man knows how great a portion of the conscience of mankind is in Flaubert and Balzac, and yet their books have been proscribed in the courts of law, and I found some time ago that our own National Library, though it had two books on the genius of Flaubert, had refused on moral grounds to have any books written by him. With these stupidities in one's memory, how can one, as many would have us, arouse the mob, and in this matter the pulpit and the newspaper are but voices of the mob, against the English theatre in Ireland upon moral grounds? If that theatre became conscientious as men of letters understand the conscience, many that now cry against it would think it even less moral, for it would be more daring, more logical, more free-spoken. The English theatre is demoralising, not because it delights in the husband, the wife, and the lover, a subject which has inspired great literature in most ages of the world, but because the illogical thinking and insincere feeling we call bad writing make the mind timid and the heart effeminate. I saw an English play in Dublin a few months ago called *Mice and Men*. It had run for five hundred nights in London, and been called by all the newspapers 'a pure and innocent play', 'a welcome relief', and so on.[3] In it occurred this incident: The typical scapegrace hero of the stage, a young soldier, who is in love with the wife of another, goes away for a couple of years, and when he returns finds that he is in love with a marriageable girl. His mistress, who has awaited his return with what is represented as faithful love, sends him a letter of welcome, and because he has grown virtuous of a sudden he returns it unopened, and with so careless a scorn that the husband intercepts it; and the dramatist approves this manner of crying off with an old love, and rings down the curtain on his marriage bells. Men who would turn out of their club a man who could so treat a letter from his mistress bring their wives and daughters to admire him upon the stage, so demoralising is a drama that has no intellectual tradition behind it. I could not endure it, and went out into the street and waited there until the end of the play, when I came in again to find the friends I had brought to hear it, but had I been accustomed to the commercial theatre I would not even have known that anything strange had happened upon the stage. If a man of intellect had written of such an incident he would have made his audience feel for the mistress that sympathy one feels for all that have suffered insult, and for that young man an ironical emotion that might have marred the marriage bells, and who knows what the curate and the journalist would have said of the man of intellect? Even Ireland would have cried out: Catholic Ireland that should remember the gracious tolerance of the Church when all nations were its children, and how Wolfram of Eschenbach sang from castle to castle of the courtesy of Parsival, the good husband, and of Gawain, the light lover, in that very Thuringia where a generation later the lap of S. Elizabeth was full of roses.[4] A Connacht

Bishop told his people a while since that they 'should never read stories about the degrading passion of love,' and one can only suppose that, being ignorant of a chief glory of his Church, he has never understood that this new puritanism is but an English cuckoo.[5]

SAMHAIN: 1903 —
AN IRISH NATIONAL THEATRE

[The performance of Mr. Synge's *Shadow of the Glen* started a quarrel with the extreme national party, and the following paragraphs are from letters written in the play's defence.[1] The organ of the party was at the time *The United Irishman,* but the first serious attack began in *The Independent. The United Irishman,* however, took up the quarrel, and from that on has attacked almost every play produced at our theatre, and the suspicion it managed to arouse among the political clubs against Mr. Synge especially led a few years later to the organised attempt to drive *The Playboy of the Western World* from the stage. —March 1908.]

When we were all fighting about the selection of books for the New Irish Library some ten years ago, we had to discuss the question, What is National Poetry?[2] In those days a patriotic young man would have thought but poorly of himself if he did not believe that *The Spirit of the Nation* was great lyric poetry, and a much finer kind of poetry than Shelley's 'Ode to the West Wind', or Keats's 'Ode on a Grecian Urn'.[3] When two or three of us denied this, we were told that we had effeminate tastes or that we were putting Ireland in a bad light before her enemies. If one said that *The Spirit of the Nation* was but salutary rhetoric, England might overhear us and take up the cry. We said it, and who will say that Irish literature has not a greater name in the world to-day than it had ten years ago?

To-day there is another question that we must make up our minds about, and an even more pressing one, What is a National Theatre? A man may write a book of lyrics if he have but a friend or two that will care for them, but he cannot write a good play if there are not audiences to listen to it. If we think that a national play must be as near as possible a page out of *The Spirit of the Nation* put into dramatic form, and mean to go on thinking it to the end, then we may be sure that this generation will not see the rise in Ireland of a theatre that will reflect the life of Ireland as the Scandinavian theatre reflects the Scandinavian life. The brazen head has an unexpected way of falling to pieces. We have a company of admirable and disinterested players, and the next few months will, in all likelihood, decide whether a great work for this country is to be accomplished. The poetry of Young Ireland, when it was an attempt to change or strengthen opinion, was rhetoric; but it became poetry when patriotism was transformed into a personal emotion by the events of life, as in that lamentation written by Doheny 'on his keeping' among the hills.[4] Literature is always personal, always one man's vision of the world, one man's experience, and it can only be popular when men are ready to welcome the visions of others. A community that is opinion-ridden, even when those opinions are in themselves noble, is likely to put its creative minds into some sort of a prison. If creative minds preoccupy themselves with incidents from the political history of Ireland, so much the better, but we must not enforce them to select those incidents. If, in the sincere working-out of their plot, they alight on a moral that is obviously and directly serviceable to the National cause, so much the better, but we must not force that moral upon them. I am a Nationalist, and certain of my intimate friends have made Irish politics the business of their lives, and this made certain thoughts habitual with me, and an accident made these thoughts take fire in such a way that I could give them dramatic expression. I had a very vivid dream one night, and I made *Cathleen ni Houlihan* out of this dream. But if some external necessity had forced me to write nothing but drama with an obviously patriotic intention, instead of letting my work shape itself under the casual impulses of dreams and daily thoughts, I would have lost, in a short time, the power to write movingly upon any theme. I could have aroused opinion; but I could not have touched the heart, for I would have been busy at the oakum-picking that is not the less mere journalism for being in dramatic form. Above all, we must not say that certain incidents which have been a part of literature in all other lands are forbidden to us. It may be our duty, as it has been the duty of many dramatic movements, to bring new kinds of subjects into the theatre, but it cannot be our duty to make the bounds of drama narrower. For instance, we are told that the English theatre is immoral, because it is preoccupied with the husband, the wife, and the lover. It is, perhaps, too exclusively preoccupied with that subject, and it is certain it has not shed any new light upon it for a considerable time, but a subject that inspired Homer and about half the great literature of the world will, one doubts not, be a necessity to our National Theatre also. Literature is, to my mind, the great teaching power of the world, the ultimate creator of all values, and it is this, not only in the sacred books whose power everybody acknowledges, but by every movement of imagination in song or story or drama that height of intensity and sincerity has made literature at all. Literature must take the responsibility of its power, and keep all its freedom: it must be like the spirit and like the wind that blows where it listeth;[5] it must claim its right to pierce through every crevice of human nature, and to describe the relation of the soul and the heart to the facts of life and of law, and to describe that relation as it is, not as we would have it be; and in so far as it fails to do this it fails to give us that foundation of understanding and charity for whose lack our moral sense can be but cruelty. It must be as incapable of telling a lie as Nature, and it must sometimes say before all the virtues, 'The greatest of these is charity'.[6] Sometimes the patriot will have to falter and the wife to desert her home, and neither be followed by divine vengeance or man's judgment. At other moments it must be content to judge without remorse, compelled by nothing but its own capricious spirit that has yet its message from the foundation of the world. Aristophanes held up the people of Athens to ridicule, and even prouder of that spirit than of themselves, they invited the foreign ambassadors to the spectacle.

I would sooner our theatre failed through the indifference or hostility of our audiences than gained an immense popularity by any loss of freedom. I ask nothing that my masters have not asked for, but I ask all that they were given. I ask no help that would limit our freedom from either official or patriotic hands, though I am glad of the help of any who love the arts so dearly that they would not bring them into even honourable captivity. A good Nationalist is, I suppose, one who is ready to give up a great deal that he may preserve to his country whatever part of her possessions he is best fitted to guard, and that theatre where the capricious spirit that bloweth as it listeth has for a moment found a dwelling-place, has good right to call itself a National Theatre.

SAMHAIN: 1903 —
THE THEATRE, THE PULPIT,
AND THE NEWSPAPERS

I was very well content when I read an unmeasured attack in *The Independent* on the Irish National Theatre.[1] There had, as yet, been no performance, but the attack was confident, and it was evident that the writer's ears were full of rumours and whisperings. One knew that some such attack was inevitable, for every dramatic movement that brought any new power into literature arose among precisely these misunderstandings and animosities. Drama, the most immediately powerful form of literature, the most vivid image of life, finds itself opposed, as no other form of literature does, to those enemies of life, the chimeras of the Pulpit and the Press. When a country has not begun to care for literature, or has forgotten the taste for it, and most modern countries seem to pass through this stage, these chimeras are hatched in every basket. Certain generalisations are everywhere substituted for life. Instead of individual men and women and living virtues differing as one star differeth from another in glory, the public imagination is full of personified averages, partisan fictions, rules of life that would drill everybody into the one posture, habits that are like the pinafores of charity-school children. The priest, trained to keep his mind on the strength of his Church and the weakness of his congregation, would have all mankind painted with a halo or with horns. Literature is nothing to him, he has to remember that Seaghan the Fool might take to drinking again if he knew of pleasant Falstaff, and that Paudeen might run after Red Sarah again if some strange chance put Plutarch's tale of Antony or Shakespeare's play into his hands, and he is in a hurry to shut out of the schools that Pandora's box, *The Golden Treasury*.[2] The newspaper he reads of a morning has not only the haloes and horns of the vestry, but it has crowns and fools' caps of its own. Life, which in its essence is always surprising, always taking some new shape, always individualising, is nothing to it, it has to move men in squads, to keep them in uniform, with their faces to the right enemy, and enough hate in their hearts to make the muskets go off. It may know its business well, but its business is building and ours is shattering. We cannot linger very long in this great dim temple where the wooden images sit all round upon thrones, and where the worshippers kneel, not knowing whether they tremble because their gods are dead or because they fear they may be alive. In the idol-house every god, every demon, every virtue, every vice, has been given its permanent form, its hundred hands, its elephant trunk, its monkey head. The man of letters looks at those kneeling worshippers who have given up life for a posture, whose nerves have dried up in the contemplation of lifeless wood. He swings his silver hammer and the keepers of the temple cry out, prophesying evil, but he must not mind their cries and their prophecies, but break the wooden necks in two and throw down the wooden bodies. Life will put living bodies in their place till new image-brokers have set up their benches.

Whenever literature becomes powerful, the priest, whose forerunner imagined S. Patrick driving his chariot-wheels over his own erring sister, has to acknowledge, or to see others acknowledge, that there is no evil that men and women may not be driven into by their virtues all but as readily as by their vices, and the politician, that it is not always clean hands that serve a country or foul hands that ruin it.[3] He may even have to say at last, as an old man who had spent many years in prison to serve a good cause said to me, 'There never was a cause so evil that it has not been served by good men for what seemed to them sufficient reasons'.[4] And if the priest or the politician should say to the man of letters, 'Into how dangerous a state of mind are you not bringing us?' the man of letters can but answer, 'It is dangerous, indeed', and say, like my Seanchan, 'When did we promise safety?'[5]

Thought takes the same form age after age, and the things that people have said to me about this intellectual movement of ours have, I doubt not, been said in every country to every writer who was a disturber of the old life. When *The Countess Cathleen* was produced, the very girls in the shops complained to us that to describe an Irishwoman as selling her soul to the devil was to slander the country. The silver hammer had threatened, as it seems, one of those personifications of an average. Someone said to me a couple of weeks ago, 'If you put on the stage any play about marriage that does not point its moral clearly, you will make it difficult for us to go on attacking the English theatre for its immorality'.[6] Again, we were disordering the squads, the muskets might not all point in the same direction.

Now that these opinions have found a leader and a voice in *The Independent,* it is easy at any rate to explain how much one differs from them. I had spoken of the capricious power of the artist and compared it to the capricious movements of a wild creature, and *The Independent,* speaking quite logically from its point of view, tells me that these movements were only interesting when 'under restraint'. The writers of the Anglo-Irish movement, it says, 'will never consent to serve except on terms that never could or should be conceded'. I had spoken of the production of foreign masterpieces, but it considers that foreign masterpieces would be very dangerous. I had asked in *Samhain* for audiences sufficiently tolerant to enable the half-dozen minds who are likely to be the dramatic imagination of Ireland for this generation to put their own thought and their own characters into their work.[7] That is to say, I had asked for the amount of freedom which every nation has given to its dramatic writers. But the newspaper hopes and believes that no 'such tolerance will be extended to Mr. Yeats and his friends'.

I have written these lines to explain our thoughts and intentions to many personal friends, who live too deep in the labour of politics to give the thought to these things that we have given, and because not only in our theatre, but in all matters of national life, we have need of a new discovery of life—of more precise thought, of a more perfect sincerity. I would see, in every branch of our National propaganda, young men who would have the sincerity and the precision of those Russian revolutionists that Kropotkin and Stepniak tell us of, men who would never use an argument to convince others which would not convince themselves, who would not make a mob drunk with a passion they could not share, and who would above all seek for fine things for their own sake, and for precise knowledge for its own sake, and not for its momentary use.[8] One can serve one's country alone out of the abundance of one's own heart, and it is labour enough to be certain one is in the right, without having to be certain that one's thought is expedient also.

SAMHAIN: 1904—
THE DRAMATIC MOVEMENT

The National Theatre Society has had great difficulties because of the lack of any suitable playhouse. It has been forced to perform in halls without proper lighting for the stage, and almost without dressing-rooms, and with level floors in the auditorium that prevented all but the people in the front row from seeing properly. These halls are expensive too, and the players of poetical drama in an age of musical comedy have light pockets. But now a generous English friend, Miss Horniman, has rearranged and in part rebuilt, at very considerable expense, the old Mechanics' Institute Theatre, now the Abbey Theatre, and given us the use of it without any charge, and I need not say that she has gained our gratitude, as she will gain the gratitude of our audience.[1] The work of decoration and alteration has been done by Irishmen, and everything, with the exception of some few things that are not made here, or not of a good enough quality, has been manufactured in Ireland. The stained glass in the entrance hall is the work of Miss Sarah Purser and her apprentices, the large copper mirror-frames are from the new metal works at Youghal, and the pictures of some of our players are by an Irish artist.[2] These details and some details of form and colour in the building, as a whole, have been arranged by Miss Horniman herself.

Having been given the free use of this theatre, we may look upon ourselves as the first endowed theatre in any English-speaking country, the English-speaking countries and Venezuela being the only countries which have never endowed their theatres; but the correspondents who write for parts in our plays or posts in the Theatre at a salary are in error. We are, and must be for some time to come, contented to find our work its own reward, the player giving* his work, and the playwright his, for nothing; and though this cannot go on always, we start our winter very cheerfully with a capital of some forty pounds. We playwrights can only thank these players, who have given us the delight of seeing our work so well performed, working with so much enthusiasm, with so much patience, that they have found for themselves a lasting place among the artists, the only aristocracy that has never been sold in the market or seen the people rise up against it.

It is a necessary part of our plan to find out how to perform plays for little money, for it is certain that every increase in expenditure has lowered the quality of dramatic art itself, by robbing the dramatist of freedom in experiment, and by withdrawing attention from his words and from the work of the players. Sometimes one friend or another has helped us with costumes or scenery, but the expense has never been very great, ten or twenty pounds being enough in most cases for quite a long play. These friends have all accepted the principles I have explained from time to time in *Samhain,* but they have interpreted them in various ways according to their temperament.

Miss Horniman staged *The King's Threshold* at her own expense, and she both designed and made the costumes. The costumes for the coming performances of *On Baile's Strand* are also her work and her gift and her design. She made and paid for the costumes in *The Shadowy Waters,* but in this case followed a colour-scheme of mine. The colour-scheme in *The Hour-Glass,* our first experiment, was worked out by Mr. Robert Gregory and myself, and the costumes were made by Miss Lavelle, a member of the company; while Mr. Robert Gregory has designed the costumes and scenery for *Kincora.*³ As we gradually accumulate costumes in all the main colours and shades, we will be able to get new effects by combin-

---

*The players, though not the playwrights, are now all paid. —March 1908. The playwrights have, for a good many years now, drawn the usual royalties. —1923.

ing them in different ways without buying new ones. Small dramatic societies, and our example is beginning to create a number, not having so many friends as we have, might adopt a simpler plan, suggested to us by a very famous decorative artist.[4] Let them have one suit of clothes for a king, another for a queen, another for a fighting-man, another for a messenger, and so on, and if these clothes are loose enough to fit different people, they can perform any romantic play that comes without new cost. The audience would soon get used to this way of symbolising, as it were, the different ranks and classes of men, and as the king would wear, no matter what the play might be, the same crown and robe, they could have them very fine in the end. Now, one wealthy theatre-goer and now another might add a pearl to the queen's necklace, or a jewel to her crown, and be the more regular in attendance at the theatre because that gift shone out there like a good deed.

We can hardly do all we hope unless there are many more of these little societies to be centres of dramatic art and of the allied arts. But a very few actors went from town to town in ancient Greece, finding everywhere more or less well-trained singers among the principal townsmen to sing the chorus that had otherwise been the chief expense. In the days of the stock companies two or three well-known actors would go from town to town finding actors for all the minor parts in the local companies. If we are to push our work into the small towns and villages, local dramatic clubs must take the place of the old stock companies. A good-sized town should be able to give us a large enough audience for our whole, or nearly our whole, company to go there; but the need for us is greater in those small towns where the poorest kind of farce and melodrama have gone and Shakespearean drama has not gone, and it is here that we will find it hardest to get intelligent audiences. If a dramatic club existed in one of the larger towns near, they could supply us not only with actors, should we need them, in their own town, but with actors when we went to the small towns and to the villages where the novelty of any kind of drama would make success certain. These clubs would play in Gaelic far better than we can hope to, for they would have native Gaelic speakers, and should we succeed in stirring the imagination of the people enough to keep the rivalry between plays in English and Irish to a rivalry in quality, the certain development of two schools with distinct though very kindred ideals would increase the energy and compass of our art.

At a time when drama was more vital than at present, unpaid actors, and actors with very little training, have influenced it deeply. The Mystery Plays and the Miracle Plays got their players at no great distance from the church door, and the classic drama of France had for a forerunner performances of Greek and Latin Classics, given by students and people of quality, and even at its height Racine wrote two of his most famous tragedies to be played by young girls at school.[5] This was before acting had got so far away from our natural instincts of expression. When the play is in verse, or in rhythmical prose, it does not gain by the change, and a company of amateurs, if they love literature, and are not self-conscious, and really do desire to do well, can often make a better hand of it than the ordinary professional company.

The greater number of their plays will, in all likelihood, be comedies of Irish country life, and here they need not fear competition, for they will know an Irish country-man as no professional can know him; but whatever they play, they will have one advantage the English amateur has not: there is in their blood a natural capacity for acting, and they have never, like him, become the mimics of well-known actors. The arts have always lost something of their sap when they have been cut off from the people as a whole; and when the theatre is perfectly alive, the audience, as at the Gaelic drama to-day in Gaelic-speaking districts, feels itself to be almost a part of the play. I have never felt that the dignity of art was imperilled when the audience at Dr. Hyde's *An Pósadh* cheered the bag of flour or the ham lent by some local shopkeepers to increase the bridal gifts. It was not merely because of its position in the play that the Greek chorus represented the people, and the old ballad-singers[†] waited at the end of every verse till their audience had taken up the chorus; while Ritual, the most powerful form of drama, differs from the ordinary form, because every one who hears it is also a player. Our modern theatre, with the seats always growing more expensive, and its dramatic art drifting always from the living impulse of life, and becoming more and more what Rossetti would have called 'soulless self-reflections of man's skill', no longer gives pleasure to any imaginative mind.[6] It is easy for us to hate England in this country, and we give that hatred something of nobility if we turn it now and again into hatred of the vulgarity of commercial syndicates, of all that commercial finish and pseudo-art she has done so much to cherish. Mr. Standish O'Grady has quoted somebody as saying, 'The passions must be held in reverence, they must not, they cannot be excited at will', and the noble using of that old hatred will win for us sympathy and attention from all artists and people of good taste, and from those of England more than anywhere, for there is the need greatest.[7]

Before this part of our work can be begun, it will be necessary to create a household of living art in Dublin, with principles that have become habits, and a public that has learnt to care for a play because it is a play, and not because it is serviceable to some cause. Our patent is not so wide* as we had hoped for, for we had hoped to have a patent as little restricted as that of the Gaiety or the Theatre Royal. We were, however, vigorously opposed by these theatres and by the Queen's Theatre, and the Solicitor-General, to meet them half-way, has restricted our patent to plays written by Irishmen or on Irish subjects or to foreign masterpieces, provided these masterpieces are not English. This has been done to make our competition against the existing theatres as unimportant as possible. It does not directly interfere with the work of our society to any serious extent, but it would have indirectly helped our work had such bodies as the Elizabethan Stage Society, which brought *Everyman* to Dublin some years ago, been able to hire the theatre from Miss Horniman, when it is not wanted by us, and to perform there without the limitations imposed by a special licence.[8]

Everything that creates a theatrical audience is an advantage to us, and the small number of seats in our theatre would have kept away that kind of drama, in whatever language, which spoils an audience for good work.[9]

The enquiry itself was not a little surprising, for the legal representatives of the theatres, being the representatives of Musical

---

*Our patent has been widened since. —1923.

Comedy, were very anxious for the morals of the town. I had spoken of the Independent Theatre, and a lawyer wanted to know if a play of mine which attacked the institution of marriage had not been performed by it recently. I had spoken of M. Maeterlinck and of his indebtedness to a theatre somewhat similar to our own, and one of our witnesses, who knew no more about it than the questioner, was asked if a play by M. Maeterlinck called *L'Intruse* had not been so immoral that it was received with a cry of horror in London. I have written no play about marriage, and the Independent Theatre died some twelve years ago, and *L'Intruse* might be played in a nursery with no worse effects than a little depression of spirits.[10] Our opponents, having thus protested against our morals, went home with the fees of Musical Comedy in their pockets.

For all this, we are better off so far as the law is concerned than we would be in England. The theatrical law of Ireland was made by the Irish Parliament, and though the patent system, the usual method of the time, has outlived its use and come to an end everywhere but in Ireland, we must be grateful to that ruling caste of free spirits, that being free themselves they left the theatre in freedom. In England there is a censor, who forbids you to take a subject from the Bible, or from politics, or to picture public characters, or certain moral situations which are the foundation of some of the greatest plays of the world. When I was at the great American Catholic University of Notre Dame I heard that the students had given a performance of *Oedipus the King,* and *Oedipus the King* is forbidden in London.[11] A censorship created in the eighteenth century by Walpole, because somebody had written against election bribery, has been distorted by a puritanism which is not the less an English invention for being a pretended hatred of vice and a real hatred of intellect.[12] Nothing has ever suffered so many persecutions as the intellect, though it is never persecuted under its own name. It is but according to old usage when a law that cherishes Musical Comedy and permits to every second melodrama the central situation of *The Sign of the Cross,* attempted rape, becomes one of the secondary causes of the separation of the English theatre from life.[13] It does not interfere with anything that makes money, and Musical Com-

edy, with its hints and innuendoes, and its consistently low view of
life, makes a great deal, for money is always respectable; but
would a group of artists and students see once again the masterpieces of the world, they would have to hide from the law as if they
had been a school of thieves; or were we to take with us to London that beautiful Nativity Play of Dr. Hyde's, which was performed
in Sligo Convent a few months ago, that holy vision of the central
story of the world, as it is seen through the minds and the traditions of the poor, the constables might upset the cradle.[14] And yet
it is precisely these stories of the Bible that have all to themselves,
in the imagination of English people, especially of the English
poor, the place they share in this country with the stories of Finn
and of Oisin and of Patrick.[15]

Milton set the story of Samson into the form of a Greek play,
because he knew that Samson was, in the English imagination, what
Herakles was in the imagination of Greece; and I have never been
able to see any other subjects for an English dramatist who looked
for some common ground between his own mind and simpler
minds.[16] An English poet of genius once told me that he would have
tried his hand in plays for the people, if they knew any story the
censor would pass, except Jack and the Beanstalk.[17]

The Gaelic League has its great dramatic opportunity because
of the abundance of stories known in Irish-speaking districts, and
because of the freedom of choice and of treatment the leaders of a
popular movement can have if they have a mind for it. The Gaelic
plays acted and published during the year selected their subjects
from the popular mind, but the treatment is disappointing. Dr.
Hyde, dragged from gathering to gathering by the necessities of the
movement, has written no new play; and Father Peter O'Leary has
thrown his dramatic power, which is remarkable, into an imaginative novel. Father Dinneen has published a little play that has
some lifelike dialogue, but the action is sometimes irrelevant, and
the motives of the principal character are vague and confused, as
if it were written in a hurry.[18] Father Dinneen seems to know that
he has not done his best, for he describes it as an attempt to provide more vivid dialogue for beginners than is to be found in the
reading-books rather than a drama. An anonymous writer has

written a play called *The Money of the Narrow Cross,* which tells
a very simple tale, like that of a child's book, simply and adequately.
It is very slight, in low relief as it were, but if its writer is a young
man it has considerable promise.[19]

A play called *Seaghán na Scuab* was described in *The United
Irishman* as the best play ever written in Irish; but though the subject of it is a dramatic old folk-tale, which has shown its vigour by
rooting itself in many countries, the treatment is confused and
conventional and there is a flatness of dialogue unusual in these
plays.[20] There is, however, an occasional sense of comic situation
which may come to something if its writer will work seriously at
his craft. One is afraid of quenching the smoking flax, but this play
was selected for performance at the Oireachtas before a vast audience in the Rotunda. It was accompanied by *The Doctor* in English and Irish, written by Mr. O'Beirne, and performed by the
Tawin players, who brought it from their seaside village in Galway.[21]
Mr. O'Beirne deserves the greatest praise for getting this company
together, as well as for all he has done to give the Tawin people a
new pleasure in their language; but I think a day will come when
he will not be grateful to the Oireachtas Committee for bringing
this first crude work of his into the midst of so many thousand people. It would be very hard for a much more experienced dramatist
to make anything out of the ugly violence, the threadbare, second-
hand imaginations that flow in upon a man out of the newspapers,
when he has founded his work on proselytising zeal, instead of his
experience of life and his curiosity about it. These two were the only
plays, out of a number that have been played in Irish, that I have
seen this year. I went to Galway Feis, like many others, to see Dr.
Hyde's *Lost Saint,* for I had missed every performance of it hitherto though I had read it to many audiences in America, and I
awaited the evening with some little excitement. Although the
Lost Saint was on the programme, an Anti-Emigration play was put
in its place.[22] I did not wait for this, but, whatever its merits, it is
not likely to have contained anything so beautiful as the old man's
prayer in the other: 'O Lord, O God, take pity on this little soft child.
Put wisdom in his head, cleanse his heart, scatter the mist from his
mind and let him learn his lessons like the other boys. O Lord, Thou

wert Thyself young one time; take pity on youth. O Lord, Thou, Thyself, shed tears; dry the tears of this little lad. Listen, O Lord, to the prayer of Thy servant, and do not keep from him this little thing he is asking of Thee. O Lord, bitter are the tears of a child, sweeten them: deep are the thoughts of a child, quiet them: sharp is the grief of a child, take it from him: soft is the heart of a child, do not harden it'.[23]

A certain number of propagandist plays are unavoidable in a popular movement like the Gaelic revival, but they may drive out everything else. The plays, while Father Peter O'Leary and Father Dinneen and Dr. Hyde were the most popular writers and the chief influence, were full of the traditional folk-feeling that is the mastering influence in all old Irish literature. Father O'Leary chose for his subjects a traditional story of a trick played upon a simple villager, a sheep-stealer frightened by what seemed to him a ghost, the quarrels between Maeve and Ailell of Cruachan; Father Dinneen chose for his a religious crisis, alive as with the very soul of tragedy, or a well sacred to the faeries; while Dr. Hyde celebrated old story-tellers and poets, and old saints, and the Mother of God with the countenance she wears in Irish eyes.[24] Hundreds of men scattered through the world, angry at the spectacle of modern vulgarity, rejoiced in this movement, for it seemed impossible for anything begun in so high a spirit, so inspired by whatever is ancient, or simple, or noble, to sink into the common base level of our thought. This year one has heard little of the fine work, and a great deal about plays that get an easy cheer, because they make no discoveries in human nature, but repeat the opinions of the audience, or the satire of its favourite newspapers. I am only speaking of the plays of a year, and that is but a short period in what one hopes may be a great movement, but it is not wise to say, as do many Gaelic Leaguers, who know the weaknesses of their movement, that if the present thinks but of grammar and propaganda the future will do all the rest. A movement will often in its first fire of enthusiasm create more works of genius than whole easy-going centuries that come after it.

Nearly everything that is greatest as English prose was written in a generation or two after the first beautiful use of prose in England: and Mistral has made the poems of modern Provence, as well as reviving and all but inventing the language: for genius is more often of the spring than of the middle green of the year. We cannot settle times and seasons, flowering-time and harvest-time are not in our hands, but we are to blame if genius comes and we do not gather in the fruit or the blossom. Very often we can do no more for the man of genius than to distract him as little as may be with the common business of the day. His own work is more laborious than any other, for not only is thought harder than action, as Goethe said, but he must brood over his work so long and so unbrokenly that he find there all his patriotism, all his passion, his religion even—it is not only those that sweep a floor that are obedient to Heaven—until at last he can cry with Paracelsus, 'In this crust of bread I have found all the stars and all the heavens'.[25]

The following new plays were produced by the National Theatre Society during the last twelve months: *The Shadow of the Glen* and *Riders to the Sea,* by Mr. J. M. Synge; *Broken Soil,* by Mr. Colm*; *The Townland of Tamney,* by Mr. Seumas MacManus; *The Shadowy Waters* and *The King's Threshold,* by myself. The following plays were revived: *Deirdre,* by A. E.; *Twenty-five,* by Lady Gregory; *Cathleen ni Houlihan, The Pot of Broth,* and *The Hour-Glass,* by myself. We could have given more plays, but difficulties about the place of performance, the shifting of scenery from where we rehearsed to where we acted, and so on, always brought a great deal of labour upon the Society. The Society went to London in March and gave two performances at the Royalty to full houses. They played there Mr. Synge's two plays, Mr. Colm's play, and my *King's Threshold* and *Pot of Broth.* We were commended by the critics with generous sympathy, and had an enthusiastic and distinguished audience.[26]

We have many plays awaiting performance during the coming winter. Mr. Synge has written us a play in three acts called *The Well of the Saints,* full, as few works of our time are, with temperament, and of a true and yet bizarre beauty. Lady Gregory has written us an historical tragedy in three acts about King Brian and a very merry

*This distinguished writer now spells his name Colum. —1923.

comedy of country life.[27] Mr. Bernard Shaw has written us a play*
in four acts, his first experiment in Irish satire; Mr. Tarpey, an Irishman whose comedy *Windmills* was successfully performed by the
Stage Society some years ago, a little play which I have not yet seen;
and Mr. Boyle, a village comedy in three acts; and I hear of other
plays by competent hands that are coming to us.[28] My own *On
Baile's Strand* is in rehearsal, and I hope to have ready for the spring
a play on the subject of *Deirdre,* with choruses somewhat in the
Greek manner. We are, of course, offered from all parts of the world
great quantities of plays which are impossible for literary or dramatic reasons. Some of them have a look of having been written
for the commercial theatre and of having been sent to us on rejection. It will save trouble if I point out that a play which seems
to its writer to promise an ordinary London or New York success
is very unlikely to please us, or succeed with our audience if it did.
Writers who have a better ambition should get some mastery of their
art in little plays before spending many months of what is almost
sure to be wasted labour on several acts.

We were invited to play in the St. Louis Exhibition, but thought
that our work should be in Ireland for the present, and had other
reasons for refusing.[29]
    A Company, which has been formed in America by Miss Wych-
erley, who played in *Everyman* during a part of its tour in America, to take some of our plays on tour, has begun with three
one-act plays of mine, *Cathleen ni Houlihan, The Hour-Glass,* and
The Land of Heart's Desire. It announces on its circulars that it is
following the methods of our Theatre.[30]
    Though the commercial theatre of America is as unashamedly
commercial as the English, there is a far larger audience interested
in fine drama than here. When I was lecturing in, I think, Philadel-
phia—one town mixes with another in my memory at times—some
one told me that he had seen *The Duchess of Malfi* played there
by one of the old stock companies in his boyhood; and *Everyman*
has been far more of a success in America than anywhere else.[31]
They have numberless University towns each with its own character

John Bull's Other Island. —March 1908.

and with an academic life animated by a zeal and by an imagination unknown in these countries. There is nearly everywhere that leaven of highly-cultivated men and women so much more necessary to a good theatrical audience to-day than were ever Ralegh and Sidney, when the groundling could remember the folk-songs and the imaginative folk-life.[32] The more an age is busy with temporary things, the more must it look for leadership in matters of art to men and women whose business or whose leisure has made the great writers of the world their habitual company. Literature is not journalism because it can turn the imagination to whatever is essential and unchanging in life.

SAMHAIN: 1904—
FIRST PRINCIPLES

Two Irish writers had a controversy a month ago, and they accused one another of being unable to think, with entire sincerity, though it was obvious to uncommitted minds that neither had any lack of vigorous thought. But they had a different meaning when they spoke of thought, for the one, though in actual life he is the most practical man I know, meant thought as Pascal, as Montaigne, as Shakespeare, or as, let us say, Emerson, understood it—a reverie about the adventures of the soul, or of the personality, or some obstinate questioning of the riddle. Many who have to work hard always make time for this reverie, but it comes more easily to the leisured, and in this it is like a broken heart, which is, a Dublin newspaper assured us lately, impossible to a busy man. The other writer had in mind, when he spoke of thought, the shaping energy that keeps us busy, and the obstinate questionings he had most respect for were, how to change the method of government, how to change the language, how to revive our manufactures, and whether it is the Protestant or the Catholic that scowls at the other with the darker scowl. Ireland is so poor, so misgoverned, that a great portion of the imagination of the land must give itself to a very passionate consideration of questions like these, and yet it is precisely these loud questions that drive away the reveries that incline the imagination to the lasting work of literature and give, together with religion, sweetness, and nobility, and dignity to life. We should desire no more from these propagandist thinkers than that they carry out their work, as far as possible, without making it more difficult for those fitted by Nature or by circumstance for another kind of thought to do their work also; and certainly it is not well that Martha chide at Mary, for they have the One Master over them.[1]

When one all but despairs, as one does at times, of Ireland welcoming a National Literature in this generation, it is because we do not leave ourselves enough of time, or of quiet, to be interested in men and women. A writer in *The Leader,* who is unknown to me, elaborates this argument in an article full of beauty and dignity. He is speaking of our injustice to one another, and he says that we are driven into injustice 'not wantonly but inevitably, and at call of the exacting qualities of the great things. Until this latter dawning, the genius of Ireland has been too preoccupied really to concern itself about men and women; in its drama they play a subordinate part, born tragic comedians though all the sons and daughters of the land are. A nation is the heroic theme we follow, a mourning, wasted land its moving spirit; the impersonal assumes personality for us'.[2] When I wrote my *Countess Cathleen,* I thought, of course, chiefly of the actual picture that was forming before me, but there was a secondary meaning that came into my mind continuously. 'It is the soul of one that loves Ireland', I thought, 'plunging into unrest, seeming to lose itself, to bargain itself away to the very wickedness of the world, and to surrender what is eternal for what is temporary', and I know that this meaning seemed natural to others, for that great orator, J. F. Taylor, who was not likely to have searched very deeply into any work of mine, for he cared little for mine, or, indeed, any modern work, turned the play into such a parable in one of his speeches.[3]

There is no use being angry with necessary conditions, or failing to see that a man who is busy with some reform that can only be carried out in a flame of energetic feeling, will not only be indifferent to what seems to us the finer kind of thinking, but that he will support himself by generalisations that seem untrue to the man of letters. A little play, *The Rising of the Moon,* which is in the present number of *Samhain,* and is among those we are to produce during the winter, has, for instance, roused the suspicions of a very resolute leader of the people, who has a keen eye for rats behind the arras. A Fenian ballad-singer partly converts a policeman, and is it not unwise under any circumstances to show a policeman in so favourable a light? It is well known that many of the younger policemen were Fenians: but it is necessary that the Dublin crowds should be kept of so high a heart that they will fight the police at any moment. Are not morals greater than literature?[4] Others have objected to Mr. Synge's *Shadow of the Glen* because Irish women, being more chaste than those of England and Scotland, are a valuable part of our national argument. Mr. Synge should not, it is said by some, have chosen an exception for the subject of his play, for who knows but the English may misunderstand him? Some even deny that such a thing could happen at all, while others that know the country better, or remember the statistics, say that it could but should never have been staged. All these arguments, by their methods, even more than by what they have tried to prove, misunderstand how literature does its work. Men of letters have sometimes said that the characters of a romance or of a play must be typical. They mean that the character must be typical of something which exists in all men because the writer has found it in his own mind. It is one of the most inexplicable things about human nature that a writer, with a strange temperament, an Edgar Allan Poe, let us say, made what he is by conditions that never existed before, can create personages and lyric emotions, which startle us by being at once bizarre and an image of our own secret thoughts. Are we not face to face with the microcosm, mirroring everything in universal nature? It is no more necessary for the characters created by a romance writer, or a dramatist, to have existed before, than for his own personality to have done so; characters and personality alike, as is perhaps true in the instance of Poe, may draw half their life not from the solid earth but from some dreamy drug. This is true even of historical drama, for it was Goethe, the founder of the historical drama of Germany, who said, 'We do the people of history the honour of naming after them the creations of our own minds'.[5] All that a dramatic writer need do is to persuade us, during the two hours' traffic of the stage, that the events of his play did really happen. He must know enough of the life of his country, or of history, to create this illusion, but no matter how much he knows, he will fail if his audience is not ready to give up something of the dead letter. If his mind is full of energy he will not be satisfied with little knowledge, but he will be far more likely to alter incidents and characters, wilfully even as it may seem, than to become a literal historian. It was one of the complaints against Shakespeare, in his own day, that he made Sir John Falstaff out of a praiseworthy old Lollard preacher.[6] One day, as he sat over Holinshed's *History of England,* he persuaded himself that Richard the Second, with his French culture, 'his too great friendliness to his friends', his beauty of mind, and his fall before dry, repelling Bolingbroke, would be a good image for an accustomed mood of fanciful, impracticable lyricism in his own mind.[7] The historical Richard has passed away for ever and the Richard of the play lives more intensely, it seems, than did ever living man. Yet Richard the Second, as Shakespeare made him, could never have been born before the Renaissance, before the Italian influence, or even one hour before the innumerable streams that flowed in upon Shakespeare's mind,[†] the innumerable experiences we can never know, brought Shakespeare to the making of him. He is typical not because he ever existed, but because he has made us know of something in our own minds we had never known of had he never been imagined.

Our propagandists have twisted this theory of the men of letters into its direct contrary, and when they say that a writer should make typical characters they mean personifications of averages, of statistics, or even personified opinions, or men and women so faintly imagined that there is nothing about them to separate them from the crowd, as it appears to our hasty eyes. We must feel that we could engage a hundred others to wear the same livery as easily as we could engage a coachman. We must never forget that we are engaging them to be the ideal young peasant, or the true patriot, or the happy Irish wife, or the policeman of our prejudices, or to express some other of those invaluable generalisations, without which our practical movements would lose their energy. Who is there that likes a coachman to be too full of human nature, when he has his livery on? No one man is like another, but one coachman should be as like another as possible, though he may assert himself a little when he meets the gardener. The patriots would impose on us heroes and heroines, like those young couples in the Gaelic plays, who might all change brides or bridegrooms in the dance and never find out the difference. The personifications need not be true even, if they are about our enemy, for it might be more difficult to fight out our necessary fight if we remembered his virtue at wrong moments; and might not Teigue and Bocach, that are light in the head, go over to his party?

Ireland is indeed poor, is indeed hunted by misfortune, and has indeed to give up much that makes life desirable and lovely, but is she so very poor that she can afford no better literature than this? Perhaps so, but if it is a Spirit from beyond the world that decides when a nation shall awake into imaginative energy, and no philosopher has ever found what brings the moment, it cannot be for us to judge. It may be coming upon us now, for it is certain that we have more writers who are thinking, as men of letters understand thought, than we have had for a century, and he who wilfully makes their work harder may be setting himself against the purpose of that Spirit.

I would not be trying to form an Irish National Theatre if I did not believe that there existed in Ireland, whether in the minds of a few people or of a great number I do not know, an energy of thought about life itself, a vivid sensitiveness as to the reality of things, powerful enough to overcome all those phantoms of the night. Everything calls up its contrary, unreality calls up reality, and, besides, life here has been sufficiently perilous to make men think. I do not think it a national prejudice that makes me believe we are harder, a more masterful race than the comfortable English of our time, and that this comes from an essential nearness to reality of those few scattered people who have the right to call themselves the Irish race. It is only in the exceptions, in the few minds, where the flame has burnt as it were pure, that one can see the permanent character of a race. If one remembers the men who have dominated Ireland for the last hundred and fifty years, one understands that it is strength of personality, the individualising quality in a man, that stirs Irish imagination most deeply in the end. There is scarcely a man who has led the Irish people, at any time, who may not give some day to a great writer precisely that symbol he may require for the expression of himself. The critical mind of Ireland is far more subjugated than the critical mind of England by the phantoms and misapprehensions of politics and social necessity, but the life of Ireland has rejected them more resolutely. Indeed, it is in life itself in England that one finds the dominion of what is not human life.

We have no longer in any country a literature as great as the literature of the old world, and that is because the newspapers, all kinds of second-rate books, the preoccupation of men with all kinds of practical changes, have driven the living imagination out of the world. I have read hardly any books this summer but Cervantes and Boccaccio and some Greek plays. I have felt that these men, divided from one another by so many hundreds of years, had the same mind. It is we who are different; and then the thought would come to me, that has come to me so often before, that they lived at times when the imagination turned to life itself for excitement. The world was not changing quickly about them. There was nothing to draw their imagination from the ripening of the fields, from the birth and death of their children, from the destiny of their souls, from all that is the unchanging substance of literature. They had not to deal with the world in such great masses that it could only be represented to their minds by figures and by abstract generalisations. Everything that their minds ran on came on them vivid with the colour of the senses, and when they wrote it was out of their own rich experience, and they found their symbols of expression in things that they had known all their life long. Their very words were more vigorous than ours, for their phrases came from a common mint, from the market, or the tavern, or from the great poets of a still older time. It is the change that followed the Renaissance, and was completed by newspaper government and the scientific movement, that has brought upon us all these phrases and generalisations, made by minds that would grasp what they have never seen. Yesterday I went out to see the reddening apples in the garden, and they faded from my imagination sooner than they would have from the imagination of that old poet who made the songs of the seasons for the Fianna, or out of Chaucer's, that celebrated so many trees.[8] Theories, opinions, these opinions among the rest, flowed in upon me and blotted them away. Even our greatest poets see the world with preoccupied minds. Great as Shelley is, those theories about the coming changes of the world, which he has built up with so much elaborate passion, hurry him from life continually. There is a phrase in some old cabalistic writer about man falling into his own circumference, and every generation we get further away from life itself, and come more and more under the influence which Blake had in his mind when he said, 'Kings and Parliament seem to me something other than human life'.[9] We lose our freedom more and more as we get away from ourselves, and not merely because our minds are overthrown by abstract phrases and generalisations, reflections in a mirror that seem living, but because we have turned the table of value upside down, and believe that the root of reality is not in the centre but somewhere in that whirling circumference. How can we create like the ancients, while innumerable considerations of external probability or social utility destroy the seeming irresponsible creative power that is life itself? Who to-day could set Richmond's and Richard's tents side by side on the battlefield, or make Don Quixote, mad as he was, mistake a windmill for a giant in broad daylight?[10] And when I think of free-spoken Falstaff I know of no audience, but the tinkers of the roadside, that could encourage the artist to an equal comedy. The old writers were content if their inventions had but an emotional and moral consistency, and created out of themselves a fantastic, energetic, extravagant art. A civilisation is very like a man or a woman, for it comes in but a few years into its beauty, and its strength, and then, while many years go by, it gathers and makes order about it, the strength and beauty going out of it the while, until in the end it lies there with its limbs straightened out and a clean linen cloth folded upon it. That may well be, and yet we need not follow among the mourners, for it may be, before they are at the tomb, a messenger will run out of the hills and touch the pale lips with a red ember, and wake the limbs to the disorder and the tumult that is life. Though he does not come, even so we will keep from among the mourners and hold some cheerful conversation among ourselves; for has not Virgil, a knowledgeable man and a wizard, foretold that other Argonauts shall row between cliff and cliff, and other fair-haired Achaeans sack another Troy?[11]

Every argument carries us backwards to some religious conception, and in the end the creative energy of men depends upon their believing that they have, within themselves, something immortal and imperishable, and that all else is but as an image in a looking-glass. So long as that belief is not a formal thing, a man will create out of a joyful energy, seeking little for any external test of an impulse that may be sacred, and looking for no foundation outside life itself. If Ireland could escape from those phantoms of hers she might create, as did the old writers; for she has a faith that is as theirs, and keeps alive in the Gaelic traditions—and this has always seemed to me the chief intellectual value of Gaelic—a portion of the old imaginative life. When Dr. Hyde or Father Peter O'Leary is the writer, one's imagination goes straight to the century of Cervantes, and, having gone so far, one thinks at every moment that they will discover his energy. It is precisely because of this reason that one is indignant with those who would substitute for the ideas of the folk-life the rhetoric of the newspapers, who would muddy what had begun to seem a fountain of life with the feet of the mob. Is it impossible to revive Irish and yet to leave the finer intellects a sufficient mastery over the more gross, to prevent it from becoming, it may be, the language of a Nation, and yet losing all that has made it worthy of a revival, all that has made it a new energy in the mind?

Before the modern movement, and while it was but new, the ordinary man, whether he could read and write or not, was ready to welcome great literature. When Ariosto found himself among the brigands, they repeated to him his own verses, and the audience in the Elizabethan theatres must have been all but as clever as an Athenian audience.[12] But to-day we come to understand great literature by a long preparation, or by some accident of nature, for we only begin to understand life when our minds have been purified of temporary interests by study.

But if literature has no external test, how are we to know that it is indeed literature? The only test that nature gives, to show when we obey her, is that she gives us happiness, and when we are no longer obedient she brings us to pain sooner or later. Is it not the same with the artist? The sign that she makes to him is that happiness we call delight in beauty. He can only convey this in its highest form after he has purified his mind with the great writers of the world; but their example can never be more than a preparation. If his art does not seem, when it comes, to be the creation of a new personality, in a few years it will not seem to be alive at all. If he is a dramatist his characters must have a like newness. If they could have existed before his day, or have been imagined before his day, we may be certain that the spirit of life is not in them in its fullness. This is because art, in its highest moments, is not a deliberate creation, but the creation of intense feeling, of pure life; and every feeling is the child of all past ages and would be different if even a moment had been left out. Indeed, is it not that delight in beauty which tells the artist that he has imagined what may never die, itself but a delight in the permanent yet ever-changing form of life, in her very limbs and lineaments? When life has given it, has she given anything but herself? Has she any other reward, even for the saints? If one flies to the wilderness, is not that clear light that falls about the soul when all irrelevant things have been taken away, but life that has been about one always, enjoyed in all its fullness at length? It is as though she had put her arms about one, crying, 'My beloved, you have given up everything for me'. If a man spend all his days in good works till there is no emotion in his heart that is not full of virtue, is not the reward he prays for eternal life? The artist, too, has prayers and a cloister, and if he do not turn away from temporary things, from the zeal of the reformer and the passion of revolution, that zealous mistress will give him but a scornful glance.

What attracts me to drama is that it is, in the most obvious way, what all the arts are upon a last analysis. A farce and a tragedy are alike in this, that they are a moment of intense life. An action is taken out of all other actions; it is reduced to its simplest form, or at any rate to as simple a form as it can be brought to without our losing the sense of its place in the world. The characters that are involved in it are freed from everything that is not a part of that action; and whether it is, as in the less important kinds of drama, a mere bodily activity, a hair-breadth escape or the like, or as it is in the more important kinds, an activity of the souls of the characters, it is an energy, an eddy of life purified from everything but itself. The dramatist must picture life in action, with an unpreoccupied mind, as the musician pictures her in sound and the sculptor in form.

But if this be true, has art nothing to do with moral judgments? Surely it has, and its judgments are those from which there is no appeal. The character, whose fortune we have been called in to see, or the personality of the writer, must keep our sympathy, and whether it be farce or tragedy, we must laugh and weep with him and call down blessings on his head. This character who delights us may commit murder like Macbeth, or fly the battle for his sweetheart as did Antony, or betray his country like Coriolanus, and yet we will rejoice in every happiness that comes to him and sorrow at his death as if it were our own.[13] It is no use telling us that the murderer and the betrayer do not deserve our sympathy. We thought so yesterday, and we still know what crime is, but everything has been changed of a sudden; we are caught up into another code, we are in the presence of a higher court. Complain of us if you will, but it will be useless, for before the curtain falls a thousand ages, grown conscious in our sympathies, will have cried *Absolvo te.*[14] Blame if you will the codes, the philosophies, the experiences of all past ages that have made us what we are, as the soil under our feet has been made out of unknown vegetations: quarrel with the acorns of Eden if you will, but what has that to do with us? We understand the verdict and not the law; and yet there is some law, some code, some judgment. If the poet's hand had slipped, if Antony had railed at Cleopatra in the tower, if Coriolanus had abated that high pride of his in the presence of death, we might have gone away muttering the Ten Commandments.[15] Yet maybe we are wrong to speak of judgment, for we have but contemplated life, and what more is there to say when she that is all virtue, the gift and the giver, the fountain whither all flows again, has given all herself? If the subject of drama or any other art were a man himself, an eddy of momentary breath, we might desire the contemplation of perfect characters; but the subject of all art is passion, and a passion can only be contemplated when separated by itself, purified of all but itself, and aroused into a perfect intensity by opposition with some other passion, or it may be with the law, that is the expression of the whole whether of Church or Nation or external

Nature. Had Coriolanus not been a law-breaker, neither he nor we had ever discovered, it may be, that noble pride of his, and if we had not seen Cleopatra through the eyes of so many lovers, would we have known that soul of hers to be all flame, and wept at the quenching of it? If we were not certain of law we would not feel the struggle, the drama, but the subject of art is not law, which is a kind of death, but the praise of life, and it has no commandments that are not positive.

But if literature does not draw its substance from history, or anything about us in the world, what is a National literature? Our friends have already told us, writers for the Theatre in Abbey Street, that we have no right to the name, some because we do not write in Irish, and others because we do not plead the National cause in our plays, as if we were writers for the newspapers. I have not asked my fellow-workers what they mean by the words National literature, but though I have no great love for definitions, I would define it in some such way as this: It is the work of writers who are moulded by influences that are moulding their country, and who write out of so deep a life that they are accepted there in the end. It leaves a good deal unsettled—was Rossetti an Englishman, or Swift an Irishman?—but it covers more kinds of National literature than any other I can think of.[16] If you say a National literature must be in the language of the country, there are many difficulties. Should it be written in the language that your country does speak or the language that it ought to speak? Was Milton an Englishman when he wrote in Latin or Italian, and had we no part in Columbanus when he wrote in Latin the beautiful sermon comparing life to a highway and to a smoke?[17] And then there is Beckford, who is in every history of English literature, and yet his one memorable book, a story of Persia, was written in French.[18]

Our theatre is of no great size, for though we know that if we write well we shall find acceptance among our countrymen in the end, we would think our emotions were on the surface if we found a ready welcome. Edgar Allan Poe and Walt Whitman are National writers of America, although the one had his first true acceptance in France and the other in England and Ireland. When

I was a boy, six persons, who, alone out of the whole world, it may be, believed Walt Whitman a great writer, sent him a message of admiration, and of those names four were English and two Irish, my father's and Professor[†] Dowden's.[19] It is only in our own day that America has begun to prefer him to Lowell, who is not a poet at all.[20]

I mean by deep life that men must put into their writing the emotions and experiences that have been most important to themselves. If they say, 'I will write of Irish country-people and make them charming and picturesque like those dear peasants my great-grandmother used to put in the foreground of her water-colour paintings', then they had better be satisfied with the word 'provincial'. If one condescends to one's material, if it is only what a popular novelist would call local colour, it is certain that one's real soul is somewhere else. Mr. Synge, upon the other hand, who is able to express his own finest emotions in those curious ironical plays of his, where, for all that, by the illusion of admirable art, every one seems to be thinking and feeling as only country-men could think and feel, is truly a National writer, as Burns was when he wrote finely and as Burns was not when he wrote 'Highland Mary' and 'The Cotter's Saturday Night'.[21]

A writer is not less National because he shows the influence of other countries and of the great writers of the world. No nation, since the beginning of history, has ever drawn all its life out of itself. Even The Well of English Undefiled, the Father of English Poetry himself, borrowed his metres, and much of his way of looking at the world, from French writers, and it is possible that the influence of Italy was more powerful among the Elizabethan poets than any literary influence out of England herself.[22] Many years ago, when I was contending with Sir Charles Gavan Duffy over what seemed to me a too narrow definition of Irish interests, Professor York Powell either said or wrote to me that the creative power of England was always at its greatest when her receptive power was greatest.[23] If Ireland is about to produce a literature that is important to her, it must be the result of the influences that flow in upon the mind of an educated Irishman to-day, and, in a greater degree, of what came into the world with himself. Gaelic can hardly fail to do a portion of the work, but one cannot say whether it may not be some French or German writer who will do most to make him an articulate man. If he really achieve the miracle, if he really make all that he has seen and felt and known a portion of his own intense nature, if he put it all into the fire of his energy, he need not fear being a stranger among his own people in the end. There never have been men more unlike an Englishman's idea of himself than Keats and Shelley, while Campbell, whose emotion came out of a shallow well, was very like that idea.[24] We call certain minds creative because they are among the moulders of their nation and are not made upon its mould, and they resemble one another in this only—they have never been foreknown or fulfilled an expectation.

It is sometimes necessary to follow in practical matters some definition which one knows to have but a passing use. We, for instance, have always confined ourselves to plays upon Irish subjects, as if no others could be National literature. Our theatre inherits this limitation from previous movements, which found it necessary and fruitful. Goldsmith and Sheridan and Burke had become so much a part of English life, were so greatly moulded by the movements that were moulding England, that, despite certain Irish elements that clung about them, we could not think of them as more important to us than any English writer of equal rank.[25] Men told us that we should keep our hold of them, as it were, for they were a part of our glory; but we did not consider our glory very important. We had no desire to turn braggarts, and we did suspect the motives of our advisers. Perhaps they had reasons, which were not altogether literary, for thinking it might be well if Irishmen of letters, in our day also, would turn their faces to England. But what moved me always the most, and I had something to do with forcing this limitation upon our organisations, is that a new language of expression would help to awaken a new attitude in writers themselves, and that if our organisations were satisfied to interpret a writer to his own countrymen merely because he was of Irish birth, the organisations would become a kind of trade union for the helping of Irishmen to catch the ear of London publishers and managers, and for upholding writers who had been beaten by abler Englishmen. Let a man turn his face to us, accepting the commercial disadvantages that would bring upon him, and talk of what is near to our hearts, Irish Kings and Irish Legends and Irish Country-men, and we would find it a joy to interpret him. Our one philosophical critic, Mr. John Eglinton, thinks we were very arbitrary, and yet I would not have us enlarge our practice.[26] England and France, almost alone among nations, have great works of literature which have taken their subjects from foreign lands, and even in France and England this is more true in appearance than reality. Shakespeare observed his Roman crowds in London, and saw, one doubts not, somewhere in his own Stratford, the old man that gave Cleopatra the asp. Somebody I have been reading lately finds the Court of Louis the Fourteenth in *Phèdre* and *Andromaque*.[27] Even in France and England almost the whole prose fiction professes to describe the life of the country, often of the districts where its writers have lived, for, unlike a poem, a novel requires so much minute observation of the surface of life that a novelist who cares for the illusion of reality will keep to familiar things. A writer will indeed take what is most creative out of himself, not from observation, but experience, yet he must master a definite language, a definite symbolism of incident and scene. Flaubert explains the comparative failure of his Salammbô by saying, 'One cannot frequent her'. He could create her soul, as it were, but he could not tell with certainty how it would express itself before Carthage fell to ruins.[28] In the small nations which have to struggle for their National life, one finds that almost every creator, whether poet or novelist, sets all his stories in his own country. I do not recollect that Björnson ever wrote of any land but Norway, and Ibsen, though he lived in exile for many years, driven out by his countrymen, as he believed, carried the little seaboard towns of Norway everywhere in his imagination.[29] So far as we can be certain of anything, we may be certain that Ireland with her long National struggle, her old literature, her unbounded folk-imagination, will, in so far as her literature is National at all, be more like Norway than England or France.

If literature is but praise of life, if our writers are not to plead the National Cause, nor insist upon the Ten Commandments, nor upon the glory of their country, what part remains for it, in the common life of the country? It will influence the life of the country immeasurably more, though seemingly less, than have our propagandist poems and stories. It will leave to others the defence of all that can be codified for ready understanding, of whatever is the especial business of sermons, and of leading articles; but it will bring all the ways of men before that ancient tribunal of our sympathies. It will measure all things by the measure not of things visible but of things invisible. In a country like Ireland, where personifications have taken the place of life, men have more hate than love, for the unhuman is nearly the same as the inhuman, but literature, which is a part of that charity that is the forgiveness of sins, will make us understand men no matter how little they conform to our expectations. We will be more interested in heroic men than in heroic actions, and will have a little distrust for everything that can be called good or bad in itself with a very confident heart. Could we understand it so well, we will say, if it were not something other than human life? We will have a scale of virtues, and value most highly those that approach the indefinable. Men will be born among us of whom it is possible to say, not 'What a philanthropist', 'What a patriot', 'How practical a man', but, as we say of the men of the Renaissance, 'What a nature', 'How much abundant life'. Even at the beginning we will value qualities more than actions, for these may be habit or accident; and should we say to a friend, 'You have advertised for an English cook', or 'I hear that you have no clerks who are not of your own faith', or 'You have voted an address to the king', we will add to our complaint, 'You have been unpatriotic and I am ashamed of you, but if you cease from doing any of these things because you have been terrorised out of them, you will cease to be my friend'. We will not forget how to be stern, but we will remember always that the highest life unites, as in one fire, the greatest passion and the greatest courtesy.

A feeling for the form of life, for the graciousness of life, for the dignity of life, for the moving limbs of life, for the nobleness of life, for all that cannot be written in codes, has always been greatest among the gifts of literature to mankind. Indeed, the Muses being women, all literature is but their love-cries to the manhood of the world. It is now one and now another that cries, but the words are the same: 'Love of my heart, what matter to me that you have been quarrelsome in your cups, and have slain many, and have given your love here and there? It was because of the whiteness of your flesh and the mastery in your hands that I gave you my love, when all life came to me in your coming'. And then in a low voice that none may overhear: 'Alas! I am greatly afraid that the more they cry against you the more I love you'.

There are two kinds of poetry, and they are commingled in all the greatest works. When the tide of life sinks low there are pictures, as in the 'Ode on a Grecian Urn' and in Virgil at the plucking of the Golden Bough.[30] The pictures make us sorrowful. We share the poet's separation from what he describes. It is life in the mirror, and our desire for it is as the desire of the lost souls for God; but when Lucifer stands among his friends, when Villon sings his dead ladies to so gallant a rhythm, when Timon makes his epitaph, we feel no sorrow, for life herself has made one of her eternal gestures, has called up into our hearts her energy that is eternal delight.[31] In Ireland, where the tide of life is rising, we turn, not to picture-making, but to the imagination of personality—to drama, gesture.

SAMHAIN: 1904—
THE PLAY, THE PLAYER,
AND THE SCENE

I have been asked to put into this year's *Samhain* Miss Horniman's letter offering us the use of the Abbey Theatre. I have done this, but as Miss Horniman begins her letter by stating that she has made her offer out of 'great sympathy with the Irish National Theatre Company as publicly explained by Mr. Yeats on various occasions', she has asked me to go more into detail as to my own plans and hopes than I have done before.[1] I think they are the plans and hopes of my fellow-dramatists, for we are all of one movement, and have influenced one another, and have in us the spirit of our time. I discussed them all very shortly in the last[†] *Samhain*. And I know that it was that *Samhain,* and a certain speech I made in front of the curtain, that made Miss Horniman entrust us with her generous gift.[2] But the last[†] *Samhain* is practically out of print, and my speech has gone even out of my own memory. I will repeat, therefore, much that I have said already, but adding a good deal to it.

First. Our plays must be literature or written in the spirit of literature. The modern theatre has died away to what it is because the writers have thought of their audiences instead of their subject. An old writer saw his hero, if it was a play of character, or some dominant passion, if it was a play of passion, like *Phèdre* or *Andromaque,* moving before him, living with a life he did not endeavour to control.[3] The persons acted upon one another as they were bound by their natures to act, and the play was dramatic, not because he had sought out dramatic situations for their own sake, but because will broke itself upon will and passion upon passion.

Then the imagination began to cool, the writer began to be less alive, to seek external aids, remembered situations, tricks of the theatre, that had proved themselves again and again. His persons no longer will have a particular character, but he knows that he can rely upon the incidents, and he feels himself fortunate when there is nothing in his play that has not succeeded a thousand times before the curtain has risen. Perhaps he has even read a certain guide-book to the stage published in France, and called *The Thirty-six Situations of Drama.*[4] The costumes will be magnificent, the actresses will be beautiful, the Castle in Spain will be painted by an artist upon the spot. We will come from his play excited if we are foolish, or can condescend to the folly of others, but knowing nothing new about ourselves, and seeing life with no new eyes and hearing it with no new ears. The whole movement of theatrical reform in our day has been a struggle to get rid of this kind of play, and the sincere play, the logical play, that we would have in its place, will always seem, when we hear it for the first time, undramatic, unexciting. It has to stir the heart in a long-disused way, it has to awaken the intellect to a pleasure that ennobles and wearies. I was at the first performance of an Ibsen play given in England. It was *A Doll's House,* and at the fall of the curtain I heard an old dramatic critic say, 'It is but a series of conversations terminated by an accident'.[5] So far, we here in Dublin mean the same thing as do Mr. Max Beerbohm, Mr. Walkley, and Mr. Archer, who are seeking to restore sincerity to the English stage, but I am not certain that we mean the same thing all through.[6] The utmost sincerity, the most unbroken logic, give me, at any rate, but an imperfect pleasure if there is not a vivid and beautiful language. Ibsen has sincerity and logic beyond any writer of our time, and we are all seeking to learn them at his hands; but is he not a good deal less than the greatest of all times, because he lacks beautiful and vivid language? 'Well, well, give me time and you shall hear all about it. If only I had Peter here now', is very like life, is entirely in its place where it comes, and when it is united to other sentences exactly like itself, one is moved, one knows not how, to pity and terror, and yet not moved as if the words themselves could sing and shine.[7] Mr. Max Beerbohm wrote once that a play cannot have style because the people must talk as they talk in daily life. He was thinking, it is obvious, of a play made out of that typically modern life where there is no longer vivid speech.[8] Blake says that a work of art must be minutely articulated by God or man, and man has too little help from that occasional collabo- rateur when he writes of people whose language has become abstract and dead.[9] Falstaff gives one the sensation of reality, and when one remembers the abundant vocabulary of a time when all but everything present to the mind was present to the senses, one imagines that his words were but little magnified from the words of such a man in real life.[10] Language was still alive then, alive as it is in Gaelic to-day, as it is in English-speaking Ireland where the schoolmaster or the newspaper has not corrupted it. I know that we are at the mere beginning, laboriously learning our craft, try- ing our hands in little plays for the most part, that we may not ven- ture too boldly in our ignorance; but I never hear the vivid, picturesque, ever-varied language of Mr. Synge's persons without feeling that the great collaborateur has his finger in our business. May it not be that the only realistic play that will live as Shakespeare has lived, as Calderón has lived, as the Greeks have lived, will arise out of the common life, where language is as much alive as if it were new come out of Eden? After all, is not the greatest play not the play that gives the sensation of an external reality but the play in which there is the greatest abundance of life itself, of the reality that is in our minds? Is it possible to make a work of art, which needs every subtlety of expression if it is to reveal what hides itself con- tinually, out of a dying, or at any rate a very ailing, language? and all language but that of the poets and of the poor is already bedridden. We have, indeed, persiflage, the only speech of educated men that expresses a deliberate enjoyment of words: but persiflage is not a true language. It is impersonal; it is not in the midst but on the edge of life; it covers more character than it discovers: and yet, such as it is, all our comedies are made out of it.

What the ever-moving, delicately moulded flesh is to human beauty, vivid musical words are to passion. Somebody has said that every nation begins with poetry and ends with algebra, and passion has always refused to express itself in algebraical terms.[11]

Have we not been in error in demanding from our playwrights personages who do not transcend our common actions any more than our common speech? If we are in the right, all antiquity has been in error. The scholars of a few generations ago were fond of deciding that certain persons were unworthy of the dignity of art. They had, it may be, an over-abounding preference for kings and queens, but we are, it may be, very stupid in thinking that the average man is a fit subject at all for the finest art. Art delights in the exception, for it delights in the soul expressing itself according to its own laws and arranging the world about it in its own pattern, as sand strewn upon a drum will change itself into different patterns, according to the notes of music that are sung or played to it. But the average man is average because he has not attained to freedom. Habit, routine, fear of public opinion, fear of punishment here or hereafter, a myriad of things that are 'something other than human life', something less than flame, work their will upon his soul and trundle his body here and there.[12] At the first performance of *Ghosts* I could not escape from an illusion unaccountable to me at the time. All the characters seemed to be less than life-size; the stage, though it was but the little Royalty stage, seemed larger than I had ever seen it. Little whimpering puppets moved here and there in the middle of that great abyss. Why did they not speak out with louder voices or move with freer gestures? What was it that weighed upon their souls perpetually? Certainly they were all in prison, and yet there was no prison.[13] In India there are villages so obedient that all the jailer has to do is to draw a circle upon the ground with his staff, and to tell his thief to stand there so many hours; but what law had these people broken that they had to wander round that narrow circle all their lives? May not such art, terrible, satirical, inhuman, be the medicine of great cities, where nobody is ever alone with his own strength? Nor is Maeterlinck very different, for his persons 'enquire after Jerusalem in the regions of the grave, with weak voices almost inarticulate, wearying repose'.[14] Is it the mob that has robbed those angelic persons of the energy of their souls? Will not our next art be rather of the country, of great open spaces, of the soul rejoicing in itself? Will not the generations to come begin again to have an over-abounding faith in kings and queens, in masterful spirits, whatever names we call them by? I had Molière with me on my way to America, and as I read I seemed to be at home in Ireland listening to that conversation of the people which is so full of riches because so full of leisure, or to those old stories of the folk which were made by men who believed so much in the soul, and so little in anything else, that they were never entirely certain that the earth was solid under the foot-sole.[15] What is there left for us, that have seen the newly discovered stability of things changed from an enthusiasm to a weariness, but to labour with a high heart, though it may be with weak hands, to rediscover an art of the theatre that shall be joyful, fantastic, extravagant, whimsical, beautiful, resonant, and altogether reckless? The arts are at their greatest when they seek for a life growing always more scornful of everything that is not itself and passing into its own fullness, as it were, ever more completely as all that is created out of the passing mode of society slips from it; and attaining that fullness, perfectly it may be—and from this is tragic joy and the perfectness of tragedy—when the world itself has slipped away in death. We, who are believers, cannot see reality anywhere but in the soul itself, and seeing it there we cannot do other than rejoice in every energy, whether of gesture, or of action, or of speech, coming out of the personality, the soul's image, even though the very laws of nature seem as unimportant in comparison as did the laws of Rome to Coriolanus when his pride was upon him.[16] Has not the long decline of the arts been but the shadow of declining faith in an unseen reality?

> If the sun and moon would doubt,
> They'd immediately go out.[17]

Second. If we are to make a drama of energy, of extravagance, of phantasy, of musical and noble speech, we shall need an appropriate stage-management. Up to a generation or two ago, and to our own generation, here and there, lingered a method of acting and of stage-management, which had come down, losing much of its beauty and meaning on the way, from the days of Shakespeare. Long after England, under the influence of Garrick, began the movement towards Naturalism, this school had a great popularity in Ireland, where it was established at the Restoration by an actor who probably remembered the Shakespearean players.[18] France has inherited from Racine and from Molière an equivalent art, and, whether it is applied to comedy or to tragedy, its object is to give importance to the words. It is not only Shakespeare whose finest thoughts are inaudible on the English stage. Congreve's *Way of the World* was acted in London last spring, and revived again a month ago, and the part of Lady Wishfort was taken by a very admirable actress, an actress of genius who has never had the recognition she deserves.[19] There is a scene where Lady Wishfort turns away a servant with many words. She cries, 'Go, set up for yourself again, do; drive a trade, do, with your three pennyworth of small ware, flaunting upon a packthread, under a brandy-seller's bulk, or against a dead wall by a ballad-monger; go, hang out an old frisoneer-gorget, with a yard of yellow colberteen again, do; an old gnawed mask, two rows of pins, and a child's fiddle; a glass necklace with the beads broken, and a quilted nightcap with one ear. Go, go, drive a trade'.[20] The conversation of an older time, of Urquhart, the translator of Rabelais, let us say, awakes with a little of its old richness.[21] The actress acted so much and so admirably that when she first played it—I heard her better a month ago, perhaps because I was nearer to the stage— I could not understand a word of a passage that required the most careful speech. Just as the modern musician, through the over-development of an art that seems exterior to the poet, writes so many notes for every word that the natural energy of speech is dis-solved and broken and the words made inaudible, so did this actress, a perfect mistress of her own art, put into her voice so many different notes, so run up and down the scale under an impulse of anger and scorn that one had hardly been more affronted by a musi-cal setting. Everybody who has spoken to large audiences knows that he must speak difficult passages, in which there is some deli-cacy of sound or of thought, upon one or two notes. The larger his audience, the more he must get away, except in trivial passages, from the methods of conversation. Where one requires the full attention of the mind, one must not weary it with any but the most needful changes of pitch and note, or by an irrelevant or obtrusive gesture. As long as drama was full of poetical beauty, full of des-cription, full of philosophy, as long as its words were the very ves-ture of sorrow and laughter, the players understood that their art was essentially conventional, artificial, ceremonious.

The stage itself was differently shaped, being more a platform than a stage, for they did not desire to picture the surface of life, but to escape from it. But realism came in, and every change towards realism coincided with a decline in dramatic energy. The proscenium was imported into England at the close of the seventeenth century, appropriate costumes a generation later. The audience were forbidden to sit upon the stage in the time of Sheridan, the last English-speaking playwright whose plays have lived.[22] And the last remnant of the platform, the part of the stage that still projected beyond the proscenium, dwindled in size till it disappeared in our own day. The birth of science was at hand, the birth-pangs of its mother had troubled the world for centuries. But now that Gargantua is born at last, it may be possible to remember that there are other giants.[23]

We can never bring back old things precisely as they were, but must consider how much of them is necessary to us, accepting, even if it were only out of politeness, something of our own time. The necessities of a builder have torn from us, all unwilling as we were, the apron, as the portion of the platform that came in front of the proscenium used to be called, and we must submit to the picture-making of the modern stage. We would have preferred to be able to return occasionally to the old stage of statue-making, of gesture. On the other hand, one accepts, believing it to be a great improvement, some appropriateness of costume, but speech is essential to us. An Irish critic has told us to study the stage-management of Antoine, but that is like telling a good Catholic to take his theology from Luther.[24] Antoine, who described poetry as a way of saying nothing, has perfected naturalistic acting and carried the spirit of science into the theatre.[25] Were we to study his methods, we might, indeed, have a far more perfect art than our own, a far more mature art, but it is better to fumble our way like children. We may grow up, for we have as good hopes as any other sturdy ragamuffin.

An actor must so understand how to discriminate cadence from cadence, and so cherish the musical lineaments of verse or prose, that he delights the ear with a continually varied music. This one has to say over and over again, but one does not mean that his speaking should be a monotonous chant. Those who have heard Mr. Frank Fay speaking verse will understand me. That speech of his, so masculine and so musical, could only sound monotonous to an ear that was deaf to poetic rhythm, and no man should, as do London managers, stage a poetical drama according to the desire of those who are deaf to poetical rhythm. It is possible, barely so, but still possible, that some day we may write musical notes as did the Greeks, it seems, for a whole play, and make our actors speak upon them—not sing, but speak. Even now, when one wishes to make the voice immortal and passionless, as in the Angel's part in my *Hour-Glass,* one finds it desirable for the player to speak always upon pure musical notes, written out beforehand and carefully rehearsed. On the one occasion when I heard the Angel's part spoken in this way with entire success, the contrast between the crystalline quality of the pure notes and the more confused and passionate speaking of the Wise Man was a new dramatic effect of great value.

If a song is brought into a play it does not matter to what school the musician belongs if every word, if every cadence, is as audible and expressive as if it were spoken. It must be good speech, and we must not listen to the musician if he promise to add meaning to the words with his notes, for one does not add meaning to the word 'love' by putting four o's in the middle, or by subordinating it even slightly to a musical note. But where can we find a musician so mild, so quiet, so modest, unless he be a sailor from the forecastle or some ghost out of the twelfth century? One must ask him for music that shall mean nothing, or next to nothing, apart from the words, and after all he is a musician.

When I heard the Aeschylean Trilogy at Stratford-on-Avon last spring I could not hear a word of the chorus, except in a few lines here and there which were spoken without musical setting.[26] The chorus was not without dramatic, or rather operatic effect; but why should those singers have taken so much trouble to learn by heart so much of the greatest lyric poetry of Greece? 'Twinkle, twinkle, little star', or any other memory of their childhood, would have served their turn.[27] If it had been comic verse, the singing-master and the musician would have respected it, and the audience would have been able to hear. Mr. Dolmetsch and Miss Florence Farr have been working for some time to find out some way of setting serious poetry which will enable us to hear it, and the singer to sing

sweetly and yet never to give a word, a cadence, or an accent that
would not be given it in ordinary passionate speech.[28] It is difficult,
for they are trying to re-discover an art that is only remembered or
half-remembered in ships and in hovels and among wandering tribes
of uncivilised men, and they have to make their experiment with
singers who have been trained by a method of teaching that professes to change a human being into a musical instrument, a creation of science, 'something other than human life'. In old days the
singer began to sing over the rocking cradle or among the wine-cups,
and it was as though life itself caught fire of a sudden; but to-day
the poet, fanatic that he is, watches the singer go up on to the platform, wondering and expecting every moment that he will punch
himself as if he were a bag. It is certainly impossible to speak with
perfect expression after you have been a bagpipes for many years,
even though you have been making the most beautiful music all the
time.

The success of the chorus in the performance of *Hippolytus* last
spring—I did not see the more recent performance, but hear upon
all hands that the chorus was too large—the expressiveness of
the greater portion as mere speech, has, I believe, re-created the
chorus as a dramatic method.[29] The greater portion of the singing,
as arranged by Miss Farr, even when four or five voices sang
together, though never when ten sang together, was altogether
admirable speech, and some of it was speech of extraordinary
beauty. When one lost the meaning, even perhaps where the whole
chorus sang together, it was not because of a defective method, but
because it is the misfortune of every new artistic method that we
can only judge of it through performers who must be for a long time
unpractised and amateurish. This new art has a double difficulty,
for the training of a modern singer makes articulate speech, as a
poet understands it, nearly impossible, and those who are masters
of speech very often, perhaps usually, are poor musicians. Fortunately, Miss Farr, who has some knowledge of music, has, it may
be, the most beautiful voice on the English stage, and is in her management of it an exquisite artist.

That we may throw emphasis on the words in poetical drama,
above all where the words are remote from real life as well as
in themselves exacting and difficult, the actors must move, for

the most part, slowly and quietly, and not very much, and there should be something in their movements decorative and rhythmical as if they were paintings on a frieze. They must not draw attention to themselves at wrong moments, for poetry and indeed all picturesque writing is perpetually making little pictures which draw the attention away for a second or two from the player. The actress who played Lady Wishfort should have permitted us to give a part of our attention to that little shop or wayside booth. Then, too, one must be content to have long quiet moments, long grey spaces, long level reaches, as it were—the leisure that is in all fine life—for what we may call the business-will in a high state of activity is not everything, although contemporary drama knows of little else.

Third. We must have a new kind of scenic art. I have been the advocate of the poetry as against the actor, but I am the advocate of the actor as against the scenery. Ever since the last remnant of the old platform disappeared, and the proscenium grew into the frame of a picture, the actors have been turned into a picturesque group in the foreground of a meretricious landscape-painting. The background should be of as little importance as the background of a portrait-group, and it should, when possible, be of one colour or of one tint, that the persons on the stage, wherever they stand, may harmonise with it or contrast with it and preoccupy our attention. Their outline should be clear and not broken up into the outline of windows and wainscoting, or lost into the edges of colours. In a play which copies the surface of life in its dialogue we may, with this reservation, represent anything that can be represented successfully—a room, for instance—but a landscape painted in the ordinary way will always be meretricious and vulgar. It will always be an attempt to do something which cannot be done successfully except in easel painting, and the moment an actor stands near to your mountain, or your forest, one will perceive that he is standing against a flat surface. Illusion, therefore, is impossible, and should not be attempted. We should be content to suggest a scene upon a canvas, whose vertical flatness we accept and use, as the decorator of pottery accepts the roundness of a bowl or a jug. Having chosen the distance from naturalism, which will keep one's composition from competing with the illusion created by the actor, who belongs to a world with depth as well as height and breadth, one must keep this distance without flinching. The distance will vary according to the distance the playwright has chosen, and especially in poetry, which is more remote and idealistic than prose, one will insist on schemes of colour and simplicity of form, for every sign of deliberate order gives remoteness and ideality. But, whatever the distance be, one's treatment will always be more or less decorative. We can only find out the right decoration for the different types of play by experiment, but it will probably range between, on the one hand, woodlands made out of recurring pattern, or painted like old religious pictures upon gold background, and upon the other the comparative realism of a Japanese print. This decoration will not only give us a scenic art that will be a true art because peculiar to the stage, but it will give the imagination liberty, and without returning to the bareness of the Elizabethan stage. The poet cannot evoke a picture to the mind's eye if a second-rate painter has set his imagination of it before the bodily eye; but decoration and suggestion will accompany our moods, and turn our minds to meditation, and yet never become obtrusive or wearisome. The actor and the words put into his mouth are always the one thing that matters, and the scene should never be complete of itself, should never mean anything to the imagination until the actor is in front of it.

If we remember that the movement of the actor, and the graduation and the colour of the lighting, are the two elements that distinguish the stage picture from an easel painting, we may not find it difficult to create an art of the stage ranking as a true fine art. Mr. Gordon Craig has done wonderful things with the lighting, but he is not greatly interested in the actor, and his streams of coloured direct light, beautiful as they are, will always seem, apart from certain exceptional moments, a new externality.[30] We should rather desire, for all but exceptional moments, an even, shadowless light, like that of noon, and it may be that a light reflected out of mirrors will give us what we need.

M. Appia and M. Fortuny are making experiments in the staging of Wagner for a private theatre in Paris, but I cannot understand what M. Appia is doing, from the little I have seen of his writing, excepting that the floor of the stage will be uneven like the ground, and that at moments the lights and shadows of green boughs will fall over the player that the stage may show a man wandering through a wood, and not a wood with a man in the middle of it.[31] One agrees with all the destructive part of his criticism, but it looks as if he himself is seeking, not convention, but a more perfect realism. I cannot persuade myself that the movement of life is flowing that way, for life moves by a throbbing as of a pulse, by reaction and action. The hour of convention and decoration and ceremony is coming again.

The experiments of the Irish National Theatre Society will have of necessity to be for a long time few and timid, and we must often, having no money and not a great deal of leisure, accept for a while compromises, and much even that we know to be irredeemably bad. One can only perfect an art very gradually; and good playwriting, good speaking, and good acting are the first necessity.

Our first season at the Abbey Theatre has been tolerably successful. We drew small audiences, but quite as big as we had hoped for,
and we end the year with a little money. On the whole, we have probably more than trebled our audiences of the Molesworth Hall.[1] The
same people come again and again, and others join them, and I do
not think we lose any of them. We shall be under more expense in
our new season, for we have decided to pay some of the company
and send them into the provinces, but our annual expenses will not
be as heavy as the weekly expenses of the most economical London manager. Mr. Philip Carr, whose revivals of Elizabethan plays
and old comedies have been the finest things one could see in a London theatre, spent three hundred pounds and took twelve pounds
during his last week; but here in Ireland enthusiasm can do half the
work, and nobody is accustomed to get much money, and even Mr.
Carr's inexpensive scenery costs more than our simple decora-
tions.[2] Our staging of *Kincora,* the work of Mr. Robert Gregory,
was beautiful, with a high, grave dignity and that strangeness
which Ben Jonson thought to be a part of all excellent beauty, and
the expense of scenery, dresses, and all was hardly above thirty
pounds.[3] If we find a good scene we repeat it in other plays, and in
course of time we shall be able to put on new plays without any
expense for scenery at all. I do not think that even the most expensive decoration would increase in any way the pleasure of an audience that comes to us for the play and the acting.

We shall have abundance of plays, for Lady Gregory has written us a new comedy besides her *White Cockade,* which is in
rehearsal; Mr. Boyle, a satirical comedy in three acts; Mr. Colum
has made a new play out of his *Broken Soil;* and I have made almost

a new one out of my *Shadowy Waters;* and Mr. Synge has practically finished a longer and more elaborate comedy than his last.[4]
Since our start last Christmas we have shown eleven plays created
by our movement and very varied in substance and form, and six
of these were new: *The Well of the Saints, Kincora, The Building
Fund, The Land, On Baile's Strand,* and *Spreading the News.*

One of our plays, *The Well of the Saints,* has been accepted for
immediate production by the Deutsches Theater of Berlin; and
another, *The Shadow of the Glen,* is to be played during the season at the National Bohemian Theatre at Prague; and my own *Cathleen ni Houlihan* has been translated into Irish and been played at
the Oireachtas, before an audience of some thousands.[5] We have
now several dramatists who have taken to drama as their most serious business, and we claim that a school of Irish drama exists, and
that it is founded upon sincere observation and experience.

As is natural in a country where the Gaelic League has created
a preoccupation with the country-man, the greatest number of our
plays are founded on the comedy and tragedy of country life, and
are written more or less in dialect. When the Norwegian National
movement began, its writers chose for their maxim, 'To understand
the saga by the peasant and the peasant by the saga'.[6] Ireland in our
day has rediscovered the old heroic literature of Ireland, and she
has rediscovered the imagination of the folk. My own preoccupation is more with the heroic legend than with the folk, but Lady
Gregory in her *Spreading the News,* Mr. Synge in his *Well of
the Saints,* Mr. Colum in *The Land,* Mr. Boyle in *The Building
Fund,* have been busy, much or little, with the folk and the folk-
imagination. Mr. Synge alone has written of the peasant as he is to
all the ages; of the folk-imagination as it has been shaped by centuries of life among fields or on fishing-grounds. His people talk a
highly-coloured musical language, and one never hears from them
a thought that is of to-day and not of yesterday. Lady Gregory has
written of the people of the markets and villages of the West, and
their speech, though less full of peculiar idiom than that of Mr.
Synge's people, is still always that vivid speech which has been
shaped through some generations of English speaking by those who
still think in Gaelic. Mr. Colum and Mr. Boyle, on the other hand,

write of the country-man or villager of the East or centre of Ireland, who thinks in English, and the speech of their people shows the influence of the newspaper and the National Schools.[7] The people they write of, too, are not the true folk. They are the peasant as he is being transformed by modern life, and for that very reason the man of the towns may find it easier to understand them. There is less surprise, less wonder in what he sees, but there is more of himself there, more of his vision of the world and of the problems that are troubling him.

It is not fitting for the showman to overpraise the show, but he is always permitted to tell you what is in his booths. Mr. Synge is the most obviously individual of our writers. He alone has discovered a new kind of sarcasm, and it is this sarcasm that keeps him, and may long keep him, from general popularity. Mr. Boyle satirises a miserly old woman, and he has made a very vivid person of her, but as yet his satire is such as all men accept; it brings no new thing to judgment.[8] We have never doubted that what he assails is evil, and we are never afraid that it is ourselves. Lady Gregory alone writes out of a spirit of pure comedy, and laughs without bitterness and with no thought but to laugh. She has a perfect sympathy with her characters, even with the worst of them, and when the curtain goes down we are so far from the mood of judgment that we do not even know that we have condoned many sins. In Mr. Colum's *Land* there is a like comedy when Cornelius and Sally fill the scene, but then he is too young to be content with laughter. He is still interested in the reform of society, but that will pass, for at about thirty every writer, who is anything of an artist, comes to understand that all a work of art can do is to show us the reality that is within our minds, and the reality that our eyes look on. He is the youngest of us all by many years, and we are all proud to foresee his future.

I think that a race or a nation or a phase of life has but few dramatic themes, and that when these have been once written well they must afterwards be written less and less well until one gets at last but 'soulless self-reflections of man's skill'.[9] The first man writes what it is natural to write, the second man what is left to him, for the imagination cannot repeat itself. The hoydenish young woman, the sentimental young woman, the villain and the hero alike ever self-possessed, of contemporary drama, were once real discoveries, and one can trace their history through the generations like a joke or a folk-tale, but, unlike these, they grow always less interesting as they get farther from their cradle. Our opportunity in Ireland is not that our playwrights have more talent—it is possible that they have less than the workers in an old tradition—but that the necessity of putting a life that has not hitherto been dramatised into their plays excludes all these types which have had their origin in a different social order.

An audience with National feeling is alive, at the worst it is alive enough to quarrel with. One man came up from the scene of Lady Gregory's *Kincora* at Killaloe that he might see her play, and having applauded loudly, and even cheered for the Dalcassians, became silent and troubled when Brian took Gormleith for his wife. 'It is a great pity', he said to the man next to him, 'that he didn't marry a quiet girl from his own district'.[10] Some have quarrelled with me because I did not take some glorious moment of Cuchulain's life for my play, and not the killing of his son, and all our playwrights have been attacked for choosing bad characters instead of good, and called slanderers of their country.[11] In so far as these attacks come from National feeling, that is to say, out of an interest or an affection for the life of this country now and in past times, as did the country-man's trouble about Gormleith, they are in the long run the greatest help to a dramatist, for they give him something to startle or to delight. Every writer has had to face them where his work has aroused a genuine interest. The Germans at the beginning of the nineteenth century preferred Schiller to Goethe, and thought him the greater writer, because he put nobler characters into his books; and when Chaucer encounters Eros in the month of May, that testy god complains that though he had 'sixty bokes† olde and newe', and all full of stories of women and the life they led, and though for every bad woman there are a hundred good, he has chosen to write only of the bad ones. He complains that Chaucer by his *Troilus* and his *Romaunt of the Rose* has brought love and women to discredit.[12] It is the same in painting as in literature, for when a new painter arises men cry out, even when he is a painter of the beautiful like Rossetti, that he has chosen the exaggerated or the ugly or the unhealthy, forgetting that it is the business of art and of letters to change the values and to mint the coinage. Without this outcry there is no movement of life in the arts, for it is the sign of values not yet understood, of a coinage not yet mastered. Sometimes the writer delights us, when we grow to understand him, with new forms of virtue discovered in persons where one had not hitherto looked for it, and sometimes—and this is more and more true of modern art— he changes the values not by the persons he sets before one, who may be mean enough, but by his way of looking at them, by the implications that come from his own mind, by the tune they dance to, as it were. Eros, into whose mouth Chaucer, one doubts not, puts arguments that he had heard from his readers and listeners, objected to Chaucer's art in the interests of pedantic mediaeval moralising; the contemporaries of Schiller commended him for reflecting vague romantic types from the sentimental literature of his predecessors; and those who object to the peasant as he is seen in the Abbey Theatre have their imaginations full of what is least observant and most sentimental in the Irish novelists.[13] When I was a boy I spent many an afternoon with a village shoemaker who was a great reader. I asked him once what Irish novels he liked, and he told me there were none he could read. 'They sentimentalised the people', he said angrily; and it was against Kickham that he complained most. 'I want to see the people', he said, 'shown up in their naked hideousness'. That is the peasant mind as I know it, a mind that delights in strong sensations whether of beauty or of ugliness, in bare facts, and is quite without sentimentality. The sentimental mind is found among the middle classes, and it was this mind which came into Irish literature with Gerald Griffin and later on with Kickham.[14]

It is the mind of the town, and it is a delight to those only who have seen life, and above all country life, with unobservant eyes, and most of all to the Irish tourist, to the patriotic young Irishman who goes to the country for a month's holiday with his head full of vague idealisms. It is not the art of Mr. Colum, born of the people, and when at his best looking at the town and not the country with strange eyes, nor the art of Mr. Synge, spending weeks and months in remote places talking Irish to fishers and islanders. I remember meeting, about twenty years ago, a lad who had a little

yacht at Kingstown. Somebody was talking of the sea paintings of
a great painter, Hook, I think, and this made him very angry.[15] No
yachtsman believed in them or thought them at all like the sea,
he said. Indeed, he was always hearing people praise pictures that
were not a bit like the sea, and thereupon he named certain of the
greatest painters of water—men who more than all others had spent
their lives in observing the effects of light upon cloud and wave.
I met him again the other day, well on in middle life, and though
he is not even an Irishman, indignant with Mr. Synge's and Mr.
Boyle's peasants. He knew the people, he said, and neither he nor
any other person that knew them could believe that they were properly represented in *The Well of the Saints* or *The Building Fund.*
Twenty years ago his imagination was under the influence of popular pictures, but to-day it was under that of the conventional
idealism writers like Kickham and Griffin substitute for the ever-
varied life of the cottages, and of that conventional idealism that
the contemporary English theatre substitutes for all life whatsoever.
I saw *Caste,* the earliest play of the modern school, a few days ago,
and found there more obviously than I expected, for I am not much
of a theatre-goer, the English half of the mischief.[16] Two of the
minor persons had a certain amount of superficial characterisation,
as if out of the halfpenny comic papers; but the central persons, the
man and woman that created the dramatic excitement, such as it
was, had not characters of any kind, being vague ideals, perfection
as it is imagined by a commonplace mind. The audience could give
them its sympathy without the labour that comes from awakening knowledge. If the dramatist had put into his play whatever man
or woman of his acquaintance seemed to come closest to perfection, he would have had to make it a study, among other things,
of the little petty faults and perverted desires that arise out of the
nature of its surroundings. He would have troubled that admiring
audience by making a self-indulgent sympathy more difficult. He
might have even seemed, like Ibsen or the early Christians, an
enemy of the human race. We have gone down to the roots, and
we have made up our minds upon one thing quite definitely—that
in no play that professes to picture life in its daily aspects shall we
admit these white phantoms. We can do this, not because we have
any special talent, but because we are dealing with a life which has

for all practical purposes never been set upon the stage before. The conventional types of the novelists do not pervert our imagination, for they are built, as it were, into another form, and no man who has chosen for himself a sound method of drama, whether it be the drama of character or of crisis, can use them. The Gaelic League and *Cumann na nGaedheal* play does indeed show the influence of the novelists; but the typical Gaelic League play is essentially narrative and not dramatic. Every artist necessarily imitates those who have worked in the same form before him, and when the preoccupation has been with the same life he almost always, consciously or unconsciously, borrows more than the form, and it is this very borrowing—affecting thought, language, all the vehicles of expression—which brings about the most of what we call decadence.

After all, if our plays are slanders upon their country; if to represent upon the stage a hard old man like Cosgar, or a rapacious old man like Shan, or a faithless wife like Nora Burke, or to select from history treacherous Gormleith for a theme, is to represent this nation at something less than its full moral worth; if every play played in the Abbey Theatre now and in times to come be something of a slander, is anybody a penny the worse?[17] Some ancient or mediaeval races did not think so. Jusserand describes the French conquerors of mediaeval England as already imagining themselves in their literature, as they have done to this day, as a great deal worse than they are, and the English imagining themselves a great deal better.[18] The greater portion of the *Divine Comedy* is a catalogue of the sins of Italy, and Boccaccio became immortal because he exaggerated with an unceasing playful wit the vices of his countryside. The Greeks chose for the themes of their serious literature a few great crimes, and Corneille, in his article on the theory of the drama, shows why the greatness and notoriety of these crimes is necessary to tragic drama.[19] The public life of Athens found its chief celebration in the monstrous caricature of Aristophanes, and the Greek nation was so proud, so free from morbid sensitiveness, that it invited the foreign ambassadors to the spectacle. And I answer to those who say that Ireland cannot afford this freedom because of her political circumstances, that if Ireland cannot

afford it, Ireland cannot have a literature. Literature has never been
the work of slaves, and Ireland must learn to say:

> Stone walls do not a prison make,
> Nor iron bars a cage.[20]

The misrepresentation of the average life, of a nation that follows of necessity from an imaginative delight in energetic characters and extreme types, enlarges the energy of a people by the
spectacle of energy. A nation is injured by the picking out of a single type and setting that into print or upon the stage as a type of
the whole nation. Ireland suffered for a century from that single
whisky-drinking, humorous type which seemed for a time the
accepted type of all. The Englishwoman is, no doubt, injured in
the same way in the minds of various Continental nations by a habit
of caricaturing all Englishwomen as having big teeth. But neither
nation can be injured by imaginative writers selecting types that
please their fancy. They will never impose a general type on the public mind, for genius differs from the newspapers in this, that the
greater and more confident it is, the more is its delight in varieties
and species. If Ireland were at this moment, through a misunderstanding terror of the stage Irishman, to deprive her writers of freedom, to make their imaginations timid, she would lower her
dignity in her own eyes and in the eyes of every intellectual nation.
That old caricature did her very little harm in the long run, perhaps
a few car-drivers have copied it in their lives, while the mind of the
country remained untroubled; but the loss of imaginative freedom
and daring would turn us into old women. In the long run, it is the
great writer of a nation that becomes its image in the minds of pos-
terity, and even though he represent no man of worth in his art, the
worth of his own mind becomes the inheritance of his people. He
takes nothing away that he does not give back in greater volume.

If Ireland had not lost the Gaelic she never would have had this
sensitiveness as of a *parvenu* when presented at Court for the first
time, or of a nigger newspaper. When Ireland had the confidence
of her own antiquity, her writers praised and blamed according
to their fancy, and even, as throughout all mediaeval Europe,

laughed when they had a mind to at the most respected persons, at the sanctities of Church and State. The story of *The Shadow of the Glen,* found by Mr. Synge in Gaelic-speaking Aran, and by Mr. Curtin in Munster; the Song of *The Red-haired Man's Wife,* sung in all Gaelic Ireland; *The Midnight Court* of MacGiolla Meidhre; *The Vision of MacCoinglinne;* the old romancers, with their Bricriu and their Conan, laughed and sang as fearlessly as Chaucer or Villon or Cervantes.[21] It seemed almost as if those old writers murmured to themselves, 'If we but keep our courage let all the virtues perish, for we can make them over again; but if that be gone, all is gone'. I remember when I was an art student at the Metropolitan School of Art a good many years ago, saying to Mr. Hughes the sculptor, as we looked at the work of our fellow-students, 'Every student here that is doing better work than another is doing it because he has a more intrepid imagination; one has only to look at the line of a drawing to see that'; and he said that was his own thought also.[22] All good art is extravagant, vehement, impetuous, shaking the dust of time from its feet, as it were, and beating against the walls of the world.

If a sincere religious artist were to arise in Ireland in our day, and were to paint the Holy Family, let us say, he would meet with the same opposition that sincere dramatists are meeting with to-day.[23] The half-educated mind is never sincere in the arts, and one finds in Irish chapels, above all in Irish convents, the religious art that it understands. A Connacht convent a little time ago refused a fine design for stained glass, because of the personal life in the faces and in the attitudes, which seemed to them ugly, perhaps even impious. They sent to the designer an insipid German chromo-lithograph, full of faces without expression or dignity, and gestures without personal distinction, and the designer, too anxious for success to reject any order, has carried out this meaningless design in glass of beautiful colour and quality. Let us suppose that Meister Stefan were to paint in Ireland to-day that exquisite Madonna of his, with her lattice of roses; a great deal that is said of our plays would be said of that picture. Why select for his model a little girl selling newspapers in the streets, why slander with that miserable little body the Mother of God? He could only answer, as the imaginative artist always answers, 'That is the way I have seen her in my mind, and what I have made of her is very living'.[24] All art is founded upon personal vision, and the greater the art the more surprising the vision; and all bad art is founded upon impersonal types and images, accepted by average men and women out of imaginative poverty and timidity, or the exhaustion that comes from labour.

Nobody can force a movement of any kind to take any pre-arranged pattern to any very great extent; one can, perhaps, mod-ify it a little, and that is all. When one says that it is going to develop in a certain way, one means that one sees, or imagines that one sees, certain energies which left to themselves are bound to give it a cer-tain form. Writing in *Samhain* some years ago, I said that our plays would be of two kinds, plays of peasant life and plays of a roman-tic and heroic life, such as one finds in the folk-tales.[25] To-day I can see other forces, and can foretell, I think, the form of technique that will arise. About fifty years ago, perhaps not so many, the play-wrights of every country in the world became persuaded that their plays must reflect the surface of life; and the author of *Caste,* for instance, made a reputation by putting what seemed to be average common life and average common speech for the first time upon the stage in England, and by substituting real loaves[†] of bread and real cups of tea for imaginary ones. He was not a very clever nor a very well-educated man, and he made his revolution superficially; but in other countries men of intellect and knowledge created that intellectual drama of real life, of which Ibsen's later plays are the ripened fruit. This change coincided with the substitution of sci-ence for religion in the conduct of life, and is, I believe, as tempo-rary, for the practice of twenty centuries will surely take the sway in the end. A rhetorician in that novel of Petronius, which satirises, or perhaps one should say celebrates, Roman decadence, complains that the young people of his day are made blockheads by learning old romantic tales in the schools, instead of what belongs to common life.[26] And yet is it not the romantic tale, the extravagant and ungovernable dream which comes out of youth; and is not that desire for what belongs to common life, whether it comes from Rome or Greece or England, the sign of fading fires, of ebbing imaginative desire? In the arts I am quite certain that it is a substitution of apparent for real truth. Mr. George Moore has a very vivid character; he is precisely one of those whose characters can be represented most easily upon the stage. Let us suppose that some dramatist had made even him the centre of a play in which the moderation of common life was carefully preserved, how very little he could give us of that headlong intrepid man, as we know him, whether through long personal knowledge or through his many books. The more carefully the play reflected the surface of life the more would the elements be limited to those that naturally display themselves during so many minutes of our ordinary affairs. It is only by extravagance, by an emphasis far greater than that of life as we observe it, that we can crowd into a few minutes the knowledge of years. Shakespeare or Sophocles can so quicken, as it were, the circles of the clock, so heighten the expression of life, that many years can unfold themselves in a few minutes, and it is always Shakespeare or Sophocles, and not Ibsen, that makes us say, 'How true, how often I have felt as that man feels'; or 'How intimately I have come to know those people on the stage'. There is a certain school of painters that has discovered that it is necessary in the representation of light to put little touches of pure colour side by side. When you went up close to that big picture of the Alps by Segantini, in Mr. Lane's Loan Exhibition a year ago, you found that the grass seeds, which looked brown enough from the other side of the room, were full of pure scarlet colour.[27] If you copy nature's moderation of colour you do not imitate her, for you have only white paint and she has light. If you wish to represent character or passion upon the stage, as it is known to the friends, let us say, of your principal persons, you must be excessive, extravagant, fantastic even, in expression; and you must be this, more extravagantly, more excessively, more fantastically than ever, if you wish to show character and passion as they would be known to the principal person of your play in the depths of his own mind. The greatest art symbolises not those things that we have observed so much as those things that we have experienced, and when the imaginary saint or lover or hero moves us most deeply, it is the moment when he awakens within us for an instant our own heroism, our own sanctity, our own desire. We possess these things—the greatest of men not more than Seaghan the Fool—not at all moderately, but to an infinite extent, and though we control or ignore them, we know that the moralists speak true when they compare them to angels or to devils, or to beasts of prey. How can any dramatic art, moderate in expression, be a true image of Hell or Heaven or the wilderness, or do anything but create those faint histories that but touch our curiosity, those groups of persons that never follow us into our intimate life, where Odysseus and Don Quixote and Hamlet are with us always?[28]

The scientific movement is ebbing a little everywhere, and here in Ireland it has never been in flood at all. And I am certain that everywhere literature will return once more to its old extravagant fantastical expression, for in literature, unlike science, there are no discoveries, and it is always the old that returns. Everything in Ireland urges us to this return, and it may be that we shall be the first to recover after the fifty years of mistake.

The antagonist of imaginative writing in Ireland is not a habit of scientific observation but our interest in matters of opinion. A misgoverned country seeking a remedy by agitation puts an especial value upon opinion, and even those who are not conscious of any interest in the country are influenced by the general habit. All fine literature is the disinterested contemplation or expression of life, but hardly any Irish writer can liberate his mind sufficiently from questions of practical reform for this contemplation. Art for art's sake, as he understands it, whether it be the art of the 'Ode on a Grecian Urn' or of the imaginer of Falstaff, seems to him a neglect of public duty.[29] It is as though the telegraph-boys botanised among the hedges with the undelivered envelopes in their pockets; a man must calculate the effect of his words before he writes them, who they are to excite and to what end. We all write if we follow the habit of the country not for our own delight but for the improvement of our neighbours, and this is not only true of such obviously propagandist work as *The Spirit of the Nation* or a Gaelic League play, but of the work of writers who seemed to have escaped from every National influence, like Mr. Bernard Shaw, Mr. George Moore, or even Mr. Oscar Wilde.[30] They never keep their head for very long out of the flood of opinion. Mr. Bernard Shaw, the one brilliant writer of comedy in England to-day, makes his comedies something less than life by never forgetting that he is a reformer, and Mr. Wilde could hardly finish an act of a play

without denouncing the British public; and Mr. Moore—God bless
the hearers!—has not for ten years now been able to keep himself from
the praise or blame of the Church of his fathers.[31] Goethe, whose mind
was more busy with philosophy than any modern poet, has said, 'The
poet needs all philosophy, but he must keep it out of his work'.[32] One
remembers Dante, and wishes that Goethe had left some commentary upon that saying, some definition of philosophy perhaps; but
one cannot be less than certain that the poet, though it may be well
for him to have right opinions, above all if his country be at death's
door, must keep all opinion that he holds to merely because he
thinks it right, out of his poetry, if it is to be poetry at all. At the inquiry
which preceded the granting of a patent to the Abbey Theatre I was
asked if *Cathleen ni Houlihan* was not written to affect opinion. Certainly it was not. I had a dream one night which gave me a story, and
I had certain emotions about this country, and I gave those emotions
expression for my own pleasure. If I had written to convince others
I would have asked myself, not 'Is that exactly what I think and feel?'
but 'How would that strike so-and-so? How will they think and feel
when they have read it?' And all would be oratorical and insincere.
If we understand our own minds, and the things that are striving
to utter themselves through our minds, we move others, not because
we have understood or thought about those others, but because all
life has the same root. Coventry Patmore has said, 'The end of art
is peace', and the following of art is little different from the following of religion in the intense preoccupation that it demands.[33] Somebody has said, 'God asks nothing of the highest soul except
attention'; and so necessary is attention to mastery in any art, that
there are moments when we think that nothing else is necessary, and
nothing else so difficult.[34] The religious life has created for itself
monasteries and convents where men and women may forget in
prayer and contemplation everything that seems necessary to the most
useful and busy citizens of their towns and villages, and one imagines that even in the monastery and the convent there are passing
things, the twitter of a sparrow in the window, the memory of some
old quarrel, things lighter than air, that keep the soul from its joy. How
many of those old religious sayings can one not apply to the life of
art? 'The Holy Spirit', wrote S. Thomas à Kempis, 'has liberated
me from a multitude of opinions'.[35] When one sets out to cast into

some mould so much of life merely for life's sake, one is tempted at every moment to twist it from its eternal shape to help some friend or harm some enemy. Alas! all men, we in Ireland more than others, are fighters, and it is a hard law that compels us to cast away our swords when we enter the house of the Muses, as men cast them away at the doors of the banqueting-hall at Tara.[36] A weekly paper, in reviewing last year's *Samhain*, convinced itself, or at any rate its readers—for that is the heart of the business in propaganda—that I only began to say these things a few months ago under I know not what alien influence; and yet I seem to have been saying them all my life.[37] I took up an anthology of Irish verse that I edited some ten years ago, and I found them there, and I think they were a chief part of an old fight over the policy of the New Irish Library.[38] Till they are accepted by writers and readers in this country it will never have a literature, it will never escape from the election rhyme and the pamphlet. So long as I have any control over the National Theatre Society it will be carried on in this spirit, call it art for art's sake if you will; and no plays will be produced at it which were written, not for the sake of a good story or fine verses or some revelation of character, but to please those friends of ours who are ever urging us to attack the priests or the English, or wanting us to put our imagination into handcuffs that we may be sure of never seeming to do one or the other.

I have had very little to say this year in *Samhain*, and I have said it badly. When I wrote *Ideas of Good and Evil* and *The Celtic Twilight*, I wrote everything very slowly and a great many times over.[39] A few years ago, however, my eyesight got so bad that I had to dictate the first drafts of everything, and then rewrite these drafts several times. I did the last *Samhain* this way, dictating all the thoughts in a few days, and rewriting them in two or three weeks; but this time I am letting the first draft remain with all its carelessness of phrase and rhythm.[40] I am busy with a practical project which needs the saying of many things from time to time, and it is better to say them carelessly and harshly than to take time from my poetry. One casts something away every year, and I shall, I think, have to cast away the hope of ever having a prose style that amounts to anything.

SAMHAIN: 1906—
LITERATURE AND THE
LIVING VOICE*

I

One Sunday, in summer, a few years ago, I went to the little village of Killeenan, that is not many miles from Galway, to do honour to the memory of Raftery, a Gaelic poet who died a little before the famine.² A headstone had been put over his grave in the half-ruined churchyard, and a priest had come to bless it, and many country-people to listen to his poems. After the shawled and frieze-coated people had knelt down and prayed for the repose of his soul, they gathered about a little wooden platform that had been put up in a field. I do not remember whether Raftery's poem about himself was one of those they listened to, but certainly it was in the thoughts of many, and it was the image reflected in that poem that had drawn some of them from distant villages.

> I am Raftery the poet,
> Full of hope and love;
> With eyes without light;
> With gentleness without misery.

*This essay was written immediately after the opening of the Abbey Theatre, though it was not printed, through an accident, until the art of the Abbey had become an art of peasant comedy.¹ It tells of things we have never had the time to begin. We still dream of them. —March 1908.

Going west on my journey
With the light of my heart;
Weak and tired
To the end of my road.

I am now,
And my face to a wall,
Playing music
To empty pockets.[3]

Some few there remembered him, and one old man came out among the reciters to tell of the burying, where he himself, a young boy at the time, had carried a candle.

The verses of other Gaelic poets were sung or recited too, and, although certainly not often fine poetry, they had its spirit, its *naïveté*—that is to say, its way of looking at the world as if it were but an hour old—its seriousness even in laughter, its personal rhythm.

A few days after I was in the town of Galway, and saw there, as I had often seen in other country towns, some young men marching down the middle of a street singing an already outworn London music-hall song, that filled the memory, long after they had gone by, with a rhythm as pronounced and as impersonal as the noise of a machine. In the shop windows there were, I knew, the signs of a life very unlike that I had seen at Killeenan: halfpenny comic papers and story papers, sixpenny reprints of popular novels, and, with the exception of a dusty Dumas or Scott strayed thither, one knew not how, and one or two little books of Irish ballads, nothing that one calls literature, nothing that would interest the few thousands who alone out of many millions have what we call culture.[4] A few miles had divided the sixteenth century, with its equality of culture, of good taste, from the twentieth, where if a man has fine taste he has either been born to leisure and opportunity or has in him an energy that is genius. One saw the difference in the clothes of the people of the town and of the village, for, as the Emerald Tablet says, outward and inner things answer to one another.[5] The village men wore their bawneens, their white flannel jackets; they had clothes that had a little memory of clothes that had once been adapted to their calling by centuries of continual slight changes. They were sometimes well dressed, for they suggested nothing but themselves and wore little that had suited another better. But in the town nobody was well dressed; for in modern life, only a few people—some few thousands—set the fashion, and set it to please themselves and to fit their lives; and as for the rest, they must go shabby—the ploughman in clothes cut for a life of leisure, but made of shoddy, and the tramp in the ploughman's cast-off clothes, and the scarecrow in the tramp's battered coat and broken hat.

II

All that love the arts or love dignity in life have at one time or another noticed these things, and some have wondered why the world has for some three or four centuries sacrificed so much, and with what seems a growing recklessness, to create an intellectual aristocracy, a leisured class—to set apart, and above all others, a number of men and women who are not very well pleased with one another or the world they have to live in. It is some comparison, like this that I have made, which has been the origin, as I think, of most attempts to revive some old language in which the general business of the world is no longer transacted. The Provençal movement, the Welsh, the Czech, have all, I think, been attempting, when we examine them to the heart, to restore what is called a more picturesque way of life—that is to say, a way of life in which the common man has some share in imaginative art. That this is the decisive element in the attempt to revive and to preserve the Irish language I am very certain. A language enthusiast does not put it that way to himself; he says, rather, 'If I can make the people talk Irish again they will be the less English'; but if you talk to him till you have hunted the words into their burrow you will find that the word 'Ireland' means to him a form of life delightful to his imagination, and that the word 'England' suggests to him a cold, joyless, irreligious and ugly life. The life of the villages, with its songs, its dances and its pious greetings, its conversations full of vivid images shaped hardly more by life itself than by innumerable forgotten poets, all that life of good-nature and improvisation grows more noble as he meditates upon it, for it mingles with the Middle Ages until he no longer can see it as it is but as it was, when it ran, as it were, into a point of fire in the courtliness of kings' houses. He hardly knows whether what stirred him yesterday was that old fiddler, playing an almost-forgotten music on a fiddle mended with twine, or a sudden thought of some king that was of the blood of that old man, some O'Loughlin or O'Byrne, listening amid his soldiers, he and they at the one table, they too, lucky, bright-eyed, while the minstrel sang of angry Cuchulain, or of him men called 'Golden salmon of the sea, clean hawk of the air'.[6] It will not please him, however, if you tell him that he is fighting the modern world, which he calls 'England', as Mistral and his fellows called it Paris, and that he will need more than language if he is to make the monster turn up its white belly. And yet the difference between what the word England means and all that the word Gaelic suggests is greater than any that could have been before the imagination of Mistral. Ireland, her imagination at its noon before the birth of Chaucer, has created the most beautiful literature of a whole people that has been anywhere since Greece and Rome, while English literature, the greatest of all literatures but that of Greece, is yet the literature of a few. Nothing of it but a handful of ballads about Robin Hood has come from the folk or belongs to them rightly, for the good English writers, with a few exceptions that seem accidental, have written for a small cultivated class; and is not this the reason?[7] Irish poetry and Irish stories were made to be spoken or sung, while English literature, alone of great literatures, because the newest of them all, has all but completely shaped itself in the printing-press. In Ireland to-day the old world that sang and listened is, it may be for the last time in Europe, face to face with the world that reads and writes, and their antagonism is always present under some name or other in Irish imagination and intellect. I myself cannot be convinced that the printing-press will be always victor, for change is inconceivably swift, and when it begins—well, as the proverb has it, everything comes in at the hole.[8] The world soon tires of its toys, and our exaggerated love of print and paper seems to me to come out of passing conditions and to be no more a part of the final constitution of things than the craving of a woman in child-bed for green apples. When a man takes a book into the corner, he surrenders so much life for his knowledge, so much, I mean, of that normal activity that gives him life and strength; he lays away his own handiwork and turns from his friend, and if the book is good he is at some pains to press all the little wanderings and tumults of the mind into silence and quiet. If the reader be poor, if he has worked all day at the plough or the desk, he will hardly have strength enough for any but a meretricious book; nor is it only when the book is on the knees that his own life must be given for it. For a good and sincere book needs the preparation of the peculiar studies and reveries that prepare for good taste, and make it easier for the mind to find pleasure in a new landscape; and all these reveries and studies have need of so much time and thought that it is almost certain a man cannot be a successful doctor, or engineer, or Cabinet Minister, and have a culture good enough to escape the mockery of the ragged art student who comes of an evening sometimes to borrow a half-sovereign.[9] The old culture came to a man at his work; it was not at the expense of life, but an exaltation of life itself; it came in at the eyes as some civic ceremony sailed along the streets, or as we arrayed ourselves before the looking-glass; or it came in at the ears in a song as we bent over the plough or the anvil, or at that great table where rich and poor sat down together and heard the minstrel bidding them pass around the wine-cup and say a prayer for Gawain* dead. Certainly it came without a price; it did not take one from one's friends and one's handiwork; but it was like a good woman who gives all for love and is never jealous and is ready to do all the talking when we are tired.

How the old is to come again, how the other side of the penny is to come up, how the spit is to turn the other side of the meat to the fire, I do not know, but that the time will come I am certain. When one kind of desire has been satisfied for a long time it becomes sleepy, and other kinds, long quiet, after making a noise begin to order life. Of the many things, desires or powers or instruments, that are to change the world, the artist is fitted to understand but two or three, and the less he troubles himself about the complexity that is outside his craft, the more will he find it all within his craft, and the more dexterous will his hand and his thought

*No, it was some other Knight of the Table. —1923.[10]

become. I am trying to see nothing in the world but the arts, and nothing in this change—which one cannot prove but only foretell—but the share my own art will have in it.

III

One thing is entirely certain. Wherever the old imaginative life lingers it must be stirred into life, and kept alive, and in Ireland this is the work, it may be, of the Gaelic movement. But the nineteenth century, with its moral zeal, its insistence upon irrelevant interests, having passed over, the artist can admit that he cares about nothing that does not give him a new subject or a new technique. Propaganda would be for him a dissipation, but he may compare his art, if he has a mind to, with the arts that belonged to a whole people, and discover, not how to imitate the external form of an epic or a folk-song, but how to express in some equivalent form whatever in the thoughts of his own age seem, as it were, to press into the future. The most obvious difference is that when literature belonged to a whole people, its three great forms, narrative, lyrical, and dramatic, found their way to men's minds without the mediation of print and paper. That narrative poetry may find its minstrels again, and lyrical poetry adequate singers, and dramatic poetry adequate players, he must spend much of his time with these three lost arts, and the more technical is his interest the better. When I first began working in Ireland at what some newspaper has called the Celtic Renaissance, I saw that we had still even in English a sufficient audience for song and speech. Certain of our young men and women, too restless and sociable to be readers, had amongst them an interest in Irish legend and history, and years of imaginative politics had kept them from forgetting, as most modern people have, how to listen to serious words. I always saw that some kind of theatre would be a natural centre for a tradition of feeling and thought, but that it must—and this was its chief opportunity—appeal to the interest appealed to by lively conversation or by oratory. In other words, that it must be made for young people who were sufficiently ignorant to refuse a pound of flesh even though the Nine Worthies offered their wisdom in return.[11] They are not, perhaps, very numerous, for they do not include the thousands of conquered spirits who in Dublin, as elsewhere, go to see *The Girl from Kay's,* or when Mr. Tree is upon tour, *The Girl from Prospero's Island;* and the peasant in Ireland, as elsewhere, has not taken to the theatre, and can, I think, be moved through Gaelic only.[12]

If one could get them, I thought, one could draw to oneself the apathetic people who are in every country, and people who don't know what they like till somebody tells them. Now, a friend has given me that theatre.[13] It is not very big, but it is quite big enough to seat those few thousands and their friends in a seven days' run of a new play; and I have begun my real business. I have to find once again singers, minstrels, and players who love words more than any other thing under heaven, for without fine words there is no literature.

IV

I will say but a little of dramatic technique, as I would have it in this theatre of speech, of romance, of extravagance, for I have written of all that so many times. In every art, when we consider that it has need of a renewing of life, we go backward till we light upon a time when it was nearer to human life and instinct, before it had gathered about it so many mechanical specialisations and traditions. We examine that earlier condition and think out its principles of life that we may be able to separate accidental from vital things. William Morris, for instance, studied the earliest printing, the founts of type that were made when men saw their craft with eyes that were still new, and with leisure, and without the restraints of commerce and custom. And then he made a type that was really new, that had the quality of his own mind about it, though it reminds one of its ancestry, of its high breeding as it were. Coleridge and Wordsworth were influenced by the publication of Percy's *Reliques* to the making of a simplicity altogether unlike that of old ballad-writers.[14] Rossetti went to early Italian painting, to Holy Families and choirs of angels, that he might learn how to express an emotion that had its roots in sexual desire and in the delight of his generation in fine clothes and in beautiful rooms. Nor is it otherwise with the reformers of churches and of the social order, for reform must justify itself by a return in feeling to something that our fathers have told us in the old time.

So it is with us. Inspired by players who played before a figured curtain, we have made scenery, indeed, but scenery that is little more than a suggestion—a pattern with recurring boughs and leaves of gold for a wood, a great green curtain with a red stencil upon it to carry the eye upward for a palace, and so on. More important than these, we have looked for the centre of our art where the players of the time of Shakespeare and of Corneille found theirs—in speech, whether it be the perfect mimicry of the conversation of two country-men of the roads, or that idealised speech poets have imagined for what we think but do not say. Before men read, the ear and the tongue were subtle, and delighted one another with the little tunes that were in words; every word would have its own tune, though but one main note may have been marked enough for us to name it. They loved language, and all literature was then, whether in the mouth of minstrels, players, or singers, but the perfection of an art that everybody practised, a flower out of the stem of life. And language continually renewed itself in that perfection, returning to daily life out of that finer leisure, strengthened and sweetened as from a retreat ordered by religion. The ordinary dramatic critic, when you tell him that a play, if it is to be of a great kind, must have beautiful words, will answer that you have misunderstood the nature of the stage and are asking of it what books should give. Sometimes when some excellent man, a playgoer certainly and sometimes a critic, has read me a passage out of some poet, I have been set wondering what books of poetry can mean to the greater number of men. If they are to read poetry at all, if they are to enjoy beautiful rhythm, if they are to get from poetry anything but what it has in common with prose, they must hear it spoken by men who have music in their voices and a learned understanding of its sound. There is no poem so great that a fine speaker cannot make it greater or that a bad ear cannot make it nothing. All the arts when young and happy are but the point of the spear whose handle is our daily life. When they grow old and unhappy they perfect themselves away from life, and life, seeing that they are sufficient to themselves, forgets them. The fruit of the tree that was in Eden grows out of a flower full of scent, rounds and ripens, until at last the little stem, that brought to it the sap out of the tree, dries up and breaks, and the fruit rots upon the ground.[15]

The theatre grows more elaborate, developing the player at the expense of the poet, developing the scenery at the expense of the player, always increasing the importance of whatever has come to it out of the mere mechanism of a building or the interests of a class, specialising more and more, doing whatever is easiest rather than what is most noble, and shaping imaginations before the footlights as behind, that are stirred to excitements that belong to it and not to life; until at last life, which knows that a specialised energy is not herself, turns to other things, content to leave it to weaklings and triflers, to those in whose body there is the least quantity of herself.

V

But if we are to delight our three or four thousand young men and women with a delight that will follow them into their own houses, and if we are to add the country-man to their number, we shall need more than the play, we shall need those other spoken arts. The player rose into importance in the town, but the minstrel is of the country. We must have narrative as well as dramatic poetry, and we are making room for it in the theatre in the first instance, but in this also we must go to an earlier time. Modern recitation is not, like modern theatrical art, an over-elaboration of a true art, but an entire misunderstanding. It has no tradition at all. It is an endeavour to do what can only be done well by the player. It has no relation of its own to life. Some young man in evening clothes will recite to you 'The Dream of Eugene Aram', and it will be laughable, grotesque and a little vulgar.[16] Tragic emotions that need scenic illusion, a long preparation, a gradual heightening of emotion, are thrust into the middle of our common affairs. That they may be as extravagant, as little tempered by anything ideal or distant as possible, he will break up the rhythm, regarding neither the length of the lines nor the natural music of the phrases, and distort the accent by every casual impulse. He will gesticulate wildly, adapting his movements to the drama as if Eugene Aram were in the room before us, and all the time we see a young man in evening dress who has become unaccountably insane. Nothing that he can do or say will make us forget that he is Mr. Robinson the bank clerk, and that the toes of his boots turn upward. We have nothing to learn here. We must go to the villages or we must go back hundreds of years to Wolfram of Eschenbach and the castles of Thuringia. In this, as in all other arts, one finds its law and its true purpose when one is near the source. The minstrel never dramatised anybody but himself. It was impossible, from the nature of the words the poet had put into his mouth, or that he had made for himself, that he should speak as another person. He will go no nearer to drama than we do in daily speech, and he will not allow you for any long time to forget himself. Our own Raftery will stop the tale to cry, 'This is what I, Raftery, wrote down in the book of the people'; or, 'I, myself, Raftery, went to bed without supper that night'.[17] Or, if it is Wolfram, and the tale is of Gawain or Parsival, he will tell the listening ladies that he sings of happy love out of his own unhappy love, or he will interrupt the story of a siege and its hardships to remember his own house, where there is not enough food for the mice. He knows how to keep himself interesting that his words may have weight—so many lines of narrative, and then a phrase about himself and his emotions. The reciter cannot be a player, for that is a different art; but he must be a messenger, and he should be as interesting, as exciting, as are all that carry great news. He comes from far off, and he speaks of far-off things with his own peculiar animation, and instead of lessening the ideal and beautiful elements of speech he may, if he has a mind to, increase them. He may speak to actual notes as a singer does if they are so simple that he never loses the speaking-voice, and if the poem is long he must do so, or his own voice will become weary and formless. His art is nearer to pattern than that of the player. It is always allusion, never illusion; for what he tells of, no matter how impassioned he may become, is always distant, and for this reason he may permit himself every kind of nobleness. In a short poem he may interrupt the narrative with a burden, which the audience will soon learn to sing, and this burden, because it is repeated and need not tell a story to a first hearing, can have a more elaborate musical notation, can go nearer to ordinary song. Gradually other devices will occur to him—effects of loudness and softness, of increasing and decreasing speed, certain rhythmic movements of his body, a score of forgotten things, for the art of speech is lost, and when we begin at it every day is a discovery. The reciter must be made exciting and wonderful in himself, apart from what he has to tell, and that is more difficult than it was in the Middle Ages. We are not mysterious to one another; we can come from far off and yet be no better than our neighbours. We are no longer like those Egyptian birds that flew out of Arabia, their claws full of spices; nor can we, like an ancient or mediaeval poet, throw into our verses the emotions and events of our lives, or even dramatise, as they could, the life of the minstrel into whose mouth we are to put our words.[18] I can think of nothing better than to borrow from the tellers of old tales, who will often pretend to have been at the wedding of the princess or afterwards 'when they were throwing out children by the basketful', and to give the story-teller definite fictitious personality and find for him an appropriate costume.[19] Many costumes and persons come into my imagination. I imagine an old country-man upon the stage of the theatre or in some little country court-house where a Gaelic society is meeting, and I can hear him say that he is Raftery or a brother, and that he has tramped through France and Spain and the whole world. He has seen everything, and he has all country love-tales at his finger-tips. I can imagine, too—and now the story-teller is more serious and more naked of country circumstance—a jester with black cockscomb and black clothes. He has been in the faery hills; perhaps he is the terrible *Amadán-na-Breena* himself; or he has been so long in the world that he can tell of ancient battles.[20] It is not as good as what we have lost, but we cannot hope to see in our time, except by some rare accident, the minstrel who differs from his audience in nothing but the exaltation of his mood, and who is yet as exciting and as romantic in their eyes as were Raftery and Wolfram to their people.

It is perhaps nearly impossible to make recitation a living thing, for there is no existing taste we can appeal to; but it should not be hard here in Ireland to interest people in songs that are made for the word's sake and not for the music, or for that only in a secondary degree. They are interested in such songs already, only the songs have little subtlety of thought and of language. One does not find in them that richness of emotion which but seems modern because it has been brought so very lately out of the cellar. At their best they are the songs of children and of country-people, eternally young for all their centuries, and yet not even in old days, as one thinks, a vintage for kings' houses. We require a method of setting to music that will make it possible to sing or to speak to notes a poem like Rossetti's translation of 'The Ballad of Dead Ladies' in such a fashion that no word shall have an intonation or accentuation it could not have in passionate speech.[21] It must be set for the speaking-voice, like the songs that sailors make up or remember, and a man at the far end of the room must be able to take it down on a first hearing. An English musical paper said the other day, in commenting on something I had written, 'Owing to musical necessities, vowels must be lengthened in singing to an extent which in speech would be ludicrous if not absolutely impossible'.[22] I have but one art, that of speech, and my feeling for music dissociated from speech is very slight, and listening as I do to the words with the better part of my attention, there is no modern song sung in the modern way that is not to my taste 'ludicrous' and 'impossible'. I hear with older ears than the musician, and the songs of country-people and of sailors delight me. I wonder why the musician is not content to set to music some arrangement of meaningless liquid vowels, and thereby to make his song like that of the birds; but I do not judge his art for any purpose but my own.* It is worthless for my purpose certainly, and it is one of the causes that are bringing about in modern countries a degradation of language. I have to find men with more music than I have, who will develop to a finer subtlety the singing of the cottage and the forecastle, and develop it more on the side of speech than that of music, until it has become intellectual and nervous enough to be the vehicle of a Shelley or a Keats. For some purposes it will be necessary to divine the lineaments of a still older art, and re-create the regulated declamations that died out

---

*I have heard musicians excuse themselves by claiming that they put the words there for the sake of the singer; but if that be so, why should not the singer sing something she may wish to have by rote? Nobody will hear the words; and the local time-table, or, so much suet and so many raisins, and so much spice and so much sugar, and whether it is to be put in a quick or a slow oven, would run very nicely with a little management. —March 1908.

when music fell into its earliest elaborations. Miss Farr has divined enough of this older art, of which no fragment has come down to us—for even the music of *Aucassin and Nicolette,* with its definite tune, its recurring pattern of sound, is something more than decla-mation—to make the chorus of *Hippolytus* and of *The Trojan Women,* at the Court Theatre or the Lyric, intelligible speech, even when several voices spoke together.[23] She used very often definite melodies of a very simple kind, but always when the thought became intricate and the measure grave and slow, fell back upon declamation regulated by notes. Her experiments have included almost every kind of verse, and every possible elaboration of sound compatible with the supremacy of the words. I do not think Homer is ever so moving as when she recites him to a little tune played on a stringed instrument not very unlike a lyre. She began at my suggestion with songs in plays, for it was clearly an absurd thing that words necessary to one's understanding of the action, either because they explained some character, or because they car-ried some emotion to its highest intensity, should be less intelligi-ble than the bustling and ruder words of the dialogue. We have tried our art, since we first tried it in a theatre, upon many kinds of audi-ences, and have found that ordinary men and women take pleasure in it and sometimes say that they never understood poetry before. It is, however, more difficult to move those—fortunately for our pur-pose but a few—whose ears are accustomed to the abstract emo-tion and elaboration of notes in modern music.

VI

If we accomplish this great work, if we make it possible again for the poet to express himself, not merely through words, but through the voices of singers, of minstrels, of players, we shall cer-tainly have changed the substance and the manner of our poetry. Everyone[†] who has to interest his audience through the voice dis-covers that his success depends upon the clear, simple and varied structure of his thought. I have written a good many plays in verse and prose, and almost all those plays I have rewritten after per-formance, sometimes again and again, and every re-writing that has succeeded upon the stage has been an addition to the masculine element, an increase of strength in the bony structure.

Modern literature, above all poetical literature, is monotonous in its structure and effeminate in its continual insistence upon certain moments of strained lyricism. William Morris, who did more than any modern to recover mediaeval art, did not in his *Earthly Paradise* copy from Chaucer, from whom he copied so much that was *naïve* and beautiful, what seems to me essential in Chaucer's art.[24] He thought of himself as writing for the reader, who could return to him again and again when the chosen mood had come, and became monotonous, melancholy, too continuously lyrical in his understanding of emotion and of life. Had he accustomed himself to read out his poems upon those Sunday evenings that he gave to Socialist speeches, and to gather an audience of average men, precisely such an audience as I have often seen in his house, he would have been forced to Chaucer's variety, to his delight in the height and depth, and would have found expression for that humorous, many-sided nature of his. I owe to him many truths, but I would add to those truths the certainty that all the old writers, the masculine writers of the world, wrote to be spoken or to be sung, and in a later age to be read aloud, for hearers who had to understand swiftly or not at all, and who gave up nothing of life to listen, but sat, the day's work over, friend by friend, lover by lover.

THE ARROW: 20 OCTOBER 1906*—
THE SEASON'S WORK

A character of the winter's work will be the large number of romantic, poetic and historical plays—that is to say, of plays which require a convention for their performance; their speech, whether it be verse or prose, being so heightened as to transcend that of any form of real life. Our first two years of the Abbey Theatre have been expended mostly on the perfecting of the Company in peasant comedy and tragedy. Every national dramatic movement or theatre in countries like Bohemia and Hungary, as in Elizabethan England, has arisen out of a study of the common people, who preserve national characteristics more than any other class, and out of an imaginative re-creation of national history or legend. The life of the drawing-room, the life represented in most plays of the ordinary theatre of to-day, differs but little all over the world, and has as little to do with the national spirit as the architecture of, let us say, St. Stephen's Green, or Queen's Gate, or of the Boulevards about the Arc de Triomphe.[2]

As we wish our work to be full of the life of this country, our stage-manager has almost always to train our actors from the beginning, always so in the case of peasant plays, and this makes the building up of a theatre like ours the work of years. We are now fairly satisfied with the representation of peasant life, and we can afford to give the greater part of our attention to other expressions of our art and of our life. The romantic work and poetical work once reasonably good, we can, if but the dramatist arrive, take up

---

*The Arrow, a briefer chronicle than Samhain, was distributed with the programme for a few months. —March 1908.[1]

the life of our drawing-rooms, and see if there is something characteristic there, something which our nationality may enable us to
express better than others, and so create plays of that life and means
to play them as truthful as a play of Hauptmann's or of Ibsen's upon
the German or Scandinavian stage. I am not myself interested in this
kind of work, and do not believe it to be as important as contemporary critics think it is, but a theatre such as we project should give
a reasonably complete expression to the imaginative interests of its
country. In any case it was easier, and therefore wiser, to begin where
our art is most unlike that of others, with the representation of country life.

It is possible to speak the universal truths of human nature
whether the speakers be peasants or wealthy men, for:

> Love doth sing
> As sweetly in a beggar as a king.[3]

So far as we have any model before us it is the national and municipal theatres in various Continental towns, and, like the best of these,
we must have in our repertory masterpieces from every great
school of dramatic literature, and play them confidently, even
though the public be slow to like that old stern art, and perhaps a
little proudly, remembering that no other English-speaking theatre
can be so catholic. Certainly the weathercocks of our imagination
will not turn those painted eyes of theirs too long to the quarter of
the Scandinavian winds. If the wind blow long from the Mediter-
ranean, the paint may peel before we pray for a change in the
weather.

THE ARROW: 23 FEBRUARY 1907—
THE CONTROVERSY OVER
THE PLAYBOY OF THE WESTERN WORLD

We have claimed for our writers the freedom to find in their own land every expression of good and evil necessary to their art, for Irish life contains, like all vigorous life, the seeds of all good and evil, and a writer must be free here as elsewhere to watch where weed or flower ripens. No one who knows the work of our Theatre as a whole can say we have neglected the flower; but the moment a writer is forbidden to take pleasure in the weed, his art loses energy and abundance. In the great days of English dramatic art the greatest English writer of comedy was free to create *The Alchemist* and *Volpone,* but a demand born of Puritan conviction and shopkeeping timidity and insincerity, for what many second-rate intellects thought to be noble and elevating events and characters, had already at the outset of the eighteenth century ended the English drama as a complete and serious art.[1] Sheridan and Goldsmith, when they restored comedy after an epoch of sentimentalities, had to apologise for their satiric genius by scenes of conventional love-making and sentimental domesticity that have set them outside the company of all, whether their genius be great or little, whose work is pure and whole. The quarrel of our Theatre to-day is the quarrel of the Theatre in many lands; for the old Puritanism, the old dislike of power and reality have not changed, even when they are called by some Gaelic name.

[On the second performance of *The Playboy of the Western World,* about forty men who sat in the middle of the pit succeeded in making the play entirely inaudible.[2] Some of them brought tin trumpets, and the noise began immediately on the rise of the curtain. For days articles in the Press called for the withdrawal of the play, but we played for the seven nights we had announced; and before the week's end opinion had turned in our favour. There were, however, nightly disturbances and a good deal of rioting in the surrounding streets. On the last night of the play there were, I believe, five hundred police keeping order in the theatre and in its neighbourhood. Some days later our enemies, though beaten so far as the play was concerned, crowded into the cheaper seats for a debate on the freedom of the stage. They were very excited, and kept up the discussion until near twelve. The last paragraphs of my opening statement ran as follows.]

From Mr. Yeats' opening Speech in the Debate on February 4, 1907, at the Abbey Theatre.

The struggle of the last week has been long a necessity; various paragraphs in newspapers describing Irish attacks on theatres had made many worthy young men come to think that the silencing of a stage at their own pleasure, even if hundreds desired that it should not be silenced, might win them a little fame, and, perhaps, serve their country. Some of these attacks have been made on plays which are in themselves indefensible, vulgar and old-fashioned farces and comedies. But the attack, being an annihilation of civil rights, was never anything but an increase of Irish disorder. The last I heard of was in Liverpool, and there a stage was rushed, and a priest, who had set a play upon it, withdrew his play and apologised to the audience. We have not such pliant bones, and did not learn in the houses that bred us a so suppliant knee. But behind the excitement of example there is a more fundamental movement of opinion. Some seven or eight years ago the National movement was democratised and passed from the hands of a few leaders into those of large numbers of young men organised in clubs and societies. These young men made the mistake of the newly-enfranchised everywhere; they fought for causes worthy in themselves with the unworthy instruments of tyranny and violence. Comic songs of a certain kind were to be driven from the stage, every one was to wear Irish cloth, every one was to learn Irish, every one was to hold certain opinions, and these ends were sought by personal attacks, by

virulent caricature and violent derision. It needs eloquence to persuade and knowledge to expound; but the coarser means come ready
to every man's hand, as ready as a stone or a stick, and where these
coarse means are all, there is nothing but mob, and the common-
est idea most prospers and is most sought for.

Gentlemen of the little clubs and societies, do not mistake the
meaning of our victory; it means something for us, but more for
you. When the curtain of *The Playboy* fell on Saturday night in the
midst of what *The Sunday Independent*—no friendly witness—
described as 'thunders of applause', I am confident that I saw the
rise in this country of a new thought, a new opinion, that we had
long needed.[3] It was not all approval of Mr. Synge's play that sent
the receipts of the Abbey Theatre this last week to twice the height
they had ever touched before.[4] The generation of young men and
girls who are now leaving schools or colleges are weary of the
tyranny of clubs and leagues. They wish again for individual sincerity, the eternal quest of truth, all that has been given up for so
long that all might crouch upon the one roost and quack or cry in
the one flock. We are beginning once again to ask what a man is,
and to be content to wait a little before we go on to that further
question: What is a good Irishman? There are some who have not
yet their degrees that will say to friend or neighbour, 'You have voted
with the English, and that is bad'; or 'You have sent away your Irish
servants, or thrown away your Irish clothes, or blacked your face
for your singing. I despise what you have done, I keep you still my
friend; but if you are terrorised out of doing any of these things,
evil things though I know them to be, I will not have you for my
friend any more'. Manhood is all, and the root of manhood is
courage and courtesy.

THE ARROW: 1 JUNE 1907—
ON TAKING *THE PLAYBOY*
TO LONDON

The failure of the audience to understand this powerful and strange work (*The Playboy of the Western World*) has been the one serious failure of our movement, and it could not have happened but that the greater number of those who came to shout down the play were no regular part of our audience at all, but members of parties and societies whose main interests are political. We have been denounced with even greater violence than on the first production of the play for announcing that we should carry it to London.[1] We cannot see that an attack, which we believe to have been founded on a misunderstanding of the nature of literature, should prevent us from selecting, as our custom is, whatever of our best comes within the compass of our players at the time, to show in some English theatres. Nearly all strong and strange writing is attacked on its appearance, and those who press it upon the world may not cease from pressing it, for their justification is its ultimate acceptance. Ireland is passing through a crisis in the life of the mind greater than any she has known since the rise of the Young Ireland party, and based upon a principle which sets many in opposition to the habits of thought and feeling come down from that party, for the seasons change, and need and occupation with them.[2] Many are beginning to recognise the right of the individual mind to see the world in its own way, to cherish the thoughts which separate men from one another, and that are the creators of distinguished life, instead of those thoughts that had made one man like another if they could, and have but succeeded in setting hysteria and insincerity in place of confidence and self-possession. To the Young Ireland writers, who have still the ear of Ireland, though not its distracted mind, truth was historical and external and not a self-consistent personal vision, and it is but according to ancient custom that the new truth should force its way amid riot and great anger.[3]

SAMHAIN: 1908—
FIRST PRINCIPLES

Some country-men in Galway, whither we carried our plays in dialect a few weeks ago, said that it was no use going in to see them because they showed people that could be seen on the road every day; but these were but a few, and we had a great popular success, crowds being turned away every evening from the doors.[1] Ireland is always Connacht to my imagination, for there more than else-where is the folk tradition that is the loftiest thing that has come down to us within the ring of Ireland. I knew an observant and cultivated French count, descendant of *émigrés,* who came for a few months in every summer to a property they had left him upon the Galway shore. He came from Paris or from Rome, but would not stay, if he could help it, even a few hours in Dublin, because Dublin was 'Shabby England'.[2] We find our most highly trained audiences of late in Dublin, but the majority of theatre-goers drift between what is Irish and what is English in confused uncertainty, and have not even begun the search for what is their own.

Somebody in *Un grand homme de province à Paris* says, with I know not what truth, that French actresses pay more for attacks than admiring criticism, for 'controversy is fame'.[3] In Ireland this would be an unnecessary expense, and many of the attacks which have followed us from the beginning in such plenty have arisen out of conceptions of life which, unknown to the journalists who have made them, are essentially English, though of an England that has begun to change its clothes since Matthew Arnold and his con-temporaries began a truer popular culture. Even at this moment the early Victorian thought is not so out of fashion that English news-papers would not revive it and talk of the duties of writers to preach and the like, all that old Utilitarianism, if the drama, let us say, were taken seriously enough for leading articles instead of being left to the criticism of a few writers who really know something of their business.[4] Some fifteen years ago, English critics themselves wrote of Ibsen very much as our more hysterical patriots write of us. These patriots, with an heretical preference for faith over works—for have not opinions and second- and third-hand[†] conceptions of life, images of what we wish to be, a substance of things hoped for, come from the pawnshop of schismatical faith?—continually attack in the interest of some point of view popularised by Macaulay and his contemporaries, or of some reflection from English novelists and the like, Irish emotion and temperament discovered by some writer in himself after years of labour, for all reality comes to us as the reward of labour.[5] Forms of emotion and thought which the future will recognise as peculiarly Irish, for no other country has had the like, are looked upon as un-Irish because of their novelty in a land that is so nearly conquered it has all but nothing of its own. English provincialism shouts through the lips of Irish patriots who have no knowledge of other countries to give them a standard of comparison, and they, with the confidence of all who speak the opinions of others, labour to thwart everybody who would dig a well for Irish water to bubble in.

In 1892, when I started the National Literary Society, and began a movement that was intended to lead up to the establishment of an Irish Dramatic School, the songs and ballads of Young Ireland were used as examples to prove the personal, and therefore Irish art of A. E., Lionel Johnson, Katharine Tynan and myself (see Lionel Johnson's essay,[†] *Poetry and Politics*), an un-Irish[†] thing.[6] And yet those songs and ballads, with the exception of a small number which are partly copied from Gaelic models, and a few, almost all by Mangan, that have a personal style, are imitations of the poetry of Burns and Macaulay and Scott.[7] All literature in every country is derived from models, and as often as not these are foreign models, and it is the presence of a personal element alone that can give it nationality in a fine sense, the nationality of its maker. It is only before personality has been attained that a race struggling towards self-consciousness is the better for having, as in primitive times, nothing but native models, for before this has been attained it can neither assimilate nor reject. It was precisely at this passive moment, attainment approaching but not yet come, that the Irish heart and mind surrendered to England, or rather to what is most temporary in England; and Irish patriotism, content that the names and the opinions should be Irish, was deceived and satisfied. It is always necessary to affirm and to reaffirm that nationality is in the things that escape analysis. We discover it, as we do the quality of saltness or sweetness, by the taste, and literature is a cultivation of taste.

The Irish novelists of the nineteenth century, who established themselves, like the Young Ireland poets, upon various English writers, without, except at rare moments—*Castle Rackrent* was, it may be, the most inspired of those moments—attaining to personality, have filled the popular mind with images of character, with forms of construction, with a criticism of life, which are all so many arguments to prove that some play that has arisen out of a fresh vision is unlike every Irish thing.[8] A real or fancied French influence is pointed out at once and objected to, but the English influence, which runs through the patriotic reading of the people, is not noticed because it is everywhere. I say, with certainty, that *The Playboy of the Western World*, so rich in observation, so full of the temperament of a unique man, has more of Ireland in its characters, in its method of art, in its conception of morals, than all the novels of Kickham;[†] Michael Banim (I have much respect for his brother John, perhaps because French influence in part annulled the influence of Mrs. Radcliffe, and so helped him to personality); Gerald Griffin, so full of amiable English sentiment; Carleton, in his longer tales, powerful spirit though he was; and, of course, much more in any page of it than in all those romances founded upon Walter Scott, which are or used to be published in Irish newspapers, to make boys and girls into patriots.[9] Here and there, of course, one finds Irish elements. In Lever, for instance, even after one has put aside all that is second-hand,[†] there is a rightful Irish gaiety, but one finds these elements only just in so far as the writers had come to know themselves in the Socratic sense.[10] Of course, too, the tradition itself was not all English, but it is impossible to divide what is new and, therefore, Irish, what is very old and, therefore, Irish, from all that is foreign, from all that is an accident of imperfect culture, before we have had some revelation of Irish character, pure enough and varied enough to create a standard of comparison. I do not speak carelessly of the Irish novelists, for when I was in London during the first years of my literary life, I read them continually, seeking in them an image of Ireland that I might not forget what I meant to be the foundations of my art, trying always to winnow as I read. I only escaped from many misconceptions when, in 1897, I began an active Irish life, comparing what I saw about me with what I heard of in Galway cottages.[11] Yet for all that, it was from the novelists and poets that I learned in part my symbols of expression. Somebody has said that all sound philosophy is but biography, and what I myself did, getting into an original relation to Irish life, creating in myself a new character, a new pose—in the French sense of the word—the literary mind of Ireland must do as a whole, always understanding that the result must be no bundle of formulas, not faggots but a fire.[12] We never learn to know ourselves by thought, said Goethe, but by action only; and to a writer creation is action.[13]

A moment comes in every country when its character expresses itself through some group of writers, painters, or musicians, and it is this moment, the moment of Goethe in Germany, of the Elizabethan poets in England, of the Van Eycks in the Low Countries, of Corneille and Racine in France, of Ibsen and Björnson in Scandinavia, which fixes the finer elements of national character for generations.[14] This moment is impossible until public opinion is ready to welcome in the mind of the artist a power, little affected by external things, being self-contained, self-created, self-sufficing, the seed of character. Generally up to that moment literature has tried to express everybody's thought, history being considered merely as a chronicle of facts, but now, at the instant of revelation, writers think the world is but their palette, and if history amuses them, it is but, as Goethe says, because they would do its personages the honour of naming after them their own thoughts.[15]

In the same spirit they approach their contemporaries when they borrow for their own passions the images of living men, and, at times, external facts will be no more to them than the pewter pot gleaming in the sunlight that started Jacob Boehme into his seven days' trance.[16]

There are moments, indeed, when they will give you more powerful and exact impressions of the outer world than any other can, but these impressions are always those which they have been the first to receive, and more often than not, to make them the more vivid, they will leave out everything that everybody can see every day. The man of genius may be Signor Mancini if he please, but never Mr. Lafayette.[17]

Just as they use the life of their own times they use past literature, their own and that of other countries, selecting here and there under what must always seem, until their revelation is understood, an impulse of mere caprice, and the more original, that is to say the more pure, the revelation, the greater the caprice. It was a moment of importance in Scandinavia when a certain pamphlet announced that an historical play could not find its justification in history alone, for it must contain an idea, meaning by an idea thought flowing out of character, as opinions are thought arising out of the necessities of organization.[18] We grow like others through opinions, but through ideas discover ourselves, for these are only true when images of our own power.

In no country has this independence of mind, this audacity I had almost said, been attained without controversy, for the men who affirm it seem the enemies of all other interests. In Ireland, in addition to the external art of our predecessors, full of the misunderstandings created by English influence, there is a preoccupation of a great part of the population with opinions and a habit of deciding that a man is useful to his country, or otherwise, not by what he is in himself or by what he does in his whole life, but by the opinions he holds on one or two subjects. Balzac in *Les Comédiens sans le savoir,* describes a sculptor, a follower of the Socialist Fourier, who has made an allegorical figure of harmony, and got into his statue the doctrine of his master by giving it six breasts, and by putting under its feet an enormous Savoy cabbage. One of his friends promises that when everybody is converted to their doctrine he will be the foremost man of his craft, but another and a wiser says of him that 'while opinions cannot give talent they inevitably spoil it', and adds that an artist's opinion ought to be a faith in works, and that there is no way for him to succeed but by work, 'while nature gives the sacred fire'.[19] In Paris, according to Balzac, it is ambition that makes artists and writers identify themselves with a cause that gives them the help of politicians, of journalists, or of society, as the case may be, but in Ireland, so far as I am able to see, they do it for sociability's sake, to have a crowd to shout with, and therefore by half deliberate sophistry they persuade themselves that the old tale is not true, and that art is not ruined so. I do not mean that the artist should not as a man be a good citizen and hold opinions like another; Balzac was a Catholic and a Monarchist. We, too, in following his great example, have not put away in anything the strong opinions that we set out with, but in our art they have no place. Every trouble of our theatre in its earlier years, every attack on us in any year, has come directly or indirectly either from those who prefer Mr. Lafayette to Signor Mancini, or from those who believe from a defective education that the writer who does not help some cause, who does not support some opinion, is but an idler, or if his air be too serious for that, the supporter of some hidden wickedness. A principal actor left us in our first year because he believed *The Hour-Glass* to be a problem play.[20] This is all natural enough in a country where the majority have been denied University teaching. I found precisely the same prejudices among the self-educated workingmen about William Morris, and among some few educated persons, generally women, who took their tune from the workingmen[†]. One woman used to repeat as often as possible that to paint pictures or to write poetry in this age was to fiddle while Rome was burning.[21] The artist who permits opinion to master his work is always insincere, always what Balzac calls an unconscious comedian, a man playing to a public for an end, or a philanthropist who has made the most tragic and the most useless of sacrifices.

Certain among the Nationalist attacks have been the work of ignorant men, untruthful, imputing unworthy motives, the kind of thing one cannot answer. But the Unionist hostility, though better mannered, has been more injurious. Our Nationalist pit has grown to understand us, and night after night we have not been able to find room for all who came, but except at rare moments and under exceptional circumstances our stalls have been almost empty, though the people who keep away from us in Ireland flock to us in London, where there is culture enough to make us a fashion. I think that tide is turning, however, for we played, before many Unionists at Galway matinées, *Cathleen ni Houlihan, The Gaol Gate,* and *The Rising of the Moon,* all plays that have been objected to at some time or another by some section or other of official Dublin, or that we have been warned against in friendlier moods.[22] When *Cathleen ni Houlihan* was first played in the Abbey I was hissed by a group of young men at the door, and we were offered a good deal of support once towards the filling of our empty stalls if we would drop it from our list. I heard a while ago we had lost financial support through *The Rising of the Moon,* but returned to tranquillity when I found that it would have been a donation to the National Literary Society—God save the mark!—given under the belief that we and it were the same body.[23]

In most modern countries when the moment has arrived for a personal impulse either for the first time or in some art hitherto external and conventional, the cry has been raised against the writer that he is preaching sexual immorality, for that is the subject upon which the newspapers, at any rate, most desire to see certain opinions always in force, and a view of the world as sexually unexciting as possible always displayed as if it were reality. Balzac in his preface to the *Comédie humaine*[†] had to defend himself from this charge, but it is not the burning question with us at present, for politics are our national passion.[24] We have to free our vision of reality from political prepossession, for entangled as it were with all that is exaggerated, lifeless, frozen in the attitudes of party, there are true thoughts about all those things that Ireland is most interested in, a reverie over the emptiness and the fullness of Irish character which is not less a part of wisdom because politics like art have their exaggerations. We cannot renounce political subjects in renouncing mere opinions, for that pleasure in the finer culture of England, that displeasure in Irish

disunions and disorders which are the root of reasoned Union-
ism, are as certainly high and natural thoughts† as the self-denying
enthusiasm that leads Michael Gillane to probable death or exile,
and Dervorgilla to her remorse, and Patrick Sarsfield of *The
White Cockade* to his sense of what a king should be; and we cannot renounce them because politicians believe that one thought or
another may help their opponents, any more than Balzac could
have refused to write the *Comédie humaine* because somebody
was afraid Madame l'Épicière might run away from her husband.[25]

At the close of my speech at one of the performances we were
asked to give to the British Association I used these words:[26]

'When I was coming up in the train the other day from Galway,
I began thinking how unlike your work was to my work, and then
suddenly it struck me that it was all the same. A picture arose before
my mind's eye: I saw Adam numbering the creatures of Eden; soft
and terrible, foul and fair, they all went before him.[27] That, I
thought, is the man of science, naming and numbering, for our
understanding, everything in the world. But then, I thought, we
writers, do we not also number and describe, though with a difference? You are busy with the exterior world, and we with the interior. Science understands that everything must be known in the
world our eyes look at; there is nothing too obscure, too common,
too vile, to be the subject of knowledge. When a man of science
discovers a new species, or a new law, you do not ask the value of
the law, or the value of the species, before you do him honour; you
leave all that to the judgment of the generations. It is your pride
that in you the human race contemplates all things with so pure,
so disinterested an eyesight that it forgets its own necessities and
infirmities, all its hopes and fears, in the contemplation of truth for
the sake of truth, reality for the sake of reality.
'We, on the other hand, are Adams of a different Eden, a more
terrible Eden, perhaps, for we must name and number the passions
and motives of men. There, too, everything must be known, everything understood, everything expressed; there, also, there is nothing common, nothing unclean; every motive must be followed

through all the obscure mystery of its logic. Mankind must be seen and understood in every possible circumstance, in every conceivable situation. There is no laughter too bitter, no irony too harsh for utterance, no passion too terrible to be set before the minds of men. The Greeks knew that. Only in this way can mankind be understood, only when we have put ourselves in all the possible positions of life, from the most miserable to those that are so lofty that we can only speak of them in symbols and in mysteries, will entire wisdom be possible. All wise government depends upon this knowledge not less than upon that other knowledge which is your business rather than ours; and we and you alike rejoice in battle, finding the sweetest of all music to be the stroke of sword.'[28]

October, 1908

A PEOPLE'S THEATRE*
A LETTER TO LADY GREGORY

I

My dear Lady Gregory—Of recent years you have done all that
is anxious and laborious in the supervision of the Abbey Theatre
and left me free to follow my own thoughts. It is therefore right that
I address to you this letter, wherein I shall explain, half for your ears,
half for other ears, certain thoughts that have made me believe that
the Abbey Theatre can never do all we had hoped. We set out to
make a 'People's Theatre', and in that we have succeeded. But I did
not know until very lately that there are certain things, dear to both
our hearts, which no 'People's Theatre' can accomplish.

II

All exploitation of the life of the wealthy, for the eye and the ear
of the poor and half-poor, in plays, in popular novels, in musical
comedy, in fashion papers, at the cinema, in *Daily Mirror* photographs, is a travesty of the life of the rich; and if it were not would
all but justify some Red Terror; and it impoverishes and vulgarises
the imagination, seeming to hold up for envy and to commend a
life where all is display and hurry, passion without emotion, emotion without intellect, and where there is nothing stern and solitary.[2]

*I took the title from a book by Romain Rolland on some French the-
atrical experiments. 'A People's Theatre' is not quite the same thing as 'A
Popular Theatre'. The essay was published in *The Irish Statesman* in the
autumn of 1919. —1923.[1]

The plays and novels are the least mischievous, for they still have the old-fashioned romanticism—their threepenny bit, if worn, is silver yet—but they are without intensity and intellect and cannot convey the charm of either as it may exist in those they would represent. All this exploitation is a rankness that has grown up recently among us and has come out of an historical necessity that has made the furniture and the clothes and the brains, of all but the leisured and the lettered, copies and travesties.

Shakespeare set upon the stage Kings and Queens, great historical or legendary persons about whom there is nothing unreal except the circumstance of their lives which remain vague and summary, because he could only write his best—his mind and the mind of his audience being interested in emotion and[†] intellect at their moment of union and[†] at their greatest intensity—when he wrote of those who controlled the mechanism of life. Had they been controlled by it, intellect and emotion entangled by intricacy and detail could never have mounted to that union which, as Swedenborg said of the marriage of the angels, is a conflagration of the whole being.[3] But since great crowds, changed by popular education with its eye always on some objective task, have begun to find reality in mechanism alone,[*] our popular commercial art has substituted for Lear and Cordelia the real millionaire and the real peeress, and seeks to make them charming by insisting perpetually that they have all that wealth can buy, or rather all that average men and women would buy if they had wealth. Shakespeare's groundlings watched the stage in terrified sympathy, while the British working-man looks perhaps at the photographs of these lords and ladies, whom he admires beyond measure, with the pleasant feeling that they will all be robbed and murdered before he dies.

III

Then, too, that turning into ridicule of peasant and citizen and all lesser men could but increase our delight when the great personi-

---

*I have read somewhere statistics that showed how popular education has coincided with the lessening of Shakespeare's audience. In every chief town before it began Shakespeare was constantly played.[4]—1919.

fied spiritual power, but seems unnatural when the great are but the rich. During an illness lately I read two popular novels which I had borrowed from the servants. They were good stories and half consoled me for the sleep I could not get, but I was a long time before I saw clearly why everybody with less than a thousand a year was a theme of comedy and everybody with less than five hundred a theme of farce. Even Rosencrantz and Guildenstern, courtiers and doubtless great men in their world, could be but foils for Hamlet because Shakespeare had nothing to do with objective truth, but we who have nothing to do with anything else, in so far as we are of our epoch, must not allow a greater style to corrupt us.[5]

An artisan or a small shopkeeper feels, I think, when he sees upon our Abbey stage men of his own trade, that they are represented as he himself would represent them if he had the gift of expression. I do not mean that he sees his own life expounded there without exaggeration, for exaggeration is selection and the more passionate the art the more marked is the selection, but he does not feel that he has strayed into some other man's seat. If it is comedy he will laugh at ridiculous people, people in whose character there is some contortion, but their station of life will not seem ridiculous. The best stories I have listened to outside the theatre have been told me by farmers or sailors when I was a boy, one or two by fellow-travellers in railway carriages, and most had some quality of romance, romance of a class and its particular capacity for adventure; and our theatre is a people's theatre in a sense which no mere educational theatre can be, because its plays are to some extent a part of that popular imagination. It is very seldom that a man or woman bred up among the propertied or professional classes knows any class but his own, and that a class which is much the same all over the world, and already written of by so many dramatists that it is nearly impossible to see its dramatic situations with our own eyes, and those dramatic situations are perhaps exhausted—as Nietzsche thought the whole universe would be some day—and nothing left but to repeat the same combinations over again.[6]

When the Abbey Manager sends us a play for our opinion and it is my turn to read it, if the handwriting of the MSS. or of the author's accompanying letter suggests a leisured life I start prejudiced. There will be no fresh observation of character, I think, no sense of dialogue, all will be literary second-hand, at best what Rossetti called the† 'soulless self-reflections of man's skill'.[7] On the other hand, until the Abbey plays began themselves to be copied, a handwriting learned in a National School† always made me expect dialogue written out by some man who had admired good dialogue before he had seen it upon paper.[8] The construction would probably be bad, for there the student of plays has the better luck, but plays made impossible by rambling and redundance have often contained some character or some dialogue that has stayed in my memory for years. At first there was often vulgarity, and there still is in those comic love scenes which we invariably reject, and there is often propaganda with all its distortion, but these weigh light when set against life seen as if newly created. At first, in face of your mockery, I used to recommend some reading of Ibsen or Galsworthy, but no one has benefited by that reading or by anything but the Abbey audience and our own rejection of all gross propaganda and gross imitation of the comic column in the newspapers.[9] Our dramatists, and I am not speaking of your work or Synge's but of those to whom you and Synge and I gave an opportunity, have been excellent just in so far as they have become all eye and ear, their minds not smoking lamps, as at times they would have wished, but clear mirrors.

Our players, too, have been vivid and exciting because they have copied a life personally known to them, and of recent years, since our Manager has had to select from the ordinary stage-struck young men and women who have seen many players and perhaps no life but that of the professional class, it has been much harder, though players have matured more rapidly, to get the old, exciting, vivid playing. I have never recovered the good opinion of one recent Manager because I urged him to choose instead some young man or woman from some little shop who had never given his or her thoughts to the theatre. 'Put all the names into a hat', I think I said, 'and pick the first that comes'.[10] One of our early players was exceedingly fine in the old woman in *Riders to the Sea*. 'She has never been to Aran, she knows nothing but Dublin, surely in that part she is not objective, surely she creates from imagination', I thought; but when I asked her she said, 'I copied from my old grandmother'.[11] Certainly it is this objectivity, this making of all from sympathy, from observation, never from passion, from lonely dreaming, that has made our players, at their best, great comedians, for comedy is passionless.

We have been the first to create a true 'People's Theatre', and we have succeeded because it is not an exploitation of local colour, or of a limited form of drama possessing a temporary novelty, but the first doing of something for which the world is ripe, something that will be done all over the world and done more and more perfectly: the making articulate of all the dumb classes each with its own knowledge of the world, its own dignity, but all objective with the objectivity of the office and the workshop, of the newspaper and the street, of mechanism and of politics.

IV

Yet we did not set out to create this sort of theatre, and its success has been to me a discouragement and a defeat. Dante in that passage in the *Convito* which is, I think, the first passage of poignant autobiography in literary history, for there is nothing in S. Augustine not formal and abstract beside it, in describing his poverty and his exile counts as his chief misfortune that he has had to show himself to all Italy and so publish his human frailties that men who honoured him unknown honour him no more.[12] Lacking means he had lacked seclusion, and he explains that men such as he should have but few and intimate friends. His study was unity of being, the subordination of all parts to the whole as in a perfectly proportioned human body—his own definition of beauty—and not, as with those I have described, the unity of things in the world; and like all subjectives he shrank, because of what he was, because of what others were, from contact with many men.[13] Had he written plays he would have written from his own thought and passion, observing little and using little, if at all, the conversation of his time—and whether he wrote in verse or in prose his style would have been distant, musical, metaphorical, moulded by antiquity. We stand on the margin between wilderness and wilderness, that which we observe through our senses and that which we can experience only, and our art is always the description of one or the other. If our art is mainly from experience we have need of learned speech, of agreed symbols, because all those things whose names renew experience have accompanied that experience already many times. A personage in one of Turgenev's novels is reminded by the odour of, I think, heliotrope, of some sweetheart that had worn it, and poetry is any flower that brings a memory of emotion, while an unmemoried flower is prose, and a flower pressed and named and numbered science; but our poetical heliotrope need bring to mind no sweetheart of ours, for it suffices that it crowned the bride of Paris, or Peleus' bride.[14] Neither poetry nor any subjective art can exist but for those who do in some measure share its traditional knowledge, a knowledge learned in leisure and contemplation. Even Burns, except in those popular verses which are as lacking in tradition, as modern, as topical, as Longfellow, was, as Henley said, not the founder but the last of a dynasty.[15]

Once such men could draw the crowd because the circumstance of life changed slowly and there was little to disturb contemplation and so men repeated old verses and old stories, and learned and simple had come to share in common much allusion and symbol. Where the simple were ignorant they were ready to learn and so became receptive, or perhaps even to pretend knowledge like the clowns in the mediaeval poem that describes the arrival of Chaucer's Pilgrims at Canterbury, who that they may seem gentlemen pretend to know the legends in the stained-glass windows.[16] Shakespeare, more objective than Dante—for, alas, the world must move—, was still predominantly subjective, and he wrote during the latest crisis of history that made possible a Theatre of his kind. There were still among the common people many traditional songs and stories, while court and university, which were much more important to him, had an interest Chaucer never shared in great dramatic persons, in those men and women of Plutarch, who made their death a ritual of passion; for what is passion but the straining of man's being against some obstacle that obstructs its unity?[17]

You and I and Synge, not understanding the clock, set out to bring again the Theatre of Shakespeare or rather perhaps of Sophocles. I had told you how at Young Ireland Societies and the like, young men when I was twenty had read papers to one another about Irish legend and history, and you yourself soon discovered the Gaelic League, then but a new weak thing, and taught yourself Irish. At

Spiddal or near it an innkeeper had sung us Gaelic songs, all new village work that though not literature had *naïveté* and sincerity.[18] The writers, caring nothing for cleverness, had tried to express emotion, tragic or humorous, and great masterpieces, 'The Grief of a Girl's Heart', for instance, had been written in the same speech and manner and were still sung.[19] We know that the songs of the Thames boatmen, to name but these, in the age of Queen Elizabeth had the same relation to great masterpieces.[20] These Gaelic songs were as unlike as those to the songs of the Music-Hall with their clever ear-catching rhythm, the work of some mind as objective as that of an inventor or of a newspaper reporter. We thought we could bring the old folk-life to Dublin, patriotic feeling to aid us, and with the folk-life all the life of the heart, understanding heart, according to Dante's definition, as the most interior being; but the modern world is more powerful than any propaganda or even than any special circumstance, and our success has been that we have made a Theatre of the head, and persuaded Dublin playgoers to think about their own trade or profession or class and their life within it, so long as the stage curtain is up, in relation to Ireland as a whole.[21] For certain hours of an evening they have objective modern eyes.

V

The objective nature and the subjective are mixed in different proportion as are the shadowed and the bright parts in the lunar phases. In Dante there was little shadow, in Shakespeare a larger portion, while you and Synge, it may be, resemble the moon when it has just passed its third quarter, for you have constant humour—and humour is of the shadowed part—much observation and a speech founded upon that of real life. You and he will always hold our audience, but both have used so constantly a measure of lunar light, have so elaborated style and emotion, an individual way of seeing, that neither will ever, till a classic and taught in school, find a perfect welcome.

The outcry against *The Playboy* was an outcry against its style, against its way of seeing; and when the audience called Synge 'decadent'—a favourite reproach from the objective everywhere—it was but troubled by the stench of its own burnt cakes.[22] How could they that dreaded solitude love that which solitude had made? And never have I heard any, that laugh the loudest at your comedies, praise that musical and delicate style that makes them always a fit accompaniment for verse and sets them at times among the world's great comedies. Indeed, the louder they laugh the readier are they to rate them with the hundred ephemeral farces they have laughed at and forgotten. Synge they have at least hated. When you and Synge find such an uneasy footing, what shall I do there who have never observed anything, or listened with an attentive ear, but value all I have seen or heard because of the emotions they call up or because of something they remind me of that exists, as I believe, beyond the world? O yes, I am listened to—am I not a founder of the Theatre?[†]—and here and there scattered solitaries delight in what I have made and return to hear it again; but some young Corkman, all eyes and ears, whose first rambling play we have just pulled together or half together, can do more than that. He will be played by players who have spoken dialogue like his every night for years, and sentences that it had been a bore to read will so delight the whole house that to keep my hands from clapping I shall have to remind myself that I gave my voice for the play's production and must not applaud my own judgment.

VI

I want to create for myself an unpopular theatre and an audience like a secret society where admission is by favour and never to many. Perhaps I shall never create it, for you and I and Synge have had to dig the stone for our statue and I am aghast at the sight of a new quarry, and besides I want so much—an audience of fifty, a room worthy of it (some great dining-room or drawing-room), half-a-dozen young men and women who can dance and speak verse or play drum and flute and zither, and all the while, instead of a profession, I but offer them 'an accomplishment'.[23] However, there are my *Four Plays for Dancers* as a beginning, some masks by Mr. Dulac, music by Mr. Dulac and by Mr. Rummel.[24] In most towns one can find fifty people for whom one need not build all on observation and sympathy, because they read poetry for their pleasure and understand the traditional language of passion. I desire a mysterious art, always reminding and half-reminding those who understand it of dearly loved things, doing its work by suggestion, not by direct statement, a complexity of rhythm, colour, gesture, not space-pervading like the intellect but a memory and a prophecy: a mode of drama Shelley and Keats could have used without ceasing to be themselves, and for which even Blake in the mood of *The Book of Thel* might not have been too obscure.[25] Instead of advertisements in the Press I need a hostess, and even the most accomplished hostess must choose with more than usual care, for I have noticed that city-living cultivated people, those whose names would first occur to her, set great value on painting, which is a form of property, and on music, which is a part of the organisation of life, while the lovers of literature, those who read a book many times, are either young men with little means or live far away from big towns.

What alarms me most is how a new art needing so elaborate a technique can make its first experiments before those who, as Molière said of the courtiers of his day, have seen so much.[26] How shall our singers and dancers be welcomed by those who have heard Chaliapin in all his parts and who know all the dances of the Russians?[27] Yet where can I find Mr. Dulac and Mr. Rummel or any to match them, but in London* or in Paris, and who but the leisured will welcome an elaborate art or pay for its first experiments? In one thing the luck might be upon our side. A man who loves verse and the visible arts has, in a work such as I imagined, the advantage of the professional player. The professional player becomes the amateur, the other has been preparing all his life, and certainly I shall not soon forget the rehearsal of *At the Hawk's Well*, when Mr. Ezra Pound, who had never acted on any stage, in the absence of our chief player rehearsed for half an hour.[28] Even the forms of subjective acting that were natural to the professional stage have ceased. Where all now is sympathy and observation no Irving can carry himself with intellectual pride, nor any Salvini in half-animal nobility, both wrapped in solitude.[29]

I know that you consider Ireland alone our business, and in that we do not differ, except that I care very little where a play of mine is first played so that it find some natural audience and good play-

---

*I live in Dublin now, and indolence and hatred of travel will probably compel me to make my experiment there after all. —1923.

ers. My rooks may sleep abroad in the fields for a while, but when
the winter comes they will remember the way home to the rook-
ery trees. Indeed, I have Ireland especially in mind, for I want to
make, or to help some man some day to make, a feeling of exclu-
siveness, a bond among chosen spirits, a mystery almost for
leisured and lettered people. Ireland has suffered more than England
from democracy, for since the Wild Geese fled, who might have
grown to be leaders in manners and in taste, she has had but political leaders.[30] As a drawing is defined by its outline and taste by its
rejections, I too must reject and draw an outline about the thing I
seek; and say that I seek, not a theatre but the theatre's anti-self,
an art that can appease all within us that becomes uneasy as the
curtain falls and the house breaks into applause.

VII

Meanwhile the Popular Theatre should grow always more objective; more and more a reflection of the general mind; more and
more a discovery of the simple emotions that make all men kin,
clearing itself the while of sentimentality, the wreckage of an
obsolete popular culture, seeking always not to feel and to imagine but to understand and to see. Let those who are all personality, who can only feel and imagine, leave it, before their presence
become a corruption and turn it from its honesty. The rhetoric of
D'Annunzio, the melodrama and spectacle of the later Maeterlinck,
are the insincerities of subjectives, who being very able men have
learned to hold an audience that is not their natural audience.[31] To
be intelligible they are compelled to harden, to externalise and
deform. The popular play left to itself may not lack vicissitude and
development, for it may pass, though more slowly than the novel
which need not carry with it so great a crowd, from the physical
objectivity of Fielding and Defoe to the spiritual objectivity of Tolstoy and Dostoyevsky, for beyond the whole we reach by unbiased
intellect there is another whole reached by resignation and the
denial of self.[32]

VIII

The two great energies of the world that in Shakespeare's day pene-
trated each other have fallen apart as speech and music fell apart
at the Renaissance, and that has brought each to greater freedom,
and we have to prepare a stage for the whole wealth of modern lyricism, for an art that is close to pure music, for those energies that
would free the arts from imitation, that would ally acting to decoration and to the dance. We are not yet conscious, for as yet we have
no philosophy, while the opposite energy is conscious. All visible history, the discoveries of science, the discussions of politics, are with
it; but as I read the world, the sudden changes, or rather the sudden
revelation of future changes, are not from visible history but from
its anti-self. Blake says somewhere in a Prophetic Book that things
must complete themselves before they pass away, and every new
logical development of the objective energy intensifies in an exact
correspondence a counter-energy, or rather adds to an always deep-
ening unanalysable longing.[33] That counter-longing, having no visible past, can only become a conscious energy suddenly, in those
moments of revelation which are as a flash of lightning. Are we
approaching a supreme moment of self-consciousness, the two
halves of the soul separate and face to face? A certain friend of mine
has written upon this subject a couple of intricate poems called 'The
Phases of the Moon' and 'The Double Vision' respectively, which are
my continual study, and I must refer the reader to these poems for
the necessary mathematical calculations.[34] Were it not for that other
gyre turning inward in exact measure with the outward whirl of its
fellow, we would fall in a generation or so under some tyranny that
would cease at last to be a tyranny, so perfect our acquiescence.[35]

> Constrained, arraigned, baffled, bent and unbent
> By these wire-jointed jaws and limbs of wood,
> Themselves obedient,
> Knowing not evil and good;
>
> Obedient to some hidden magical breath.
> They do not even feel, so abstract are they,
> So dead beyond our death,
> Triumph that we obey.[36]

Prefaces and Note

[PREFACE]
IN *THE COLLECTED WORKS IN VERSE*
AND PROSE (1908)

The Irish dramatic movement began in May, 1899, with the performance of certain plays by English actors who were brought to Dublin for the purpose; and in the spring of the following year and in the autumn of the year after that, performances of like plays were given by like actors at the Gaiety Theatre, Dublin.[1] In the third year I started SAMHAIN to defend the work, and on re-reading it and reading it for the first time throughout, have found it best to reprint my part of it unchanged.[2] A number has been published about once a year till very lately, and the whole series of notes are a history of a movement which is important because of the principles it is rooted in whatever be its fruits, and these principles are better told of in words that rose out of the need, than were I to explain all again and with order and ceremony now that the old enmities and friendships are ruffled by new ones that have other things to be done and said.[3]

March, 1908

PREFACE
TO *PLAYS AND CONTROVERSIES*
(1923)

I have gathered into this book two plays, written before the foundation of the Irish Theatre though much corrected since, and four plays written but the other day and intended for performance in drawing-room and studio, and a long series of dramatic notes.[1] I begin the book with these notes, which are taken for the most part from an occasional publication called *Samhain,* started in the third year of 'The Irish Dramatic Movement' to defend that movement, and long out of print. In a little while Dáil Éireann and our Dublin newspapers will consider, as I hope, the foundation of an Irish State Theatre; and I would put these old notes into evidence.[2] Though often about foolish quarrels, or plays but little better, they may keep their use even when that occasion passes; being passionately written, and at a moment when Ireland was preparing, in that dark portion of the mind which is like the other side of the moon, for insurrection and anarchic violence; and all in some measure a plea for intellectual spontaneity against unyielding, mechanical, abstract principles. I ask indulgence if I overrate their value, for it may be that I cannot judge sentences that call up memories of the time when I was most alive, having most friends and enemies. All needful explanations are in Lady Gregory's book, *Our Irish Theatre.*[3]

The plays are so abundantly annotated and prefaced that I need say nothing more except that the first was planned and partly written when I was little more than a boy, and that it gives me more pleasure in the memory than any of my plays. It was all thought out in the first fervour of my generation's distaste for Victorian rhetoric; that rhetoric once away, every poetical virtue seemed possible.

Dublin

February 1923

NOTE IN *MYTHOLOGIES*
(EDITION DE LUXE PROOFS,
1931–32)

The Irish Dramatic Movement is part of the contents of *Samhain, Beltaine, The Arrow,* occasional publications connected with the Irish Theatre.[1] A very active irascible friend of mine once wrote that these publications 'made a man of W. B. Yeats', meaning, I suppose, that they had rescued me from such thoughts as occupy the rest of this volume.[2] I do not agree with him; I doubt the value of the embittered controversy that was to fill my life for years, but certainly they rang down the curtain so far as I was concerned on what was called 'The Celtic Movement'. An 'Irish Movement' took its place. —(1931).

Uncollected
Contributions
to Beltaine,
Samhain, and
The Arrow

1899–1909

BELTAINE: MAY 1899— PLANS AND METHODS

Norway has a great and successful school of contemporary drama, which grew out of a national literary movement very similar to that now going on in Ireland.[1] Everywhere critics and writers, who wish for something better than the ordinary play of commerce, turn to Norway for an example and an inspiration. Spain and Germany, indeed, though they have a taste for bad dramatists, which Norway has not, have good dramatists, whom they admire. Elsewhere one finds the literary drama alone, when some great work, old enough to be a national superstition, is revived, with scenery and costumes so elaborate that nobody need listen to the words unless he likes; and in little and inexpensive theatres, which associations of men of letters hire from time to time that they may see upon the stage the plays of Henrik Ibsen, Maurice Maeterlinck, Gerhart Hauptmann, José Echegaray, or some less famous dramatist who has written, in the only way literature can be written, to express a dream which has taken possession of his mind.[2] These associations, the Théâtre Libre and the Independent Theatre especially, in the face of violent opposition, have trained actors who have become famous, and have had a powerful influence even upon those plays which are written to please as many people as possible, that they may make as much money as possible.[3]

*

*   *

The Irish Literary Theatre will attempt to do in Dublin something of what has been done in London and Paris; and, if it has even a small welcome, it will produce, somewhere about the old festival of Beltaine, at the beginning of every spring, a play founded upon an Irish subject. The plays will differ from those produced by associations of men of letters in London and in Paris, because times have changed, and because the intellect of Ireland is romantic and spiritual rather than scientific and analytical, but they will have as little of a commercial ambition. Their writers will appeal to that limited public which gives understanding, and not to that unlimited public which gives wealth; and if they interest those among their audience who keep in their memories the songs of Callanan and Walsh, or old Irish legends, or who love the good books of any country, they will not mind greatly if others are bored.[4]

*

*   *

The Committee think of producing in 1900 Denis Florence MacCarthy's translation of Calderón's *St. Patrick's Purgatory,* a play about the conversion of Ireland.[5] Miss Fiona Macleod has written, or is writing, three plays, *The Hour of Beauty, Fand and Cuchullain,* and *The Tanist,* an Irish historical play, and Mr. Standish O'Grady has promised an Irish historical play.[6] Others, too, have written or are writing plays, so that there will be no lack of work to select from. In all or almost all cases the plays must be published before they are acted, and no play will be produced which could not hope to succeed as a book.

*

*   *

In a play like Mr. Martyn's, where everything is subordinate to the central idea, and the dialogues as much like the dialogues of daily life as possible, the slightest exaggeration of detail, or effort to make points where points were not intended, becomes an insincerity.[7] An endeavour has therefore been made to have it acted as simply and quietly as possible. The chief endeavour with Mr. Yeats' play has been to get it spoken with some sense of rhythm.[8]

*

*   *

The two lyrics, which we print on a later page, are not sung, but spoken, or rather chanted, to music, as the old poems were probably chanted by bards and rhapsodists.[9] Even when the words of a song, sung in the ordinary way, are heard at all, their own proper rhythm and emphasis are lost, or partly lost, in the rhythm and emphasis of the music. A lyric which is spoken or chanted to music should, upon the other hand, reveal its meaning, and its rhythm so become indissoluble in the memory. The speaking of words, whether to music or not, is, however, so perfectly among the lost arts that it will take a long time before our actors, no matter how willing, will be able to forget the ordinary methods of the stage or to perfect a new method.

*
* *

Mr. Johnson, in the interpretative argument which he has written for *The Countess Cathleen,* places the events it describes in the sixteenth century. So Mr. Yeats originally wrote, but he has since written that he tried to suggest throughout the play that period, made out of many periods, in which the events in the folk-tales have happened.[10] The play is not historic, but symbolic, and has as little to do with any definite place and time as an *auto* by Calderón.[11] One should look for the Countess Cathleen and the peasants and the demons not in history, but, as Mr. Johnson has done, in one's own heart; and such costumes and scenery have been selected as will preserve the indefinite.

*
* *

There are many allusions in *The Countess Cathleen* to old Celtic legends. Usheen, or Oisin, was a legendary poet who journeyed to the Land of Youth with Niamh, an immortal woman. Adene, or Etain, was a legendary queen who left the world and found an immortal husband. Fergus was the poet of the Red Branch cycle of legends, as Oisin was of the Fenian cycle. He was the King of Uladh, but, as the legend was shaped by Ferguson, whom Mr. Yeats has followed in his lyric, he gave up his throne that he might live at peace, hunting in the woods.[12] 'The Shee', 'The Sheogues', 'The Danaan Nations', 'The People of the Raths' are different names for the faery people, the great gods of an earlier time. A Thivish is a ghost, a wandering and earthbound spirit. A Sowlth is a misshapen or shapeless spirit, sometimes identified with the Jack o' Lanthorn. 'Barach the traitor' was the man who made the feast for Fergus that the sons of Usna might lack his protection. The Clan Cailitin was a family of wizards among the troops of Maeve, who at last brought about the death of Cuchulain, 'Sualtam's and old Dectera's child'. 'The great king' who 'killed Naoise and broke Deirdre's heart', was, of course, Conchubar. Orchil was a Celtic goddess, who is always imagined as a kind of Lilith in Mr. Yeats' poetry. 'The bright spear' which Aleel sees in his frenzy driven through the eye of Balor, the old Celtic divinity of cold and darkness, is, of course, the spear flung by Lugh, the god of warmth and light and order. The battle of Moytura was to the old Celts the battle in which the gods of light and life overcame the gods of cold and darkness and chaos. It is necessary to explain these things, as the old Irish mythology is still imperfectly known in modern Ireland.[13]

*

* *

If any money is made by the performances it will be paid into the funds of the National Literary Society, to go towards the expenses of the Irish Literary Theatre in future years.

EDITOR OF 'BELTAINE'.

BELTAINE: MAY 1899—
THE THEATRE

I remember, some years ago, advising a distinguished, though too little recognised, writer of poetical plays to write a play as unlike ordinary plays as possible, that it might be judged with a fresh mind, and to put it on the stage in some small suburban theatre, where a small audience would pay its expenses.[1] I said that he should follow it the year after, at the same time of the year, with another play, and so on from year to year; and that the people who read books, and do not go to the theatre, would gradually find out about him. I suggested that he should begin with a pastoral play, because nobody would expect from a pastoral play the succession of nervous tremours which the plays of commerce, like the novels of commerce, have substituted for the purification that comes with pity and terror to the imagination and intellect. He followed my advice in part, and had a small but perfect success, filling his small theatre for twice the number of performances he had announced; but instead of being content with the praise of his equals, and waiting to win their praise another year, he hired immediately a big London theatre, and put his pastoral play and a new play before a meagre and unintelligent audience. I still remember his pastoral play with delight, because, if not always of a high excellence, it was always poetical; but I remember it at the small theatre, where my pleasure was magnified by the pleasure of those about me, and not at the big theatre, where it made me uncomfortable, as an unwelcome guest always makes one uncomfortable.[2]

Why should we thrust our works, which we have written with imaginative sincerity and filled with spiritual desire, before those quite excellent people who think that Rossetti's women are 'guys',

147

that Rodin's women are 'ugly', and that Ibsen is 'immoral', and who
only want to be left at peace to enjoy the works so many clever men
have made especially to suit them?[3] We must make a theatre for ourselves and our friends, and for a few simple people who understand
from sheer simplicity what we understand from scholarship and
thought. We have planned the Irish Literary Theatre with this hos-
pitable emotion, and, that the right people may find out about us,
we hope to act a play or two in the spring of every year; and that
the right people may escape the stupefying memory of the theatre
of commerce which clings even to them, our plays will be for the
most part remote, spiritual, and ideal.

A common opinion is that the poetic drama has come to an end,
because modern poets have no dramatic power; and Mr. Binyon,
in an article in *The Dome* for March, seems to accept this opinion
when he says, 'It has been too often assumed that it is the manager
who bars the way to poetic plays. But it is much more probable that
the poets have failed the managers. If poets mean to serve the stage,
their dramas must be dramatic'.[4] I find it easier to believe that audiences, who have learned, as I think, from the life of crowded cities
to live upon the surface of life, and actors and managers, who study
to please them, have changed, than that imagination, which is the
voice of what is eternal in man, has changed. The arts are but one
Art; and why should all intense painting and all intense poetry have
become not merely unintelligible but hateful to the greater number of men and women, and intense drama move them to pleasure?
The audiences of Sophocles and of Shakespeare and of Calderón
were not unlike the audiences I have heard listening in Irish cabins
to songs in Gaelic about 'an old poet telling his sins', and about 'the
five young men who were drowned last year', and about 'the
lovers that were drowned going to America', or to some tale of Oisin
and his three hundred years in *Tír na nÓg*.[5] Mr. Bridges' *Return of
Ulysses,* one of the most beautiful and, as I think, dramatic of modern plays, might have some success in the Aran Islands, if the
Gaelic League would translate it into Gaelic, but I am quite certain
that it would have no success in the Strand.[6]

Blake has said that all Art is a labour to bring again the Golden
Age, and all culture is certainly a labour to bring again the simplicity
of the first ages, with knowledge of good and evil added to it.[7] The

drama has need of cities that it may find men in sufficient numbers, and cities destroy the emotions to which it appeals, and therefore the days of the drama are brief and come but seldom. It has one day when the emotions of cities still remember the emotions of sailors and husbandmen and shepherds and users of the spear and the bow; as the houses and furniture and earthen vessels of cities, before the coming of machinery, remember the rocks and the woods and the hillside; and it has another day, now beginning, when thought and scholarship discover their desire. In the first day, it is the Art of the people; and in the second day, like the dramas acted of old times in the hidden places of temples, it is the preparation of a Priesthood. It may be, though the world is not old enough to show us any example, that this Priesthood will spread their Religion everywhere, and make their Art the Art of the people.

When the first day of the drama had passed by, actors found that an always larger number of people were more easily moved through the eyes than through the ears. The emotion that comes with the music of words is exhausting, like all intellectual emotions, and few people like exhausting emotions; and therefore actors began to speak as if they were reading something out of the newspapers. They forgot the noble art of oratory, and gave all their thought to the poor art of acting, that is content with the sympathy of our nerves; until at last those who love poetry found it better to read alone in their rooms what they had once delighted to hear sitting friend by friend, lover by beloved. I once asked Mr. William Morris if he had thought of writing a play, and he answered that he had, but would not write one, because actors did not know how to speak poetry with the half-chant men spoke it with in old times. Mr. Swinburne's *Locrine* was acted a month ago, and it was not badly acted, but nobody could tell whether it was fit for the stage or not, for not one rhythm, not one cry of passion, was spoken with a musical emphasis, and verse spoken without a musical emphasis seems but an artificial and cumbersome way of saying what might be said naturally and simply in prose.[8]

As audiences and actors changed, managers learned to substitute meretricious landscapes, painted upon canvas and upon cardboard, for the descriptions of poetry, until the painted scenery, which had in Greece been a charming explanation of what was least important in the story, became as important as the story. It needed some imagination, some gift for day-dreams, to see the horses and the fields and flowers of Colonus as one listened to the elders gathered about Œdipus, or to see 'the pendent bed and procreant cradle' of the 'martlet' as one listened to Duncan before the castle of Macbeth; but it needs no imagination to admire a painting of one of the more obvious effects of nature painted by somebody who understands how to show everything to the most hurried glance.[9] At the same time the managers made the costumes of the actors more and more magnificent, that the mind might sleep in peace, while the eye took pleasure in the magnificence of velvet and silk and in the physical beauty of women. These changes gradually perfected the theatre of commerce, the masterpiece of that movement towards externality in life and thought and Art, against which the criticism of our day is learning to protest.

Even if poetry were spoken as poetry, it would still seem out of place in many of its highest moments upon a stage, where the superficial appearances of nature are so closely copied; for poetry is founded upon convention, and becomes incredible the moment painting or gesture remind us that people do not speak verse when they meet upon the highway. The theatre of Art, when it comes to exist, must therefore discover grave and decorative gestures, such as delighted Rossetti and Madox Brown, and grave and decorative scenery, that will be forgotten the moment an actor has said 'It is dawn', or 'It is raining', or 'The wind is shaking the trees'; and dresses of so little irrelevant magnificence that the mortal actors and actresses may change without much labour into the immortal people of romance.[10] The theatre began in ritual, and it cannot come to its greatness again without recalling words to their ancient sovereignty.

It will take a generation, and perhaps generations, to restore the theatre of Art; for one must get one's actors, and perhaps one's scenery, from the theatre of commerce, until new actors and new painters have come to help one; and until many failures and imperfect successes[†] have made a new tradition, and perfected in detail the ideal that is beginning to float before our eyes. If one could call one's painters and one's actors from where one would, how easy it would be. I know some painters, who have never painted scenery, who could paint the scenery I want, but they have their own work to do; and in Ireland I have heard a red-haired orator repeat some bad political verses with a voice that went through one like flame, and made them seem the most beautiful verses in the world; but he has no practical knowledge of the stage, and probably despises it.[11]

(Reprinted from 'The Dome'.)

BELTAINE: FEBRUARY 1900—
PLANS AND METHODS

Our plays this year have a half deliberate unity. Mr. Martyn's
Maeve, which I understand to symbolise Ireland's choice between
English materialism and her own natural idealism, as well as
the choice of every individual soul, will be followed, as Greek
tragedies were followed by satires and Elizabethan masques by
antimasques, by Mr. George Moore's *The Bending of the Bough,*
which tells of a like choice and of a contrary decision. Mr. Moore's
play, which is, in its external form, the history of two Scottish cities,
the one Celtic in the main and the other Saxon in the main, is
a microcosm of the last ten years of public life in Ireland. I know,
however, that he wishes it to be understood that he has in no
instance consciously satirised individual men, for he wars, as
Blake claimed to do, with states of mind and not with individual
men.[1] If any person upon the stage resembles any living person it
will be because he is himself a representative of the type. Mr.
Moore uses for a symbol of any cause, that seeks the welfare of the
nation as a whole, that movement for financial equity which has
won the support of all our parties. If the play touches the imagination at all, it should make every man see beyond the symbol the
cause nearest his heart, and its struggle against the common fail-
ings of humanity and those peculiar to Ireland. I do not think the
followers of any Nationalist leader, on the one hand, or of Mr. Lecky
or Mr. Plunkett, on the other, can object to its teaching, for it is aimed
against none but those persons and parties who would put private
or English interests before Irish interests.[2] As Allingham wrote
long since,

We are one at heart if you be Ireland's friend,
Though leagues asunder our opinions tend:
There are but two great parties in the end![3]

*

*   *

The Last Feast of the Fianna has an antiquarian as well as an artistic interest. Dr. Hyde is of opinion that the Oisin and Patrick dialogues were spoken in character by two reciters, and that had Irish literature followed a natural development a regular drama would have followed from this beginning.[4] Miss Milligan has added other characters while preserving the emotions and expressions of the dialogues; and if her play were acted without scenery it would resemble a possible form of old Irish drama.[5] But for the extreme difficulty of the metre of the dialogues we would have acted this play in Irish, but the translator gave up after a few verses. We are anxious to get plays in Irish, and can we do so will very possibly push our work into the western counties, where it would be an important help to that movement for the revival of the Irish language on which the life of the nation may depend.

*

*   *

Mr. Moore and Mr. Martyn have put into their plays several eloquent things about the Celtic race, and certainly, if one were to claim that there is something in sacred races, and that the Celt is of them, and to found one's claim on Mr. Nutt's pamphlets alone, one would not lack arguments.[6] I am myself, however, more inclined to agree with Renan and to set store by a certain native tradition of thought that is passed on in the conversations of father and son, and in the institutions of life, and in literature, and in the examples of history.[7] It is these that make nations and that mould the foreign settler after the national type in a few years; and it is these, whether they were made by men of foreign or of Celtic blood, that our theatre would express. If I call them Celtic—and I think Mr. Moore and Mr. Martyn would say the same—it is because of common usage, because the men who made them have less foreign than Celtic blood, and because it is the only word that describes us and those people of Western Scotland who share our language and all but what is most modern in our national traditions.

*

*   *

Prophecies are generally unfortunate, and I made some last year that have not come true; but I think I may say that we will have no difficulty in getting good plays for next year.[8] Mr. Martyn has finished a new play, Mr. Bernard Shaw promises us a play which he describes as an Irish Rogue's Comedy, and Mr. George Moore and myself are half through a three-act play in prose on the legend of Diarmuid and Grania.[9] I have also finished a play in verse, but I rather shrink from producing another verse play unless I get some opportunity for private experiment with my actors in the speaking of verse.[10] The acting of the poetical drama should be as much oratory as acting, and oratory is a lost art upon the stage. Time too will, doubtless, bring us other plays to choose among, and we have decided to have a play in Irish if we can get it.

*

*   *

Mr. Moore and Mr. Martyn have sent me articles that see the decline of England in the decline of her drama.[11] Shelley had a like thought when he said, 'In periods of the decay of social life the drama sympathises with that decay. . . . It[†] is indisputable that the highest perfection of human society has ever corresponded with the highest dramatic excellence; and that the corruption or the extinction of the drama in a nation, where it has once flourished, is a mark of the corruption of manners and an extinction of the energies which sustain the soul of social life'.[12] I myself throw the blame for that decline of the spiritual and intellectual energies of which Mr. Martyn and Mr. Moore are convinced, as were Ruskin and Morris and Arnold and Carlyle, upon that commercialism and materialism on which these men warred; and not upon race as do certain of my countrymen.[13] It should be our business to bring Ireland from under the ruins, appealing to her, as Grattan appealed to her in his speech on the tythes, by her own example and her own hopes.[14]

*

*   *

If any money should be made by our plays, which is extremely unlikely, it will be paid into a fund for the production of plays in future years.

*

*   *

The Irish Literary Theatre works under the auspices of the National Literary Society.

EDITOR OF 'BELTAINE'.

BELTAINE: FEBRUARY 1900—
MAEVE, AND CERTAIN
IRISH BELIEFS

I think I remember Mr. Martyn telling me that he knew nothing, or next to nothing, about the belief in such women as Peg Inerny among the Irish peasants.[1] Unless the imagination has a means of knowledge peculiar to itself, he must have heard of this belief as a child and remembered it in that unconscious and instinctive memory on which imagination builds. Biddy Early,* who journeyed with the people of faery when night fell, and who cured multitudes of all kinds of sickness, if the tales that one hears from her patients are not all fancy, is, I think, the origin of his Peg Inerny; but there were, and are, many like her.[2] Sometimes, as it seems, they wander from place to place begging their bread, but living all the while a noble second life in faery. They are sometimes called 'women from the North', because witchcraft, and spirits, and faeries come from the North. A Kiltartan woman said to a friend who has got me many tales, 'One time a woman from the North came to our house, and she said a great deal of people are kept below there in the lisses. She had been there herself, and in the night-time, in one moment, they'd be all away at Cruachma, wherever that may be—down in the North, I believe. And she knew everything that was in the house, and told us about my sister being sick, and that there was a hurling match going on that day, and that it was at the Isabella Wood. I'd have picked a lot of stories out of her, but my mother got nervous when she heard the truth coming out, and told me to be quiet.

*See my article in the *Contemporary Review* for September, 1899.

She had a red petticoat on her, the same as any country-woman, and she offered to cure me, for it was that time I was delicate, and her ladyship sent me to the salt water. But she asked a shilling, and my mother said she hadn't got it. "You have", said she, "and heavier metal than that you have in the house". So then my mother gave her the shilling, and she put it in the fire and melted it, and, says she, "after two days you'll see your shilling again"; but we never did. And the cure she left, I never took it; it's not safe, and the priests forbid us to take their cures. No doubt at all she was one of the ingentry (I have never heard this word for the faeries from anybody else) that can take the form of a woman by day and another form by night'.[3] Another woman in the same neighbourhood said, 'I saw myself, when I was but a child, a woman come to the door that had been seven years with the good people, and I remember her telling us that in that seven years she'd often been glad to come outside the houses and pick the bits that were thrown into the trough for the pigs; and she told us always to leave a bit about the house for those that could not come and ask for it: and though my father was a cross man, and didn't believe in such things, to the day of his death we never went up to bed without leaving a bit of food outside the door!' Sometimes, however, one hears of their being fed with supernatural food, so that they need little or none of our food.

I have two or three stories of women who were queens when in faery; I have many stories of men and women, and have even talked with some four or five among them, who believed that they had had supernatural lovers. I met a young man once in the Burren Hills who remembered an old Gaelic poet, who had loved Maeve, and was always very sorrowful because she had deserted him. He had made lamentation for her, but the young man could only remember that it was sorrowful, and that it called her 'beauty of all beauty'; a phrase that makes one think that she had become a symbol of ideal beauty, as the supernatural lover is in Mr. Martyn's play.[4] One of the most lovely of old Gaelic poems is the appeal of such a lover to his beloved. Midhir, who is called King of the Sidhe (the faeries), sang to the beautiful Etain, wife of the King who was called Eochaid the ploughman. 'O beautiful woman, come with me to the marvellous land where one listens to a sweet music, where one has spring flowers in one's hair, where the body is like snow from head to foot, where no one is sad or silent, where teeth are white and eyebrows are black . . . . cheeks red, like fox-glove in flower. . . . . Ireland is beautiful, but not so beautiful as the Great Plain I call you to. The beer of Ireland is heady, but the beer of the Great Plain is much more heady. How marvellous is the coun-try I am speaking of: Youth does not grow old there; streams of warm blood flow there, sometimes mead, sometimes wine. Men are charming, and without a blot there. O woman, when you come into my powerful country, you will wear a crown of gold upon your head. I will give you the flesh of swine, and you will have beer and milk to drink, O beautiful woman. O beautiful woman, come with me!'[5]

Maeve (Medb is the Irish spelling) is continually described as the queen of all the western faeries, and it was probably some mem-ory of her lingering in western England, or brought home by adventurers from Ireland, that gave Shakespeare his Queen Mab.[6] But neither Maeve, nor any of our Irish faeries are like the faeries of Shakespeare; for our faeries are never very little, and are some-times taller and more beautiful than mortals. The greatest among them were the gods and goddesses of ancient Ireland, and men have not yet forgotten their glory.

I recently described in the *North American Review* a vision of Queen Maeve that came to an old Mayo woman.[7] 'She was stand-ing in the window of her master's house, looking towards a moun-tain, when she saw "the finest woman you ever saw" travelling right across from the mountain and straight to her. The woman had a sword by her side and a dagger lifted up in her hand, and was dressed in white with bare arms and feet. She looked "very strong, and fierce, but not wicked"—that is, not cruel. (She was one of 'the fair, fierce women' of the Irish poem quoted in Mr. Martyn's play.)[8] The old woman had seen the Irish giant, and "though he was a fine man" he was nothing to this woman, "for he was round and could not have stepped out so soldierly". "She was like Mrs.—," naming a stately lady of the neighbourhood; "but she had no stomach on her, and was slight, and broad in the shoulders, and was handsomer than any one you ever saw; she looked about thirty". The old woman covered her eyes with her hands, and when she uncovered them the apparition had vanished. The neighbours were wild with her for not waiting to see if there was a message, for they were sure it was Queen Maeve, who often shows herself to the pilots. I asked the old woman if she had seen others like Queen Maeve, and she said, "some of them have their hair down, but they look quite different, like the sleepy-looking ladies one sees in the papers. Those with their hair up are like this one. The others have long white dresses; but those with their hair up have short dresses, so that you can see their legs right up to the calf". After some careful questioning I found that they wore what appear to be buskins. She went on, "They are fine and dashing-looking, like the men one sees riding their horses in twos and threes on the slopes of the mountains with their swords swinging". She repeated, over and over, "There is no such race living now, none so finely proportioned", or the like, and then said, "The present queen is a nice, pleasant-looking woman, but she is not like her.⁹ What makes me think so little of the ladies is that I see none as they be", meaning the spirits. "When I think of her and of the ladies now, they are like little children running about without knowing how to put their clothes on right. Is it the ladies? Why, I would not call them women at all!"' This old woman, who can neither read nor write, has come face to face with heroic beauty, that 'highest beauty', which Blake says, 'changes least from youth to age', a beauty that has been fading out of the arts, since that decadence, we call progress, set voluptuous beauty in its place.¹⁰

BELTAINE: FEBRUARY 1900—
[NOTE] TO ALICE MILLIGAN'S
THE LAST FEAST OF THE FIANNA

The emotion which a work of art awakens in an onlooker has commonly little to do with the deliberate purpose of its maker, and must vary with every onlooker.[1] Every artist who has any imagination builds better than he knows. Miss Milligan's little play delighted me because it has made, in a very simple way and through the vehicle of Gaelic persons, that contrast between immortal beauty and the ignominy and mortality of life, which is the central theme of ancient art.

EDITOR OF 'BELTAINE'.

BELTAINE: FEBRUARY 1900— THE IRISH LITERARY THEATRE, 1900

Mr. Moore has given reasons elsewhere why the founders of the Irish Literary Theatre believe good plays more possible in Ireland than in London; but I think he makes too much of these reasons when he makes them our chief impulse.[1] I know that he and Mr. Martyn and myself, and those who are working with us, believe that we have things to say to our countrymen which it is our pleasure and our duty to say. If we write plays that are literature, and find people to like them, it will be because that strong imaginative energy, which is needed to fill with life the elaborate circumstance of a play, has not often come except as from a Sinai to some nation wandering as in a wilderness; but that strong imaginative energy comes among men, as I think, not because they have followed it from country to country, but because a genius greater than their own, and, it may be, without their knowledge or their consent, has thrown its shadow upon them.[2] Dionysius, the Areopagite, wrote that 'He has set the borders of the nations according to His angels'.[3] It is these angels, each one the genius of some race about to be unfolded, that are the founders of intellectual traditions; and as lovers understand in their first glance all that is to befall them, and as poets and musicians see the whole work in its first impulse, so races prophesy at their awakening whatever the generations that are to prolong their traditions shall accomplish in detail. It is only at the awakening—as in ancient Greece, or in Elizabethan England, or in contemporary Scandinavia—that great numbers of men understand that a right understanding of life and of destiny is more important than amusement. In London, where all the intellectual traditions gather to die, men hate a play if they are told it is literature, for they will not endure a spiritual superiority; but in Athens, where so many intellectual traditions were born, Euripides once changed hostility to enthusiasm by asking his playgoers whether it was his business to teach them, or their business to teach him.[4] New races understand instinctively, because the future cries in their ears, that the old revelations are insufficient, and that all life is revelation beginning in miracle and enthusiasm, and dying out as it unfolds itself in what we have mistaken for progress. It is one of our illusions, as I think, that education, the softening of manners, the perfecting of law —countless images of a fading light—can create nobleness and beauty, and that life moves slowly and evenly towards some perfection. Progress is miracle, and it is sudden, because miracles are the work of an all-powerful energy, and nature in herself has no power except to die and to forget. If one studies one's own mind, one comes to think with Blake, that "every time less than a pulsation of the artery is equal to 6000 years, for in this period the poet's work is done; and all the great events of time start forth and are conceived in such a period, within a pulsation of the artery".[5]

Scandinavia is, as it seems, passing from her moments of miracle; and some of us think that Ireland is passing to hers. She may not produce any important literature, but because her moral nature has been aroused by political sacrifices, and her imagination by a political pre-occupation with her own destiny, she is ready to be moved by profound thoughts that are a part of the unfolding of herself. Mr. Martyn lit upon one of them in his *Heather Field,* which shares it with old Celtic legends. He describes a man who attained the Divine vision as his brain perished, and our Irish playgoers sympathised with this man so perfectly that they hissed the doctors who found that he was mad. The London playgoers, whose life, as must be wherever success is too highly valued, is established in a contrary thought, sympathised with the doctors, and held the Divine vision a dream. This year Mr. Martyn will return to the same thought with his *Maeve,* which tells of an old woman who begs her way from door to door in life, and is a great and beautiful queen in faery, and who persuades a young girl to renounce life and seek perfection in what unfolds as death. Miss Milligan, not influenced by Mr.

Martyn, or by anything but old legends, has the same thought in her *The Last Feast of the Fianna*, which, as I think, would make one remember the mortality and indignity of all that lives. Her bard Oisin goes to faery, and is made immortal like his songs; while the heroes and Grania, the most famous of the beautiful, sink into querulous old age. Mr. Moore, in his *The Bending of the Bough*, the longest and most elaborate of our three plays, has written of the rejection of a spiritual beauty, which his play expounds, as the ideal hope, not of individual life, but of the race—its vision of itself made perfect—and the acceptance of mere individual life. His story, which pretends to describe the relations between two towns, one in the Celtic north and one in the Saxon south of a Scotland as vague as the sea-coast of Bohemia,[6] really describes the war of this vision with surrounding circumstance, and its betrayal by the light-souled and the self-seeking. It shows many real types of men and women in the fire of an impassioned satire, and will perhaps awaken some sleeping dogs. This thought of the war of immortal upon mortal life has been the moving thought of much Irish poetry, and may yet, so moving and necessary a thought it is, inspire many plays which, whether important or unimportant, shall have the sincerity of youth. It has come upon us, not because we have sought it out, but because we share, as I think, a moiety of the blood and the intellectual traditions of the race that gave romance and the kingdom of faery to European literature, and which has always waited with amorous eyes for some impossible beauty. Our daily life has fallen among prosaic things and ignoble things, but our dreams remember the enchanted valleys.

(Reprinted from THE DOME.)

BELTAINE: APRIL 1900 — THE LAST FEAST OF THE FIANNA, MAEVE, AND THE BENDING OF THE BOUGH, IN DUBLIN

I remember somebody, who has nothing to do with any propaganda, saying once that everything becomes a reality when it comes to Ireland.[1] We have brought the 'literary drama' to Ireland, and it has become a reality. If you produce the literary drama in London, you can get an audience for a night or two, but this audience will be made up of the professed students of the drama, of people who are, like yourself, in protest against their time, and who have no personal relations with that which moves upon the stage. In Ireland, we had among our audience almost everybody who is making opinion in Ireland, who is a part of his time, and numbers went out of the playhouse thinking a little differently of that Ireland which their work is shaping: some went away angry, some delighted, but all had seen that upon the stage at which they could not look altogether unmoved. Miss Milligan's little play, whose persons are the persons of numberless Irish folk tales; Mr. Martyn's *Maeve*, whose heroine typifies Ireland herself wavering between idealism and commercialism; and Mr. Moore's *Bending of the Bough*, which leaves no class, no movement, that has had any part in these last ten years of disillusionment, out of the wide folds of its satire, touched the heart as greater drama on some foreign theme could not, because they had found, as I think the drama must do in every country, those interests common to the man of letters and the man in the crowd, which are more numerous in a country that has not passed from its time of storm, than in a long-settled country like England.[2] As

I came out of the theatre, after the first night of *The Bending of the Bough,* I heard these three sentences, in which there was perhaps a little of the extravagance of the Celt, spoken by three men, one of whom is among the most influential in Ireland. 'I wonder will people dare to come and see so terrible a satire'. 'I feel, as I have never felt before in my life, that there is a new soul come into Ireland'. 'No young man who came into this theatre to-night will go out of it the same man'. The cheaper parts of the house were the loudest in their applause, for our enthusiasts are poor; and their applause did not pick out mere obvious patriotic thoughts, but was discriminate and subtle. The gallery, which sang Gaelic songs between the acts, applauded thoughts like these: 'At all events we have no proof that spiritual truths are illusory, whereas we know that the world is'. 'Respectable causes, is a cause ever respectable'; and this thought very loudly: 'There is always a right and a wrong way, and the wrong way always seems the most reasonable'.³ All the Irish papers, with the exception of the *Irish Times,* and our little Society papers, which are proud to represent what they believe to be English interests, have written of all three plays with enthusiasm and at great length.⁴ The *Daily Independent* described Mr. Moore's play as 'the most remarkable drama which has been given to the nation for many years', and said, when our week was over, 'a new intellectual life has arisen in Ireland'; and the other papers had as much, or nearly as much, to say.⁵ I do not speak of these opinions because I would agree with them, for I am too closely associated with this movement to measure the worth of the plays it has produced; but to show that we have made the literary drama a reality. The only correspondents of English papers who were present do not differ from the Dublin papers upon this point. The correspondent of the *Times* said of the reception of *The Last Feast of the Fianna* and of *Maeve,* 'The plays were enthusiastically received'; and the correspondent of the *Observer* said of the reception of *The Bending of the Bough,* 'People really had to go to see it. Never, it was said, had such an Irish play been seen on the boards of an Irish theatre. If the business of a dramatist is to hold the mirror up to nature, here, said everybody, it was held up in our faces unflinchingly. . . . When the curtain falls every one feels that there has been no such serious commentary on Irish life and Irish politics given to the world in our time; and on the whole no such just commentary either'.[6] The English critics who have read the play and not seen it, and who do not know Ireland, have not understood it, for you must know Ireland and her special temptations to understand perfectly even such a sentence as, 'There is always a right and a wrong way, and the wrong way always seems the most reasonable'. On the whole, therefore, I have a good hope that our three years of experiment, which is all we proposed to ourselves at the outset, will make literary drama permanent in Ireland during our time, and give the Irish nation a new method of expression.

SAMHAIN: 1901 —
FROM WINDLESTRAWS

The names I have crossed out are the names of three eminent authorities on education.[1] They no longer matter to us Irish, for we have for good and all taken over the intellectual government of our country, and if the degeneration of England goes on as quickly as it has these last years, we shall take over for certain generations the intellectual government of that country also whether we will or no; and because we believe, when others have ceased to believe, we have, I think, taken up the wheel of life in our hands that we may set it to whirl upon a new axle tree.

As Dr. Douglas Hyde does not reserve the Irish acting rights of his play, any friends of the language who like may play it after October 26th.[2]

*

* *

I have called this little collection of writings *Samhain*, the old name for the beginning of winter, because our plays this year are in October, and because our Theatre is coming to an end in its present shape. The profits on the sale of *Samhain* will be given to the Gaelic League. The three numbers of *Beltaine* may still be had from the Unicorn Press, bound together into one volume. They contain a record of our first two years, and a good deal of dramatic criticism.[3]

SAMHAIN: 1901 —
[NOTE] TO GEORGE MOORE'S
"THE IRISH LITERARY THEATRE"

*I do not want dramatic blank verse to be chanted, as people understand that word, but I do not want actors to speak as prose what I have taken much trouble to write as verse. Lyrical verse is another matter, and that I hope to hear spoken to musical notes in some theatre some day.[1]—Editor of SAMHAIN.

SAMHAIN: 1902—
FROM NOTES

Sealy, Bryers & Walker have still a few copies of last year's *Samhain*, and the three numbers of its forerunner[†], *Beltaine,* can still be got, bound up in one volume, for a shilling, from the Unicorn Press, Cecil Court, St. Mark's Lane, London.[1] They record the rise of the Irish dramatic movement. Any money made by the sale of the present number of *Samhain* will be spent on the production of plays on Irish subjects.

SAMHAIN: 1902—
[NOTE] TO AE'S "THE DRAMATIC TREATMENT OF HEROIC LITERATURE"

*I think it was his *History of Ireland, Heroic Period,* that started us all; it stirred others, too. Burne-Jones said to somebody, I forget who now, that it had made an epoch in his life; and I remember hearing William Morris praise it once.[1]

SAMHAIN: 1903—
FROM NOTES

A part of the essay which follows was printed in the *United Irish-man* last spring. It is a summary, as far as I can remember, of a lecture I gave after the performance of *The Hour-Glass*.[1] It repeats a good deal that has been said before in SAMHAIN or *Beltaine,* but only things that one must repeat over and over, not perhaps to convince those who do not believe us, but, as Blake said, to protect those who do.[2]

*
* *

I think that there must be some who will be glad of Mr. W. Fay's Portrait. We owe our National Theatre Society to him and his brother, and we have always owed to his playing our chief successes.[3]

SAMHAIN: 1904—
[INTERPOLATIONS]

Reader of this book, I have been watching you from the wings of the stage, and have seen you buy your SAMHAIN *with your programme. You have thought to read it through between the acts, but you have not done so.*[1]

 I have at this moment, at the end of three days' dictation, said to my typewriter, 'This is a very easy sort of writing; I wish creative writing were as easy'. And my typewriter has said, 'It is always easy to find fault with one's neighbours, and that is what you have been doing all the time'.[2]

SAMHAIN: 1904—
MISS HORNIMAN'S OFFER
OF THEATRE AND THE SOCIETY'S
ACCEPTANCE

[COPY.]   H 1 MONTAGU MANSIONS,
LONDON, W.,
April [1904].

DEAR MR. YEATS,

I have a great sympathy with the artistic and dramatic aims of the Irish National Theatre Company, as publicly explained by you on various occasions.[1] I am glad to be able to offer you my assistance in your endeavours to establish a permanent Theatre in Dublin.

I am taking the Hall of the Mechanic's Institute in Abbey Street, and an adjoining building in Marlborough Street, which I propose to turn into a small Theatre, with a proper Entrance Hall, Green-room, and Dressing-rooms. As the Company will not require the Hall constantly, I propose to arrange to let it for lectures and entertainments at a rental proportionate to its seating capacity.

The Company can have the building rent free whenever they want it, for rehearsals and performances, except when it is let. The Green-room I hope to arrange to be kept for their sole use. They must pay for their own electric light and gas, as well as for the repair of damages done during their occupation. The building will be insured, and any additions to the lighting for special occasions or plays must be permitted by the Insurance Company, formally in writing.

If any President, Vice-President, or member of the Company wants the Hall for a lecture, concert, or entertainment, the rent must be paid to me as by an ordinary person. If a lecture be given on a dramatic or theatrical subject, and the gross receipts go to the Irish National Theatre, then the President, Vice-President, or member of the Company can have the Hall for nothing. But it must be advertised clearly as being for the sole benefit of the Irish National Theatre, pecuniarily, as well as in aid of its artistic objects.

The prices of the seats can be raised, of course, but not lowered, neither by the Irish National Theatre, nor by anyone who will hire the Hall.

This is to prevent cheap entertainments from being given, which would lower the letting value of the Hall. I hope to be able to arrange to number most of the seats and to sell the tickets beforehand, with a small fee for booking. The entrance to the more expensive seats will be from Marlborough Street, where there will be a Cloak Room.

The situation, being near to the Tramway Terminus, is convenient for people living in any part of Dublin. I shall take every possible means to insure the safety and convenience of the public. I can only afford to make a very little Theatre, and it must be quite simple. You all must do the rest to make a powerful and prosperous Theatre, with a high artistic ideal.

A copy of this letter will be sent to each Vice-President and another to the Stage Manager for the Company.

Yours sincerely,

A. E. F. HORNIMAN.

––––––

[COPY.]   34 LOWER CAMDEN STREET,
                              DUBLIN: 11th May, 1904.
DEAR MISS HORNIMAN,

We, the undersigned members of the Irish National Theatre Company, beg to thank you for the interest you have evinced in the work of the Society and for the aid you propose giving to our future work by securing a permanent Theatre in Abbey Street.

We undertake to abide by all the conditions laid down in your letter to the company, and to do our utmost to forward the objects of the Society.[2]

W. B. Yeats

F. J. Fay

William G. Fay

James G. Starkey

Pɲoınɲıaɲ Mac Sıúƀłaıʒ
  (Frank Walker)

Adolphus Wright

Máɲʒec Ní ʒáɲƀaıʒ
  (Miss Garvey)

Vera Esposito

Dora L. Ainnesley

George Roberts

An Cɲaoıƀín Aoıƀín
  (Douglas Hyde)

Thomas G. Koehler

Harry F. Norman

Helen S. Laird

George Russell

Máıɲe Níc Sıúƀłaıʒ
  (Miss Walker)

J. M. Synge

Sara Allgood

Frederick Ryan

Páoɲaıʒ MacCuıłım
  (Patrick Colm)

Stephen Gwynn

Augusta Gregory

SAMHAIN: 1904—
FROM AN OPINION

One of our propagandist newspapers says that we should not quote Mr. Walkley, or any other English critic, because an Englishman is an enemy, and we should not value the criticism of an enemy.[1] Mr. Walkley is a very well read, very intelligent, very sympathetic person, whose knowledge of the drama is greater than that of most living men, and he has said charming things about us—but he is an enemy. Mr Frank Hugh O'Donnell has, if I remember, rightly, called my Countess Cathleen 'a meandering decadent with a diseased brain', but he is an Irishman, and, therefore, presumably a friend.[2]

Perhaps it is necessary for the public good to go on believing this kind of thing—I am never certain upon the point—but, if it is, literature, poor creature, will go somewhere else, for she has an unlucky craving for reality.—'He who sees Jehovah dies'.[3]

THE ARROW: 20 OCTOBER 1906—
FROM THE SEASON'S WORK

I have been so busy finishing *Deirdre,* a play in verse, that I have put off *Samhain* for a month or so; but THE ARROW is not meant as a substitute, for we hope that the queen with the wolf dog has one in her quiver for every month.[1] It will interpret or comment on particular plays, make announcements, wrap up the programme and keep it from being lost, and leave general principles to *Samhain.* We are at the outset of our first season of tolerably constant playing, for, besides our seven nights of a new play every month, there will be a new play or an old one every Saturday throughout the season. There is a list on another page including Irish historical and peasant plays, one play of industrial life, one of lower middle class life in a small country town, besides certain world-famous masterpieces.[2] When this list has run out another will be announced, containing translations of *Œdipus the King,* from the Greek, of *Phèdre,* from the French, and some native plays, *The Heather Field* of Mr. Edward Martyn, my rewritten *Shadowy Waters*—Mr. Robert Gregory has made a very beautiful stage scene for this play—,[†] *The Jackdaw,* a new comedy by Lady Gregory,[†] a new version of her *Kincora.*[3]

THE ARROW: 20 OCTOBER 1906—
A NOTE ON *THE MINERAL WORKERS*

Mr. Boyle has used the struggles of an Irish-American engineer who is trying to smelt ore in Ireland, as a symbol to represent the difficulties of any enthusiast who attempts, in a country demoralized by failure, to change anything or establish anything that would mean a break with settled habits and interests. He knows the country well—or rather the country-side where he was born and bred, and no man knows more of the world than that, if the knowledge one means† is that instinctive kind that goes to making plays of character. His people are individuals, but they are also types, and there is something of the national tragedy in the play. Every man is ready, in Mr. O'Grady's phrase, to break ranks and go hunting hares, because no man believes that the marching is going to bring him to anything better than a night's sleep.¹ But if you have no mind for meanings, you can take the play, and I hope any play we produce, as a story, and be content.

THE ARROW: 20 OCTOBER 1906—
THE *IRISH PEASANT*
ON *HYACINTH HALVEY*

The *Irish Peasant,* in a long article signed 'Pat', on the first production of *Hyacinth Halvey,*† describes that play as 'a realistic
comedy of current life on a background of implicit criticism'.¹ It
considered that the play is an exposure of the lack of any genuine
public opinion in Ireland, where 'popularity' is 'the only standard
of human worth', which results in 'all sorts of despicable characters being set upon stilts for standards'; and it winds up with 'Did
Lady Gregory intend the sermon? I think not. The thorough success of her play as a play indicates that she was concerned with the
dramatic interest of her theme and nothing else, deriving her
motive from the determining features of the life around her as every
dramatist has a right to do'. In the performance 'nothing is ever
overdone, there is never the least appeal to the gallery, the faults
are never of the fixed kind that limit progress, and there is never
an attempt to magnify a part at the expense of the artistic symmetry
of the whole. Accordingly the audiences most worth having in
Dublin, from an artistic point of view, are to be met at the Abbey
Theatre, whatever their numbers'.

THE ARROW: 20 OCTOBER 1906—
[NOTES]

The Doctor in Spite of Himself is now played with all the 'business', traditional from Molière, sent to us through the courtesy of a principal actor at the Comédie Française.[1] We had not this 'business' in time for our first production of the play, but it does not greatly differ from that invented by Mr. William Fay. One of the Dublin papers was shocked at the roughness and simplicity of the play, and the writer of the article, although he admitted he had never read Molière's text, accused us of putting these things into it. Now it is precisely this roughness and simplicity, as of some old humourous folk-tale, that has made it a world-famous masterpiece, for it can be translated into almost any language, or adapted into any social order that is not too complex. I saw in some paper the other day that it is popular in Persia.[2]

The Eloquent Dempsy is a satire on a politician in a small Irish town, who shifts with the wind and holds his own by rhetoric, good humour and an almost brazen impudence.[3] The play is full of politics, but the playwright does not take a side, for he knows that nothing concerns him but human life.

Riders to the Sea and *Cathleen ni Houlihan* have been played so many times that they need no comment, except that I draw attention to the heightening of the emotion of the words by music in *Cathleen ni Houlihan* and in *The Gaol Gate*.[4] This play is Lady Gregory's first use of peasant dialect for tragic purposes.

W. B. Y.

Henceforth there will be Sixpenny Seats in a part of the Pit.[5]
The Heating Apparatus has been improved and carefully tested.
The Secretary of the Theatre will be much obliged if theatre-goers, who wish to receive notices of the plays, will give their names and addresses at the Box Office. Almost our principal expense is advertisement, and it is of the first importance for a theatre that cannot for some time expect a large following, to lessen this expense. To all who leave their names and addresses, will be sent a free copy of The Arrow *every month, and this will contain the names and dates of our plays.*

THE ARROW: 24 NOVEMBER 1906—
[NOTES]

We started THE ARROW very largely that we might reply to hostile criticism of the kind we faced in its abundance last winter; but we have made no new enemies of late, and have played to large and growing audiences.[1] We have more need of announcements than of arguments, and the principal of these is that a distinguished Irish actress, Miss Darragh, is now—to use the German term—'the guest of the Company'.[2] Some among our audience will have seen her as the chief character in *The Walls of Jericho*, or in *Salomé*, in London lately. She has brought to us her great experience and talent out of enthusiasm for the work of the Company. I have only seen her as a most distinguished and passionate Salomé.[3] Her presence has helped us to play not merely *Deirdre*, but my new *Shadowy Waters*, and our larger audiences have encouraged us to risk this latter play, and Mr. Boyle's *Building Fund* for a week in December. This change postpones *The White Cockade, The Shadow of the Glen*, and *The Hour-Glass* till after Mr. Synge's *Playboy*.[4]

* * *

The entrance of people, after the commencement of a play, is a constant annoyance in Irish and English Theatre. Several complaints have reached us, that, at a recent performance of Mr. Synge's *Riders to the Sea*, the effect of the play was all but destroyed, by the opening and shutting of the door to the Stalls. At Bayreuth, nobody is allowed to enter the auditorium until the Act is over.[5] All work, whether it be spoken or sung, which depends for its effect upon slowly elaborated sentiment, or gradually increasing crisis, is all but ruined by interruption. English managers sometimes get out of the difficulty by beginning with a farce. We would appeal to our audience to endeavour to be seated before the rise of the curtain at 8.15.

THE ARROW: 24 NOVEMBER 1906—
DEIRDRE

The legend on which *Deirdre* is founded is, perhaps, the most famous of all Irish legends. The best version is that in Lady Gregory's *Cuchulain of Muirthemne,* and is made up out of more than a dozen old texts.[1] All these texts differ more or less, sometimes in essential things, and in arranging the story for the bounds of a one-act play, I have had to leave out many details, even some important persons, that are in all the old versions. I have selected certain things which seem to be characteristic of the tale as well as in themselves dramatic, and I have separated these from much that needed an epic form or a more elaborate treatment. Deirdre was the Irish Helen, and Naoise her Paris, and Concobar her Mene laus, and the events took place, according to the conventional chronology of the Bards, about the time of the birth of Christ.[2] Concobar was High King of Ulster, and Naoise King of one of the sub-kingdoms, and the scene of the play is laid in a guest-house among woods in the neighbourhood of Armagh, where Concobar had his palace.[3]

Fergus, who in the old poems is a mixture of chivalry and folly, had been High King before Concobar, but had been tricked into abdicating in his favour. I have made no use of this abdication in my play, except that it helps to justify the popular influence I have attributed to him. I have introduced three wandering musicians, who are not in the legend, and Mr. Arthur Darley has written the music of their songs. The scenery has been designed by Mr. Robert Gregory.[4]

THE ARROW: 24 NOVEMBER 1906—
THE SHADOWY WATERS

I began *The Shadowy Waters* when I was a boy, and when I published a version of it six or seven years ago, the plot had been so
often re-arranged and was so overgrown with symbolical ideas that
the poem was obscure and vague.[1] It found its way on to the stage
more or less by accident, for our people had taken it as an exercise
in the speaking of verse, and it pleased a few friends, though it must
have bewildered and bored the greater portion of the audience.[2] The
present version is practically a new poem, and is, I believe, sufficiently simple, appealing to no knowledge more esoteric than is necessary for the understanding of any of the more characteristic love
poems of Shelley or of Petrarch. If the audience will understand it
as a faery-tale, and not look too anxiously for a meaning, all will
be well.

Once upon a time, when herons built their nests in old men's
beards, Forgael, a Sea-King of ancient Ireland, was promised by certain human-headed birds love of a supernatural intensity and happiness. These birds were the souls of the dead, and he followed them
over seas towards the sunset, where their final rest is. By means of
a magic harp, he could call them about him when he would and listen to their speech. His friend Aibric, and the sailors of his ship,
thought him mad, or that this mysterious happiness could come after
death only, and that he and they were being lured to destruction.
Presently they captured a ship, and found a beautiful woman
upon it, and Forgael subdued her and his own rebellious sailors by
the sound of his harp. The sailors fled upon the other ship, and Forgael and the woman drifted on alone following the birds, awaiting

death and what comes after, or some mysterious transformation of the flesh, an embodiment of every lover's dream.

The scenery and the lighting have been arranged by Mr. Robert Gregory.

SAMHAIN: 1906—
NOTES

I have re-printed from the *Contemporary Review* with the kind permission of the Editor, an essay of mine on the art of the Player, the Singer, and the Reciter, in relation to literature and to the art of the Abbey Theatre. It was written shortly after the opening of the Theatre, though through an accident it was not published until October of this year, and it gives a better account than anything I have written of certain dreams I hope the Theatre may in some measure fulfil.[1] Our work has developed more quickly upon one side, and more slowly upon another, than I had foreseen. We have done little, though we have done something, to find music that would not obscure the meaning and the rhythm of words, and we have done nothing for the story-tellers, but now that our country comedies, with their abundant and vivid speech, are well played and well spoken, we may try out the whole adventure. We cannot of a certainty try it all at one time, and it will be easier for our audience to follow fragmentary experiments, now that the dream is there upon the paper.

* *
*

Our main business is to create an Irish dramatic literature, and a list of plays from the outset of our movement, printed at the end of *Samhain* will show that we have done something towards it.[2] The movement was begun by the Irish Literary Theatre, which produced or promoted the performance of Irish plays with English players, there being no others to be had at the time, for one week a year, for three years, Mr. Benson's Company playing for it in its last year.[3] After that, a company of Irish players, with Mr. William Fay to stage-manage them, and Mr. Frank Fay to teach them elocution, took up the work, and Lady Gregory and Mr. Synge and myself have been responsible or mainly responsible for the choice of plays and the general policy of the National Theatre Society, as this Company is now called, from the opening of the Abbey Theatre, the Company's first permanent home, in 1904. We have a small subsidy from Miss Horniman, the generous friend who has given us the free use of the Theatre, and are the only directors of an English-speaking Theatre who can say, as the artist can in every other art, 'we will give you nothing that does not please ourselves, and if you do not like it, and we are still confident that it is good, we will set it before you again, and trust to changing taste'. All true arts, as distinguished from their commercial and mechanical imitation, are a festival where it is the fiddler who calls the tune.

THE ARROW: 23 FEBRUARY 1907—
FROM THE CONTROVERSY
OVER THE PLAYBOY

I have reprinted in the present ARROW my speech at the Debate
in the Abbey Theatre on the 4th February upon *The Playboy,* and
the measures taken to preserve order, and certain extracts from
the *Samhain* of 1905, and from patriotic papers of various dates.[1]
These quotations show how old is the attack and how old the
defence, and that no satirical writer of the Theatre—certainly not
Mr. Boyle, who has left us because we fought Mr. Synge's battle—
has escaped a misunderstanding unavoidable where certain crude
general ideas and propagandist emotions have taken the place of
every other kind of thought. If we had withdrawn the play those
that hissed or cried 'stage Irishman' at the performance of *The
Mineral Workers* would have tried to drown the next play of Mr.
Boyle's, that they objected to, by the stamping of their feet and
the blowing of tin trumpets.[2]

THE ARROW: 23 FEBRUARY 1907—
FROM MR. YEATS' OPENING SPEECH AT THE DEBATE OF FEBRUARY 4TH, AT THE ABBEY THEATRE

'During the performances every now and then some one got up in his place and tried to make a speech.¹ On Saturday night an old gentleman stood up in the front row of the pit after the opening of the third act, and is probably very indignant that the police did not allow him to speak. I hope he is here to-night, and all those other speakers. We have never desired anything but the most free discussion that we may get at last some kind of sound criticism in this country. But before the discussion commences I will do my best to answer a few of the more obvious arguments, for there is no use wasting our time on stupidities or on misunderstandings of each other's point of view. I see it said again and again that we have tried to prevent the audience from the reasonable expression of dislike. I certainly would never like to set plays before a theatrical audience that was not free to approve or disapprove, even very loudly, for there is no dramatist that does not desire a live audience. We have to face something quite different from reasonable expression of dislike. On Tuesday and on Monday night it was not possible to hear six consecutive lines of the play, and this deafening outcry was not raised by the whole theatre, but almost entirely by a section of the pit, who acted together and even sat together. It was an attempt to prevent the play from being heard and judged. We are under contract with our audiences, we receive money on the understanding that the play shall be heard and seen; we consider it is our duty to carry out our contract.

'It has been said in to-day's *Freeman* that the forty dissentients in the pit were doing their duty because there is no government censor in Ireland.[2] The public, it is said, is the censor where there is no other appointed to the task. But were these forty—we had them counted upon Monday night and they were not more—alone the public and the censor? What right had they to prevent the far greater number who wished to hear from hearing and judging? They themselves were keeping the plays from the eyes and ears of its natural censor. We called to our aid the means which every community possesses to limit the activities of small minorities who set their interests against those of the community—we called in the police. There is no stalwart member of the *Sinn Féin* party who would not do the same if he were to find a representative of that active minority—the burglars—fumbling with the lid of his strong box.[3] We think it folly to say that we cannot use the laws common to all civilised communities to protect ourselves and our audience against the tyranny of cliques. At no time would we have ever hesitated to do what we have done. When *The Countess Cathleen* was denounced with an equal violence we called in the police.[4] That was in '99, when I was still President of the '98 Association of Great Britain.[5]

'I would indeed despise myself if for the sake of popularity or of a vague sentiment I were to mar the task I have set my hands to, and to cast the precious things of the soul into the trodden mire. A deputation of young Catholic students came to see me the other day, and the one who spoke their thoughts the most thanked us especially for this, for he said that the little domineering cliques presume upon the fear of lost popularity that keeps a Nationalist from calling to his aid those powers which hold together every community of the world, and silence the rattling bells on the cap of the fool.[6]

The only practical suggestion made in the long disorderly debate that followed was that the management of the Theatre might have tired out the opposition, and so get a hearing for the play without calling in the police. Mr. Yeats replied to this as follows—'Have you any idea as to the effect of all that noise and insult upon the nerves of the players? Do you think we would submit them to all that wear and tear of nerve night after night when we had the means of ending it? Our business was to secure quiet and silence, and we secured it as soon as possible'.

THE ARROW: 1 JUNE 1907—
FROM [NOTES]

I need add but little to the argument raised by the production of
The Playboy in Dublin, for my own statement, made in *The
Arrow* at that time, is on sale in the theatre.[1]

The plays we bring to London are a selection from a considerable
number which have been produced at the Abbey Theatre, and sometimes we have had to choose some particular one, not because it is
the best, but because it suits our players or as many as can travel.
I would myself sooner have been represented by *Deirdre* or *The
King's Threshold,* than by *The Shadowy Waters,* which may not
seem a play to any but the lovers of lyric poetry, or *On Baile's Strand,*
which is part of a cycle of plays on the life of the ancient hero Cuchulain.[2] The training of verse speakers has become the most laborious part of our work, for a player may be excellent in all else and
yet have all to learn in verse or be altogether unfitted for it. In the
first state of our theatre it proved to be impossible, no matter how
great the enthusiasm of individuals,[†] to keep to work so arduous
and prolonged players who had to earn their living in some workshop or office. Even yet we have only made a beginning, and with
the exception of one or two speakers, cannot claim more than the
rightness of our methods. Good speech of some kind has always,
whatever the play, been our principal pre-occupation—for only
when there is musical, finely articulated, delicate, varied, deliberate speech, can style, whether the play be in verse, or, as are the
greater number of ours, in dialect have any effect upon the fortunes
of a play, and as Sainte-Beuve has said, style is the only thing that

is immortal in literature.[3] It is to set arbitrary limits to the office of the player, to grant it gesture and facial expression, but to deny it, as some do, a fine speaking of fine things, or to think that the stage has become more really the stage, more consistent with itself, in forgetting the feeling for fine oratory that made possible the rogues and clowns of Ben Jonson and the Princes of Corneille and of Shakespeare.

SAMHAIN: 1908—
EVENTS

There has been no *Samhain* for a couple of years, principally because an occasional publication, called *The Arrow*, took its place for a time.[1]

* *
*

Some twelve months ago Mrs. Patrick Campbell was so well pleased by some performances of our Company that she offered to come and play with it in my *Deirdre;* coming, I need hardly say, for the love of our people's art, and bringing her service as a gift. She let me announce this from the stage, and afterwards announced it herself from the stage of the Gaiety in kind and gracious words.[2] We all feel that this great actress who has played in the one play with Bernhardt, will confer upon us in November a supreme honour.[3] When we and all our players are with the dead players of Henley's rhyme, some historian of the Theatre, remembering her coming and giving more weight to the appreciation of a fellow artist than even to the words of fine critics, will understand that if our people were not good artists one of the three or four great actresses of Europe would never have come where the oldest player is but twenty-six.[4] To the sincere artist the applause of those who have won greatness in his own craft is often his first appreciation, and always the last that he forgets. When I had just published my first book, I met William Morris in Holborn Viaduct, and he began to praise it with the words, 'That is my kind of poetry', and promised to write about it, and would have said I do not know how much more if he had not suddenly caught sight of one of those decorated lamp posts, and waving his umbrella at the post, raged at the

Corporation. As the years pass I value those words of his not less but more, understanding, as I could not at that time, how much I learned from the daily spectacle of that great, laborious, joyous man.[5]

* *
*

The *Freeman* of September 18th contained a leading article on the passing of the Gaiety Theatre and the Theatre Royal into the hands of a trust. After pointing out the way in which all such trusts lead in the long run to musical comedy, and this alone, and regretting what it thinks to be the errors of 'the only independent theatre left to us', the article wound up with: 'The Abbey patent expires in 1910, so there is no time to lose, ... would it one day be possible for the Corporation to take it over as a municipal theatre? Municipalisation is the method by which the Germans have successfully fought monopoly and saved their stage from decadence. But is dangerous even to mention such a thing in these days of punctilious auditors.'[6]

* *
*

[†]At the expiration of our patent our present arrangement with Miss Horniman will also have come to an end. We hope, however, before that day comes, to have made the theatre either self-supporting or nearly so, and to be able to hand it over to some management that will work it as a business, while keeping its artistic aim. We shall be able to hand over to that management a great mass of plays, and we shall have accustomed audiences and dramatists alike to the freedom necessary for vigorous literature. Whatever form of organization takes the place of the present, it is not likely to be subsidized, or at any rate subsidized to any large extent, and will, therefore, be much more in the hands of the public than we are. Before that time, however, all the plays which have caused disturbance with us will have been accepted as matters of course; *The Playboy* and *The Piper* will trouble their audiences no more than *The Well of the Saints,* at one time so much disliked, or *The Shadow of the Glen,* against which a newspaper once used all its resources.[7] We know that we have already created a taste for sincere and original drama and for sincere, quiet,[†]

simple acting. Ireland possesses something which has come out of its own life, and the many failures of dramatic societies which have imitated our work without our discipline and our independence, show that it could not have been made in any other way. But when the new management comes we hope that we, the present Directors, may be able to return to our proper work without the ceaseless distraction of theatrical details.

*   *
*

Before the present Patent of our Theatre comes to an end we hope to visit America. We believe that the success of our players here and in England would repeat itself in America, and upon a larger scale. In fact it was a part of our original calculation when we set out to form an Irish stock company, that it would spend a certain portion of every year among the Irish in America. It has been lack of money that has prevented us going there, and kept us playing a greater number of months in Dublin than we had thought possible. A good deal of touring is desirable, for it is difficult with a company so small as ours to put on new plays at short enough intervals to hold a Dublin audience for nine or ten months in the year. If we were to do no worse than we already do during the most fortunate part of each Dublin season, for, say ten months in the year, we should be more than independent of subsidy. Some three months touring every year with the same amount of success we have had in London, and Oxford, Glasgow and Manchester, and somewhat better stalls in Dublin than we get at present, would pay expenses and allow for all necessary widening of activity.

*   *
*

Last spring the hoardings of New York showed placards announcing that The Irish National Theatre Company of Dublin was performing there. A great many who had seen or had heard of our work in Ireland crowded to the theatre, and some of them have written to us of their disappointment, for *The Pot of Broth* and *The Rising of the Moon* were given, not by our whole company, but by three of our players who had left us, and by other players who, though they had played in a few of our performances, had been in America for many years. We allowed Mr. William Fay to take these plays to America, as his engagement with Mr. Frohman was conditional on his getting them, but it was on the understanding that Mr. Frohman was not to use the name of our Society. Not only was it used (at first with the alteration of a word) but a programme headed with the words 'Mr. Frohman presents the Irish National Theatre Company of Dublin', was otherwise copied so accurately from our Dublin programme that the names of actors who never left the Abbey Theatre were set down as playing in New York.[8] Everything was done by Mr. Frohman's agent through advertisements, interviews and portraits to identify the New York experiment with us, and after the programmes had been stopped in New York under threat of legal proceedings, and the plays had been withdrawn, 'Mr. Frohman presented the Irish National Theatre Society' (not Company this time) in a play by Mr. William Boyle to the people of Chicago.[9] The speculation was a failure. The plays were produced on large stages and in large theatres, instead of the little theatres they are written for, and as curtain-raisers to some French farce that drew its own audience; and the section of the literary and the Irish public who had heard something about us expected our whole company and a selection of plays as representative as we send to London and Oxford and Cambridge. We had hoped to have gone to America this autumn, but this failure has delayed us.

* *

*

Last January Mr. William Fay, his wife and brother, left us, but, great as their loss has been, their places have been taken by other players, and the general efficiency of the Company has not suffered. We have never produced so many plays in so short a time as we did last spring, nor had such good audiences as in August, September and October this year.

When Mr. Fay was leaving us I wrote this paragraph for a SAMHAIN we had thought to bring out immediately, read it to him, and, with his approval, published it in certain papers at the time:

'We are about to lose our principal actor. William Fay has had enough of it, and we don't wonder, and is going to some other country where his exquisite gift of comedy and his brain teeming

with fancy will bring him an audience, fame, and a little money. He has worked with us now since 1902, when he formed his company "to carry on the work of the Irish Literary Theatre", and feels that he must leave to younger men the long laborious battle. We have his good wishes, and he will return to us if at all possible to play his old parts for some brief season, or seasons, and may possibly rejoin us for a London or an American tour. We believe that William Fay is right to go, and he will have our good will and good wishes with him, though we have lost in losing him the finest comedian of his kind upon the English-speaking stage.'
—*Irish Times,* Jan. 5, 1908.[10]

* *
*

Last May a performance of *Measure for Measure* was given by the Elizabethan Stage Society at Stratford. Mr. Poel asked us to lend him Miss Sara Allgood to play the part of Isabella. I confess that she surprised me very much. I had not thought her capable of tragedy unless where, as in *Dervorgilla* and *Cathleen ni Houlihan,* she has a character element to help her, and was altogether astonished at a performance full of simplicity and power, where the elements were purely passionate.[11]

* *
*

One of our hopes for the Abbey Theatre was that it would encourage Irish dramatic enterprise apart from our own company. Rivalry should be a help in matters of art, for every good work increases the public interest in all similar work. This hope has only been fulfilled by the two visits of the Ulster Literary Theatre, which have given us a very great pleasure. I was away at the time of their last visit, but I remember vividly in the performance of a year ago the absence of the ordinary conventions, the novelty of movement and intonation.[12] I saw a play of Cockney life the other day. The actors were incomparably more experienced, the playwright was one of the new school who go directly to life, and one felt that the players were conscientious enough to do their best to go to life also. But I felt that though there was observation in detail, there was in every case a traditional representation in the player's mind. He hung his observation about some old type as a dressmaker hangs a new dress upon the *Mannequin d'Osier* that is in every dress-maker's room. [13] I believe, furthermore, that these Ulster players, like ourselves, are doing something to bring to an end the charlatanism of International acting. I saw a while ago a performance of *The Corsican Brothers,* which, but for its Corsican peasantry, had been excellent. The Brothers themselves, essentially traditional types of romance, were played with sincerity, but when the other Corsicans began to quarrel, I went straight back to the days when my uncles and aunts helped me to dress up in old tablecloths. [14] When we have a sincere dramatic art there will be in every country actors who have made a study of the characteristics of its different classes. This will make 'adaptions from the French', let us say, more difficult, but not more than the translation of a fine poem, which somebody says is impossible. [15] You can re-create it, making an English poem of a French or a German, and in the same way it will be necessary to re-create drama as we do when we play *Le Médecin malgré lui* in 'Kiltartanese'. [16] The inaccuracy of detail, the persistence of conventional types, has arisen from the same causes, which have destroyed in modern drama eloquence, poetry, beauty, and all the reveries of widsom, and given us in their place a more or less logical mechanism. When I saw the Ulster players, upon the other hand, it was in their mechanism that their playwrights failed. It was in their delight in the details of life that they interested one. I hear, however, that their plays upon their last visit showed much more unity. In any case it is only a matter of time, where one finds so much sincere observation, for the rest to follow.

*   *

*

The Ulster players are the only dramatic society, apart from our own, which is doing serious artistic work. Two other performances were lamentable; that of the Independent Theatre Society showed little sign of work or purpose. One or two of the players had a gift for acting, and working upon new material among hard workers might have struck out something new and forcible. But the performance as a whole made me wonder why so much trouble was taken to put on something not finer at its finest moments and much worse at every other moment than a third-rate touring company. The Theatre of Ireland made me indignant, because

although the playwrights had found more of themselves than
Count Markiewicz struggling with the difficulties of a strange language and strange circumstance, there was even less evidence of
work and purpose.[17] Such adventures can do nothing but injury to
the drama in Ireland. They all show talent here and there, for Ireland has talent in plenty, but it is brought to nothing by lack of work
and lack of subordination to a single aim. Though I used to speak
with the greatest freedom of the performances given by the Gaelic
League, I have not hitherto touched upon the work of these societies, and would not now, but for my real pleasure in the Ulster Theatre. One feels that in a country like this, where there is so little
criticism with any special knowledge behind it, it is a wrong to the
few fine workers to omit anything that may help to separate them
from the triflers. I have a right to speak, for I asked our own company to give up two of our Saturday performances that we might
give the Independent Theatre and the Theatre of Ireland the most
popular days.[18] I see some talk in the papers of those two societies
uniting. If they do so, there is only one means of success, the
appointment of some competent man who will be able to cast parts
with no thought but efficiency, and to insist upon regular attendance
at rehearsals. The Gaelic League companies must do the same if they
would raise the Gaelic drama out of its present decline, for theatres
cannot be democracies. The Gaelic League has difficulties one
must respect, for the Gaelic League can hardly spare many of its
thoughts for any art till its battle is more nearly won, and this single purpose gives to even their most clumsy performance a little simplicity and entire lack of pretense. The same excuse applies to the
National Players, whose representation of *Robert Emmet* in St.
Cecilia's Hall some years ago, interested me and touched me.[19] It
was frankly propagandist, had the dignity of a long national tradition, and carried my imagination to Davis and to Mitchel.[20] All
work which is done without selfishness for something beyond
one's self has moral beauty.

SAMHAIN: 1908—
ALTERATIONS IN *DEIRDRE*

There are two passages in this play as published which I always knew to be mere logic, mere bones, and yet after many attempts I thought it impossible to alter them. When, however, Mrs. Campbell offered to play the part my imagination began to work again. I think they are now as they should be.[1]

SAMHAIN: 1908—
DATES AND PLACES
OF THE FIRST PERFORMANCE
OF PLAYS PRODUCED BY THE
NATIONAL THEATRE SOCIETY
AND ITS PREDECESSORS[1]

1899.   Irish Literary Theatre at Antient Concert Rooms.
May 8th. *The Countess Cathleen,* by W. B. Yeats.
May 9th. *The Heather Field,* by Edward Martyn.

1900.   Irish Literary Theatre at the Gaiety Theatre.
February 19th. { *The Last Feast of the Fianna,* by Alice Milligan.
{ *Maeve,* by Edward Martyn.
February 20th.   *The Bending of the Bough,* by George Moore.

1901.
{ *Diarmuid and Grania,* by W. B. Yeats and
October 21st. {   George Moore.
{ *The Twisting of the Rope,* by Douglas Hyde
(first Gaelic play produced in a Theatre).[2]

**1902.   Mr. W. G. Fay's Irish National Dramatic Company at
St. Teresa's Hall, Clarendon Street.**
April 2nd. { *Deirdre,* by A. E.
{ *Cathleen ni Houlihan,* by W. B. Yeats.

Irish National Dramatic Company at Antient Concert Rooms.

October 29th. { *The Sleep of the King*, by Seamus O'Cuisin.
{ *The Laying of the Foundations*, by Fred Ryan.

October 30th. *The Pot of Broth*, by W. B. Yeats.

October 31st. *The Racing Lug*, by Seamus O'Cuisin.

1903. Irish National Theatre Society, Molesworth Hall.[*]

March 14th. { *The Hour-Glass*, by W. B. Yeats.
{ *Twenty-five*, by Lady Gregory.

October 8th. { *The King's Threshold*, by W. B. Yeats.
{ *In the Shadow of the Glen*, by J. M. Synge.

December 3rd. *Broken Soil*, by P. Colm.

1904.

January 14th. { *The Shadowy Waters*, by W. B. Yeats.
{ *The Townland of Tamney*, by Seumas
McManus.

February 25th. *Riders to the Sea*, by J. M. Synge.

Irish National Theatre Society at the Abbey Theatre.

December 27th. { *On Baile's Strand*, by W. B. Yeats.
{ *Spreading the News*, by Lady Gregory.

1905.

February 4th. *The Well of the Saints*, by J. M. Synge.

March 25th. *Kincora*, by Lady Gregory.

April 25th. *The Building Fund*, by William Boyle.

June 9th. *The Land*, by P. Colm.

National Theatre Society, Ltd.

December 9th. *The White Cockade*, by Lady Gregory.

*The first prospectus of this Society, dated March, 1903, and signed by Mr. Fred Ryan, began as follows: 'The Irish National Theatre Society was formed to continue on a more permanent basis the work of the Irish Literary Theatre'.[3] I quote this sentence as there has been some dispute as to the original objects of this Society. —W. B. Y.

1906.

January 20th.	*The Eloquent Dempsy,* by William Boyle.
February 19th.	*Hyacinth Halvey,* by Lady Gregory.
October 20th.	{ *The Gaol Gate,* by Lady Gregory. { *The Mineral Workers,* by William Boyle.
November 24th.	*Deirdre,* by W. B. Yeats.
December 8th.	{ *The Canavans,* by Lady Gregory. { New Version of *The Shadowy Waters,* by W. B. Yeats.

1907.

January 26th.	*The Playboy of the Western World,* by J. M. Synge.
February 23rd.	*The Jackdaw,* by Lady Gregory.
March 9th.	*The Rising of the Moon,* by Lady Gregory.
April 1st.	*The Eyes of the Blind,* by Miss W. M. Letts.
April 3rd.	*The Poorhouse,* by Douglas Hyde and Lady Gregory.
April 20th.[†]	*Fand,* by Wilfrid Scawen Blunt.
October 3rd.	*The Country Dressmaker,* by George Fitzmaurice.
October 31st.	*Dervorgilla,* by Lady Gregory.
November 21st.	*The Unicorn from the Stars,* by W. B. Yeats and Lady Gregory.

1908.

February 13th.	{ *The Man Who Missed the Tide,* by W. F. { Casey. { *The Piper,* by Norreys Connell.
March 19th.	{ *The Pie-Dish,* by George Fitzmaurice. { *The Golden Helmet,* by W. B. Yeats.
April 20th.	*The Workhouse Ward,* by Lady Gregory.
October 1st.	*The Suburban Groove,* by W. F. Casey.
October 8th.	*The Clancy Name,* by S. L. Robinson.
October 15th.	*When the Dawn Is Come,* by Thomas MacDonagh.

October 22nd.[†]   New Version of[†] *The Man Who Missed the
Tide*, by W. F. Casey.

Many of the above plays have been produced from 50 to 100
times.

Translations of the following have been produced.

1906.
April 16th. *The Doctor in Spite of Himself* (Molière). Translated by Lady Gregory.

1907.
March 23rd.[†] *Interior* (Maeterlinck).

1908.
March 19th.   *Teja* (Sudermann). Translated by Lady Gregory.
April 4th.   *The Rogueries of Scapin* (Molière). Translated
by Lady Gregory.

THE ARROW: 25 AUGUST 1909—
THE SHEWING-UP OF BLANCO POSNET:
STATEMENT BY THE DIRECTORS

On Sunday night the following explanation was issued on behalf of the Abbey Theatre Company:

The statement communicated to certain of Saturday's papers makes the following explanation necessary:

During the last week we have been vehemently urged to withdraw Mr. Shaw's play, which had already been advertised and rehearsed, and have refused to do so.[1] We would have listened with attention to any substantial argument; but we found, as we were referred from one well-meaning personage to another, that no one would say the play was hurtful to man, woman or child. Each said that someone else had thought so, or might think so. We were told that Mr. Redford had objected, that the Lord Chamberlain had objected, and that, if produced, it would certainly offend excited officials in London, and might offend officials in Dublin, or the law officers of the Crown, or the Lord Lieutenant, or Dublin society, or Archbishop Walsh, or the Church of Ireland, or 'rowdies up for the Horse Show', or newspaper editors, or the King.[2]

In these bewilderments and shadowy opinions there was nothing to change our conviction (which is also that of the leading weekly paper of the Lord Lieutenant's own party), that so far from containing offence for any sincere and honest mind, Mr. Shaw's play is a high and weighty argument upon the working of the Spirit of God in man's heart, or to show that it is not a befitting thing for us to set upon our stage the work of an Irishman, who is also the most famous of living dramatists, after that work had been silenced in London by what we believe an unjust decision.[3]

One thing, however, is plain enough, an issue that swallows up all else, and makes the merit of Mr. Shaw's play a secondary thing. If our patent is in danger, it is because the decisions of the English Censor are being brought into Ireland, and because the Lord Lieutenant is about to revive on what we consider a frivolous pretext, a right not exercised for 150 years, to forbid, at the Lord Chamberlain's pleasure, any play produced in any Dublin theatre, all these theatres holding their patents from him.

We are not concerned with the question of the English censorship, now being fought out in London, but we are very certain that the conditions of the two countries are different, and that we must not, by accepting the English Censor's ruling, give away anything of the liberty of the Irish theatre of the future.[4] Neither can we accept, without protest, the revival of the Lord Lieutenant's claim at the bidding of the Censor or otherwise. The Lord Lieutenant is definitely a political personage holding office from the party in power, and what would sooner or later grow into a political censorship cannot be lightly accepted.

W. B. Yeats, *Managing Director*.

A. Gregory, *Director and Patentee*.

Abbey Theatre, *August 22nd, 1909*.

THE ARROW: 25 AUGUST 1909—
FROM [NOTE]

The Managing Director of the Abbey Theatre has received a letter from Mr. Bernard Shaw, dated August 22nd, which contains the following passage:[1]

THE ARROW: 25 AUGUST 1909—
THE RELIGION OF BLANCO
POSNET

The meaning of Mr. Shaw's play, as I understand it, is that natural man, driven on by passion and vain glory, attempts to live as his fancy bids him but is awakened to the knowledge of God by finding himself stopped, perhaps suddenly, by something within himself.[1] This something which is God's care for man, does not temper the wind to the shorn lamb, as a false and sentimental piety would have it, but is a terrible love that awakens the soul amidst catastrophes and trains it by conquest and labour.

The essential incidents of the play are Blanco's giving up the horse, the harlot's refusal to name the thief, and the child's death of the croup. Without the last of these Mr. Shaw's special meaning would be lost, for he wants us to understand that God's love will not do the work of the Doctor, or any work that man can do, for it acts by awakening the intellect and the soul whether in some man of science or philosopher or in violent Posnet.

Textual Matters

and

Notes

HISTORY OF THE TEXT

Very little pre-publication material survives for *Beltaine, Samhain,* or *The Arrow*. From what we have and from references in the published correspondence, we can assume that Yeats composed his own contributions at a rather late date and that he read proofs of the volumes as a whole. Doubtless he was often assisted in one or both tasks by others, especially Lady Gregory. Considering the ephemeral nature of the publications as well as the relative haste with which they had to be produced, the original pamphlets have rather fewer misprints than one might expect.

As copy for *The Irish Dramatic Movement* in the *Collected Works in Verse and Prose* (1908), Yeats used pages from the various *Samhain*s and presumably from *The Arrow* as well. He omitted only a small portion of his contributions. In the Preface, Yeats claimed in regard to *Samhain* that he had "found it best to reprint my part of it unchanged," but this assertion is simply not accurate. For example, in the 1908 volume Yeats

- Printed the second part of "The Reform of the Theatre" from the 1903 *Samhain* as a separate essay, under the title "Moral and Immoral Plays."
- Placed after the 1903 *Samhain* two letters first published in *The United Irishman* on 10 and 17 October 1903.
- Constructed "The Controversy Over *The Playboy of the Western World*" from parts of two essays in *The Arrow* for 23 February 1907.
- Added a number of footnotes.

In addition to these changes, Yeats made a number of verbal revisions. Although fewer in number compared with his usual practice, at least some are significant. In the 1901 *Samhain*, for example, Yeats had indicated that "In Dublin the other day I saw a poster

advertising a play by a Miss Lefanu, under the patronage of certain lords and ladies"; in 1908 this becomes "In Dublin the other
day I saw a poster advertising a play by a Miss . . . under the patronage of certain titled people." Again, in the same *Samhain* Yeats had
concluded the penultimate paragraph of "Windlestraws" with
"We thought our plays inoffensive last year and the year before,
but we were accused the one year of sedition, and the other of
heresy. We await the next accusation with a cheerful curiosity." In
1908, doubtless with the disturbances surrounding *The Playboy
of the Western World* in mind, the last sentence disappears.

The major textual problem with the 1908 version of *The Irish
Dramatic Movement* concerns the running heads. To maintain the
chronological arrangement, the material from the *The Arrow* of 20
October 1906 should have preceded the 1906 *Samhain,* which was
not published until November.[1] However, presumably to avoid having the final items in the volume oscillate from *Samhain* to *The
Arrow* and back to *Samhain,* the 20 October 1906 material is placed
after the last *Samhain* and, with later items added, concludes *The
Irish Dramatic Movement.* The edition had used a running head of
"IRISH DRAMATIC MOVEMENT" on the left-hand page and
"SAMHAIN: 190x" on the right.[2] Page 225 has no running head
but begins with the title "THE ARROW: 1906," with the page number above that in parentheses, rather than flush with the outside
margin and without parentheses, as on all other pages. The next
right-hand running head, on page 227, is "THE ARROW: 1906,"
but the text on that page is the title and beginning of "The Controversy Over *The Playboy of the Western World,*" which is of
course derived from material published in *The Arrow* for 23 February 1907. The incorrect running head appears again on page 229,
even though page 228 uses the subtitle *"From Mr. Yeats' opening
speech in the Debate on February 4, 1907, at the Abbey Theatre."*
What should have been the running head on pages 227 and 229
("THE ARROW: 1907") finally appears on page 231 as the last one
in the collection, on the page with the title and opening of "On Taking *The Playboy* to London." This error was to persist in one form
or another in all later texts, including *Explorations* (1962).

At some point after publication, Yeats made a handful of corrections to *The Irish Dramatic Movement* in his own copy of the

Collected Works in Verse and Prose. Typically, he made such revisions either when he first received a volume or, more often, at the moment when a new edition was about to be produced; but since he was hoping for an expanded version as early as 1913, it is impossible to date these changes with any confidence. The material which was submitted to Macmillan in 1920 and was presumably eventually used for *Plays and Controversies* (1923) was probably a set of sheets from the 1908 printing, as it is unlikely that Yeats would have trusted his only copy of the volume itself to the post or to the printers. In addition to some new footnotes in the 1923 text, Yeats again made a number of verbal revisions. Some of these correspond to, or are related to, the corrections in the 1908 edition, so it is reasonably certain that Yeats consulted that volume while preparing copy. For instance, in the 1904 *Samhain* as well as the *Collected Works,* the play *Windmills* was "successfully prepared by the Stage Society"; in 1908 this was revised to "successfully produced," but the 1923 text reads "successfully performed." Likewise, the reference in the 1905 *Samhain* to being "under the conventional idealisms" was revised to "overpowered by the conventional idealisms" in the corrected copy but becomes "under that of the conventional idealism" in *Plays and Controversies.*[3]

There are two major textual problems with the 1923 edition. The first concerns the spacing between paragraphs. In the original pamphlets, Yeats had used a triangle of asterisks to separate sections, some of which included more than one paragraph. The *Collected Works in Verse and Prose* maintained that spacing, except for two added spaces (pages 131 and 161) and one deleted space (page 132), changes which one can assume were made at Yeats's direction. Inevitably, some of the spaces in the published volume coincided with a page break, and in those instances *Plays and Controversies* typically ignores the break.[4] This problem surfaces on the second page of *The Irish Dramatic Movement,* when the opening two paragraphs of the 1901 *Samhain* are not separated by a space.

The second problem with *Plays and Controversies* derives from the 1908 error in the running heads. In the 1923 text, the running head on both left- and right-hand pages is simply "IRISH DRAMATIC MOVEMENT." However, page 189 has as a title "THE ARROW: 1906" and there is no indication of a later date until page

197, which is headed "On Taking *The Playboy* to London"; thus
the incorrect 1906 date is implicitly assigned to "The Controversy
Over *The Playboy of the Western World.*"

Doubtless Yeats submitted a copy of *Plays and Controversies* to
be used for the Edition de Luxe in 1931 (or perhaps simply
instructed Macmillan to follow that text). The proofs for that project were produced on 30 September–26 October 1931, corrected
by Yeats between 23 June and 5 July 1932, and returned to the publishers on the latter date. They are now in the National Library of
Ireland (MS. 30,030). The fullest attempt to date at a description
of these proofs is as follows:

> The 1931 page proofs had been read very carefully by Thomas Mark,
> who made many corrections and queries to Yeats in light blue ink.
> (Occasionally they are written over pencil, perhaps indicating that
> he had skimmed the proofs and noted a few points before under-
> taking full-scale correction.) Yeats's responses and comments are in
> dark blue or blue-black ink. In addition, there are throughout the
> proofs a considerable number of queries and a few unqueried
> changes in pencil. The half-title of the proofs bears the note
> "Marked by Sutherland," and it may have been this (unidentified)
> reader who was responsible for the penciled notes. It is possible that
> a few of the penciled notes were also made by Mark; but, while Yeats
> responded to almost all of Mark's queries in [ink, there are no cer-
> tain responses in Yeats's hand to the queries in] pencil—a fact
> which may indicate that the latter group, whether by Sutherland,
> Mark, or someone else, were added after Yeats had returned the
> proofs with his own responses.[5]

Unfortunately, the editors of *The Secret Rose* fail to note that
there are also markings on the proofs in both blue pencil (though
not significant) and red ink (one of which is significant).[6] More
important, by examining some later materials, it is possible to be
more precise about the status of the pencil markings.

It seems clear that few if any of the pencil corrections are by
Thomas Mark.[7] For instance, lowercase "i" begins with a down-
stroke when in ink but an upstroke when in pencil, as in "ital" (e.g.,
Proofs 390, 394). The ink "P" in "Parsival" (Proofs 343) is quite

distinct from the pencil "P" in "Phases" (Proofs 476). And, of course, the indication of "Marked by Sutherland" is unlikely to refer to the handful of marks in blue pencil and/or red ink. For convenience, the pencil notations will hereafter be assigned to "Sutherland." In any case, however, the important point is that the pencil markings would not have been present when Yeats reviewed the proofs.

Mark was—quite understandably—very concerned to make the process of proofreading as simple as possible for Yeats. His usual procedure was to go through a text and mark in pencil any possible revisions. He would then go back and use ink for those that he wanted Yeats to consider or be aware of (sometimes first erasing the pencil version, sometimes writing over it); those that he had decided needed no correction were simply erased. It is simply inconceivable that he would have sent Yeats a set of proofs with both his own ink markings and those in pencil by Sutherland, some of which did not even offer Yeats the opportunity to simply accept or reject a suggested revision but are rather indications of Sutherland's confusion or uncertainty. Nor would Yeats have failed to respond to Sutherland's direct queries had they been present on the proofs he read: for instance, the very first penciled query in *The Irish Dramatic Movement,* whether the "dialogue of Oisin and Patrick" was "a title?", which goes unanswered by Yeats.

In theory, the penciled corrections could have been added when Mark received the proofs back from Yeats and before the second proof (not known to be extant) was prepared. However, the proofs were in Mark's hand for no more than a day (at best), so this is extremely improbable.[8] Nor would he have been likely to send the proofs in their current state to the printers, given that they included a plethora of unanswered queries. Clearly, then, the most logical time for the addition of the penciled corrections would have been the next occasion when *The Irish Dramatic Movement* was to be put into production, namely after Yeats's death, when the Edition de Luxe had been expanded to eleven volumes and the work had been moved from *Mythologies* to *Essays.* At that time Mark presumably enlisted Sutherland to check the second proof (that of 8 July 1932) against the first proof of *Mythologies,* both to see that the corrections had been made and to check for further errors or inconsistencies. Mark would then have drawn on Sutherland's work to prepare a corrected set of *The Irish Dramatic Movement* section of the second proof to be submitted as partial copy for the proof of *Essays,* which was produced and eventually sent to Mrs. Yeats on 26 June 1939. Although this proof of *Essays* is not known to be extant, an examination of the surviving fourth proof of *The Irish Dramatic Movement* section, dated 24–29 August 1939, indicates that a substantial portion of Sutherland's suggestions had been incorporated.[9] In short, Sutherland's penciled comments have no authority in establishing the text of *The Irish Dramatic Movement.*

The base-text for the present edition is therefore the 1931–32 page proofs of *Mythologies* without the penciled markings—in other words, the proofs as they stood when Yeats returned them to Macmillan on 5 July 1932 with the indication that he "need not see [them] again" (BL 55003/129). Material absent from the proofs has been taken from the original publications.[10]

In addition to a selection of the penciled corrections, the 24–29 August 1939 proofs incorporate a substantial number of the ink corrections on the 1931–32 proofs, both those which Yeats accepted and those which he did not comment on. Other changes, however, were ignored, either accidentally or deliberately. And of course the proofs themselves were subject to further revision, most likely in 1939.[11] For example, on the title page of the 1931–32 proofs Mark had asked whether "S." or "St." should be used.

> S. is used for Saint in the beginning of Vol. I [*The Poems*] and elsewhere.
> St. is used in Vol. II.
> Which form should be followed in this edition?

Yeats wrote "Yes" after the first sentence; he then canceled this less-than-clear response and indicated "use S." below. Moreover, at each of the four places on the proofs which read "St." followed by the name of a saint, Yeats clearly indicated a preference for "S." Such is the form printed on the 1939 proofs. However, on those proofs Mark proceeded to revise to "Saint," noting on page 319 "as in other vols.," referring to what had by then been renamed the Coole Edition. Another instance in which Mark did not follow what seems to have been Yeats's preference in 1932 concerns "countrymen" vs. "country-men." On page 389 of the *Mythologies* proofs Mark had asked whether "Countrymen" should be "Country-men," "as elsewhere," noting that "Vol. I usually has country-men, but it is a very small point." Yeats crossed out the question mark, thus accepting the hyphenated form. Presumably Yeats intended to use "country-men" when referring to the residents of rural Ireland and "countrymen" when referring to all the inhabitants of the nation. This is precisely the kind of change which he would have been confident Mark could institute throughout the text without further ado. However, the 1939 proofs do not use the hyphenated form, even in the reference to "Country-men" which Yeats had explicitly approved. On a more positive note, the proofs do correct the misprint found in both *Plays and Controversies* and the 1931–32 proofs of "The Faces of the Moon" for "The Phases of the Moon." For the correction of this error, overlooked by both Yeats and Mark, we have to thank the elusive Sutherland and his penciled notation.

In any case, by far the most significant change on the 1939 proofs was the explicit decision by Mrs. Yeats to include "First Principles" from the 1908 *Samhain* and the implicit decision not to include "Events" from the same publication. Whether this decision should be followed in a new edition is an open question. On the one hand, it is not altogether easy to believe that Yeats simply overlooked the existence of the 1908 *Samhain* when submitting copy for both *Plays and Controversies* and *Mythologies,* especially when "First Principles" concludes with one of his most powerful statements on the function of the artist, in this instance contrasted with the work of the scientist: "We, on the other hand, are Adams of a different Eden, a more terrible Eden, perhaps, for we must name and number the passions and motives of men," and so on. One could thus argue that the 1908 essay should be excluded from the main body of any new edition. On the other hand, Yeats did occasionally forget, for instance, the last time he had revised a particular text. If, as argued, the copy for the expanded edition of *The Irish Dramatic Movement* which he had projected as early as

1913 consisted of sheets from the *Collected Works in Verse and Prose,* then he might well have lost sight of the 1908 *Samhain.* On balance, and given that Mrs. Yeats's decision in 1939 produced a text which has been in wide circulation since 1962, "First Principles" has been retained in *The Irish Dramatic Movement* in this edition.[12]

The exclusion of "Events" presents an even more difficult question. As noted, Yeats omitted very little material from the various *Samhain*s when preparing the 1908 version of *The Irish Dramatic Movement.* Indeed, in both the [Note] in the *Collected Works in Verse and Prose* and in the Preface to *Plays and Controversies,* he defended the reprinting of some admittedly ephemeral materials, arguing in the latter edition that

> Though often about foolish quarrels, or plays but little better, they may keep their use even when that occasion passes; being passionately written, and at a moment when Ireland was preparing, in that dark portion of the mind which is like the other side of the moon, for insurrection and anarchic violence; and all in some measure a plea for intellectual spontaneity against unyielding, abstract principles. I ask indulgence if I overrate their value, for it may be that I cannot judge sentences that call up memories of the time when I was most alive, having most friends and enemies.

One could thus argue with considerable support that if Yeats had remembered (or been reminded) that *The Irish Dramatic Movement* did not include any material from the 1908 *Samhain,* he would have added not only "First Principles" but also most if not all of "Events."[13] On the other hand, there is something approaching a precedent for the non-inclusion of "Events," namely the omission of "Notes" from the 1906 *Samhain* (though admittedly "Events" is over five times longer than "Notes"). Again giving considerable weight to the received text of *The Irish Dramatic Movement* since 1962, I have resisted (but just) the temptation to add "Events" to the main text. Any future electronic edition of *The Irish Dramatic Movement* will want to offer at least three versions: the last contents approved by Yeats, as on the 1931–32 *Mythologies* proofs; the last contents approved by Mrs. Yeats, as on the 24–29 August

1939 proofs and eventually in *Explorations*; and an expanded edition which places the 20 October 1906 excerpt from *The Arrow* in the proper chronological position and inserts "Events" ahead of the 1908 "First Principles."

Of *Explorations* itself little need be said, as it is the printing furthest away from the last version approved by Yeats. The galley proofs, based on the 1939 proofs, survive, dated 24 November–8 December 1961 (BL 55896). These show a moderate number of changes, instigated by Thomas Mark and/or Lovat Dickson at Macmillan, and carrying an uncertain degree of involvement and/or approval of Mrs. Yeats—who is described on the title page as having "Selected" the contents of the volume. One interesting change, that of "nigger" to "negro" in the 1905 *Samhain,* has been noted in the Introduction. Here I will add but one more: in all texts published or produced during Yeats's lifetime, from *The Arrow* of 20 October 1906 through the proofs of *Mythologies,* we are told in "The Season's Work" that

> It is possible to speak of the universal truths of human nature whether the speakers be peasants or wealthy men, for—

> > Love doth sing
> > As sweetly in a beggar as a king.

After revision on the 1961 proofs, this becomes

> Is it possible to speak of the universal truths of human nature whether the speakers be peasants or wealthy men, for—

> > Love doth sing
> > As sweetly in a beggar as a king?

This is the text found in *Explorations,* published in London on 23 July 1962, just over forty years after Yeats had last corrected the text of *The Irish Dramatic Movement.* It is awkward at least, if not quite senseless. More to the point, it is not what Yeats wrote.

TEXTUAL EMENDATIONS
AND CORRECTIONS

Although Yeats was never inattentive to the details of any of his texts, it is clear that he was less concerned with the proofreading of his prose than with that, say, of his poetry or plays. As noted in the Introduction, when Yeats returned the proofs of *Mythologies* to Macmillan in 1932, he indicated that Thomas Mark could see to the remaining details (at the time, Yeats anticipated a steady stream of proofs for other volumes in the Edition de Luxe). Moreover, the state of the contemporary proofs as well as the posthumous proofs and published text do not show Mark and his colleagues at Macmillan, London, at their finest hour.[1] Given those facts as well as the likely interests of most readers of this edition, a more liberal policy of emendation than that used in, for instance, *The Poems*, 2nd ed. (1997), has seemed advisable. It has also seemed useful not to clutter the text with emendation signals and to keep the textual apparatus to a minimum.

For reasons explained in the "History of the Text," the base-text for the major part of this edition is the corrected page proofs of *Mythologies* (1931–32), Manuscript 30,030 in the National Library of Ireland. The proofs show four categories of revision, which have been treated as follows.

A. Changes in ink by Thomas Mark followed by a query. Yeats replied to almost all of these, in most cases accepting Mark's suggestion. Revisions not explicitly rejected are incorporated into the present text and are not considered emendations.

B. Changes in ink by Thomas Mark not followed by a query. Many of these were simple corrections of errors, which obviously did not require a response from Yeats. Yeats did not comment on these changes, and thus they have been treated as in A.

C. Changes in red ink, possibly but not certainly by Mark. It is probable that these are the result of a preliminary checking of the proofs against the copy submitted to the printer. Of the three red ink markings in *The Irish Dramatic Movement,* two concern the spacing between letters. The single substantive change, the correction in the 1901 *Samhain* of the misprint "must say" to "may say" (the reading of all previous texts), has been treated as in A.

D. Suggested changes in pencil by "Sutherland." As argued in the "History of the Text," these markings would not have been present when Yeats reviewed the proofs in 1932 and thus they have not been incorporated in the present text as a matter of course. In some instances, of course, these revisions will coincide with the changes listed below.

In sum, the base-text consists of the *Mythologies* proofs with their ink corrections (of whatever color) as accepted, rejected, or modified by Yeats, but without the pencil markings.

GLOBAL EMENDATIONS

A. The source and date of each item from the 1899–1909 publications is included, as in "*THE ARROW:* 20 October 1906—The Season's Work." As noted in the "History of the Text," the running heads in the *Collected Works* (1908) attempted to provide this information, albeit imperfectly. The later texts have "SAMHAIN/ SAMHAIN" only for the 1901 essay and then the imprecise "THE ARROW: 1906."[2] The two items from the 1903 *United Irishman* have been headed "*SAMHAIN,*" as it is clear that both *Plays and Controversies* and the Edition de Luxe proofs omit any reference to the original printings and implicitly assign the works to the 1903 *Samhain.* Yeats's own note to "A People's Theatre" cites the first publication of that essay.

B. The spacing between sections follows that in the *Collected Works,* with spaces coinciding with page breaks determined by reference to the original pamphlets; in addition, on the proofs of *Mythologies* Yeats decided to retain a space which had been accidentally introduced into "The Dramatic Movement" (*Samhain,* 1904). As noted in the "History of the Text," many of the original spaces were lost in successive reprintings of *The Irish Dramatic Movement.* In this edition a space coincides with a page break at the bottom of pages 23 and 180.

C. Quotations introduced by "he said" or similar constructions are preceded by a comma; other quotations are preceded by a colon (without a following dash). On the title page of the *Mythologies* proofs Mark had asked "'He said' etc., before quoted speech, are followed either by a comma or a colon in the text of this volume. Is it worth while to aim at any uniformity in this detail, as suggested in the margins?" Yeats replied "I leave this ~~the~~ to Macmillan[']s reader. I have accepted his suggestions ~~where eve~~ where ever he has made the correction but I am a babe in such things. ~~Bullen~~ Some printer[']s reader put in those colons[.]"

D. "S." has been used before the names of saints. As noted in "History of the Text," Yeats indicated his preference for this form on the *Mythologies* proofs. However, names of buildings (St. Teresa's Hall) and places (St. Stephen's Green) have been printed in their standard form. It is very unlikely indeed that Yeats anticipated "S." being used in those instances. The first was queried only in pencil on the *Mythologies* proofs; it was revised to "Saint" on the 1939 proofs (the erroneous "Theresa's" continues into *Explorations*). "St. Stephen's Green" was unchallenged on the *Mythologies* proofs and indeed survived intact through the galley proofs of *Explorations,* on which it also was changed to "Saint."

E. As explained in "History of the Text," "country-man" and similar forms have been used when Yeats refers to the inhabitants of rural Ireland.

F. The footnotes that Yeats added to the *Collected Works in Verse and Prose* are variously dated "March 1908," "1908," or undated; these have been regularized to "March 1908." The single footnote in the periodical version of "A People's Theatre" has been dated "1919." Yeats's footnote numbers have been changed to asterisks, so as to avoid confusion with the numbers for the editorial notes.

Specific Emendations

The following specific emendations are indicated in the text by a †. The table below lists a short title, the page on the Edition de Luxe proofs (when applicable), and the page number in this edition; the reading of the base-text; the emended reading; and the authority (if any) for the emendation. CW is volume four of the 1908 *Collected Works*, P&C the 1923 *Plays and Controversies*.

Title page—Proofs [301]

[1.2]	1919.	1919	no contemporary authority

S1902—Proofs 315

11.13	vol. i.	Vol. I	cf. *Samhain* (1902), CW

S1903—Proofs 330

21.23	ill-done	ill done	Proofs 306

S1903—Proofs 331

22.11	*Broth,* and	*Broth* and	no contemporary authority

S1903Reform—Proofs 338

26.26	faery	Faery	Proofs 98

S1904Dramatic—Proofs 359

43.30	ballad singers	ballad-singers	Proofs 373

S1904First—Proofs 375

55.16	mind;	mind,	no contemporary authority

S1904Play—Proofs 394

68.10	in last	in the last	no contemporary authority

S1904Play—Proofs 394

68.13	But last	But the last	no contemporary authority

S1905—Proofs 416

83.31	bookkes	bokes	Middle English spelling

S1905—Proofs 424

89.21	loves	loaves	all previous editions

S1908First

116.7	second and third hand	second- and third-hand	cf. Proofs 465 ("second-hand")

S1908First
116.28   Essay   essay   no contemporary evidence

S1908First
116.28   unIrish   un-Irish   earlier in essay

S1908First
117.25   Kickham,   Kickham;   rest of sentence

S1908First
117.34   secondhand   second-hand   Proofs 465

S1908First
120.27   working men.   workingmen.   earlier in sentence

S1908First
121.27   *Humaine,*   *humaine*   no contemporary evidence

S1908First
122.2   thoughts, as   thoughts as   no contemporary evidence

PeoplesTheatre—Proofs 462
125.13   &   and   holograph revision

PeoplesTheatre—Proofs 462
125.14   &   and   holograph revision

PeoplesTheatre—Proofs 465
127.2   'The soulless   the 'soulless   text in Rosetti

PeoplesTheatre—Proofs 465
127.4   national school   National School   cf. Proofs 413

PeoplesTheatre—Proofs 471
131.13   theatre   Theatre   earlier in essay

BMay1899Theatre
150.35   successors   successes   *Ideas of Good and Evil*
                                                    (1903)

BFebruary1900Plans
154.19   it   It   text in Shelley

S1902Notes
169.2   forerunners   forerunner   no contemporary authority

A20October1906Note
177.17   play—*The*   play—, *The*   elsewhere in sentence

A20October1906Note
177.18   Gregory; a   Gregory, a   elsewhere in sentence

A20October1906Note
178.8   means, is   means is   no contemporary authority

A20October1906Note
179.2   Hyacinth   *Hyacinth Halvey*   no contemporary authority

A1June1907Notes
193.16   individuals   individuals,   no contemporary authority

S1908Events
196.17   [no asterisks]   [asterisks]   page break

S1908Events
196.34   quiet   quiet,   no contemporary authority

S1908Dates
205.18   April 27th.   April 20th.   error in dating

S1908Dates
206.1   Oct. 21.   October 22nd.   error in dating

S1908Dates
206.1   Version, *The*   Version of *The*   earlier in list

S1908Dates
206.10   Mar 16.   March 23rd.   error in dating

CORRECTIONS AND REGULARIZATIONS

The following are corrections of obvious errors and misprints as well as regularizations to Yeats's preferred form of certain Irish names. See also note 2 to "Miss Horniman's Offer of Theatre and the Society's Acceptance" (page 173) and note 1 to "Dates and Places of the First Performance of Plays produced by the National Theatre Society and its Predecessors" (page 203).

adequately	adequately.
Agusta Gregory	Augusta Gregory
An Posadh	*An Pósadh*
Arran	Aran
Baile's Strand	*On Baile's Strand*
Bjornsen	Björnson
Calderon, Calderon's	Calderón, Calderón's
Callinan's	Callanan's
Campany	Company
Casadh an t-Sugain	*Casadh an tSúgáin*
Catharine Tynan	Katharine Tynan
Les Comediens sans le Savoir	*Les Comédiens sans le savoir*
Concobar	Conchubar
Connaught	Connacht
Creadeamh agus Gorta	*Creideamh agus Gorta*
Cuchullain	Cuchulain
Cumann na n-Gaedheal	*Cumann na nGaedheal*
Curtain	Curtin
Dail Eireann	Dáil Éireann
Dermot	Diarmuid
Dineen	Dinneen
The Doctor in spite of Himself	*The Doctor in Spite of Himself*
The Doll's House	*A Doll's House*
Dostoievsky	Dostoyevsky
Drama Breithe Chriosta	*Dráma Breite Críosta*
the *Duchess of Malfi*	*The Duchess of Malfi*
Eisenbach	Eschenbach
Elis agus an bhean deirce	*Eilis agus an Bhean Déirce*
emigrés	*émigrés*
Englsih	English
"The Faces of the Moon"	"The Phases of the Moon"
faëry, fairy	faery
fairies	faeries
Fion	Finn
Fortuni	Fortuny

Fourrier	Fourier
the *Gaol Gate*	*The Gaol Gate*
Gerard Hauptmann	Gerhart Hauptmann
Un Grand Homme de Province à Paris	*Un grand homme de province à Paris*
The Hawk's Well	*At the Hawk's Well*
The Hour-glass	*The Hour-Glass*
the *Hour-Glass*	*The Hour-Glass*
Hour Glass	*Hour-Glass*
Inghinidhe h-Eireann	*Inghinidhe na hÉireann*
Inghinidhe na h-Eireann	*Inghinidhe na hÉireann*
Jose Echegeray	José Echegaray
judgement	judgment
Kathleen Ni Houlihan	*Cathleen ni Houlihan*
Kitarton	Kiltartan
Le Medecin Malgre Lui	*Le Médecin malgré lui*
Love Songs of Connaught	*Love Songs of Connacht*
Lug	Lugh
MacGinlay	MacGinley
of *MacGiolla Meidhre*	of MacGiolla Meidhre
Madame L'Epicier	Madame l'Épicière
The Man who missed the Tide	*The Man Who Missed the Tide*
The Man who Missed the Tide	*The Man Who Missed the Tide*
Maive	Maeve
Maive	*Maeve*
matinees	matinées
Mechanic's	Mechanics'
Medhir	Midhir
meed	mead
Naisi	Naoise
naïvete	*naïveté*
An Naom ar Iarriad	*An Naomh ar Iarraidh*
Niam	Niamh
ov.	November
Patric	Patrick
pecuniarly	pecuniarily
Phedre	*Phèdre*
The Piedish	*The Pie-Dish*
the *Piper*	*The Piper*
Play, Plays	play, plays
the *Playboy*	*The Playboy*
the *Playboy of the Western World*	*The Playboy of the Western World*
Players	players
Poël	Poel

Poor House	Poorhouse
A Pot of Broth	The Pot of Broth
the Pot of Broth	The Pot of Broth
Produced	produced
Raleigh	Ralegh
the Rising of the Moon	The Rising of the Moon
Rummell	Rummel
"Salome"	Salomé
Seaghan na Scuab	Seaghán na Scuab
the Shadow of the Glen	The Shadow of the Glen
St. Beuve	Sainte-Beuve
Sinn Fein	Sinn Féin
Tadg Saor	Tadgh Saor
Tain bo Cuailgne	Táin Bó Cuailgne
Teer nan Oge	Tír na nÓg
Theatre.)	Theatre).
Theresa's	Teresa's
Tincear agus Sidheog	An Tincéir agus an tSidheóg
M. Trebulet Bonhommie	M. Tribulat Bonhomet
the Trojan Women	The Trojan Women
Twenty-Five	Twenty-five
unbiassed	unbiased
the United Irishman	The United Irishman
Usheen	Oisin
the Well of the Saints	The Well of the Saints
When The Dawn is Come	When the Dawn Is Come
Wilfred	Wilfrid
Withcherly	Wycherley
Workhouse Ward	The Workhouse Ward
Yeates	Yeats

OTHER TEXTUAL MATTERS

A. Ambiguous line-end hyphenation in the base-texts has been adjudicated by the form of the word used elsewhere in Yeats's canon, when possible in *The Irish Dramatic Movement*. In the single instance of a unique word, "anti-/masques" in "Plans and Methods" from the February 1900 *Beltaine*, the form used by Robert Browning in *The Ring and the Book* has been adopted. All hyphenated forms in this edition are therefore to be considered authorial, unless listed as a specific emendation.

B. Yeats's signature or initials have not been included, except in "[Notes]" from the 20 October 1906 *Arrow*, where the initials may delimit Yeats's authorship of the item; in "Dates and Places of the First Performance of Plays produced by the National Theatre Society and Its Predecessors" from the 1908 *Samhain,* where Yeats is likely responsible only for the initialed note; and in "*The Shewing-Up of Blanco Posnet:* Statement by the Directors" from the 25 August 1909 *Arrow,* where the signature is followed by a title.

C. Large initial letters, caps, or small caps at the beginning of some essays have not been reproduced, except for the salutations in "A People's Theatre" and "Miss Horniman's Offer . . ."

The remaining matters follow the typographical and format conventions of *The Collected Works of W. B. Yeats.*

D. The presentation of headings is standardized. Main headings are set in full capitals (capitals and small capitals for subtitles). Section numbers are in roman capitals. All headings are centered and have no concluding full point.

E. The placement of quotation marks has been regularized to British usage in Yeats's texts.

F. Quotations that are set off from the text and indented are not placed within quotation marks.

G. Except in headings, titles of stories and poems are placed within quotation marks; titles of books, plays, long poems, periodicals, operas, statues, paintings, and drawings are set in italics.

H. Regardless of its length in the base-text, a dash is set as an unspaced em rule when used as punctuation.

NOTES

These notes attempt to elucidate all specific allusions, though some have eluded our search. Figures on the order of Sophocles or Shakespeare are identified only in the Index. Other names are usually identified fully only at their first mention. Rather than offering notes that simply direct the reader to other notes, some material has been repeated.

Samhain: 1901

1. Yeats met the Irish dramatist, folklorist, and translator Lady Gregory (1852–1932) in 1894; in 1897 he stayed with her during the summer at Coole Park, her estate in County Galway, as he would for many summers to come. They enjoyed a mutually creative friendship that lasted until her death. Along with the Irish playwright Edward Martyn (1859–1923), in 1897 they began to plan for an Irish Literary Theatre. Martyn provided considerable financial support for the venture.

2. The Irish writer George Moore (1852–1933), a cousin of Edward Martyn, began to be involved with the Irish Literary Theatre at the end of 1898.

3. Oisín is the poet-hero of the Fionn or Ossianic cycle of Irish tales; Saint Patrick (? d. 493) is the patron saint of Ireland. Many of the Fionn tales depict acrimonious debates between Oisín and St. Patrick on the virtues of Christianity.

4. The Irish scholar and cultural activist Douglas Hyde (1860–1949) was one of the founders and the first president of the Gaelic League. Father Patrick S. Dinneen (1860–1934) was an Irish writer and scholar, Peter MacGinley (*Peadar Mac Fhionnghaile*, 1857–1940) an Irish writer.

   The competition was held at the 1901 Oireachtas, the annual festival of the Gaelic League, on 28–31 May 1901. *The United Irishman* noted on 18 May 1901 that "The competition for the One-Act Drama has brought forth ten competitors, which is certainly encouraging, considering the difficulty which the Literary Theatre has experienced during the last three years in obtaining a suitable play in Irish" (1). Yeats's lack of knowledge about the winner is understandable, as on

8 June 1901 *The United Irishman* noted only that the entry from County Cork "came out in the front rank" (1), without providing either author or title. However, *The Freeman's Journal* for 31 May 1901 reported that the competition was won by "Miss Minnie Sheehy, Clonakilty, Co. Cork," with a "special prize" to "D. O'Connell, Mill street, Co. Cork": "This competition was a distinct success. Out of ten, four were well qualified to obtain a prize, and some of the pieces sent in were fairly suited for stage production. The language, on the whole, was good. With practise the four names put forward on the list would do very well" (6). Neither play was apparently published.

5. Along with his brother, the Irish actor Frank J. Fay (1870–1931), the Irish actor and producer W. G. Fay (1872–1947) had founded an amateur dramatic company, eventually called the Ormond Dramatic Society. The Fays joined forces with the Daughters of Erin (*Inghinidhe na hÉireann*), a nationalist political and cultural organization founded in 1900 by Maud Gonne (1866–1953), an Irish nationalist and Yeats's beloved, to produce *An Tobar Draoidheachta* (*The Enchanted Well*) by Patrick S. Dinneen in 1900 and *Eilis agus an Bhean Déirce* (*Lizzie and the Beggarwoman*) by Peter MacGinley in Dublin on 27 August 1901 (a possible earlier production outside of Dublin is untraced). Macroom is in County Cork, Letterkenny in County Donegal.

6. The conversation with Death by the Irish poet Anthony Raftery (Antoine Raiftearí, 1779–1835) occurs in his poem "Vision"; Yeats is misremembering his "Argument with Whiskey." Both poems are discussed by Lady Gregory in "The Poet Raftery," published in *Argosy* for January 1901 and later revised for her *Poets and Dreamers* (London: John Murray, 1903). A *feis* is a festival.

7. The Claddagh was an Irish-speaking enclave in Galway.

8. Sir Frank Robert Benson (1858–1939) was an English actor and manager.

9. *The Deliverance of Red Hugh* by the Irish writer Alice Milligan (1866–1953) was first produced in Dublin by the Ormond Dramatic Society for the Daughters of Erin on 27 August 1901. *Tadgh Saor* (Tadgh the Smith) by the Irish writer Father Peter O'Leary (*An tAthair Peader Ó Laoghaire*, 1839–1920) was first produced in Macroom on 13 May 1900.

10. Dion Boucicault (1820–90), Irish actor and playwright; Henry Arthur Jones (1851–1929) and Sydney Grundy (1848–1914), English playwrights. The *Táin Bó Cuailgne* (*Cattle Raid of Cooley*) is the central saga of the Ulster cycle of heroic tales.

11. Hyde's *Casadh an tSúgáin*, a play about Raftery, was included in this issue of *Samhain* with a translation by Lady Gregory as *The Twisting of the Rope*. *Diarmuid and Grania* was a collaboration between Yeats and George Moore. Both were first produced by the Irish Literary Theatre in Dublin on 21 October 1901.

12. Yeats is quoting from a letter from his father, the Irish painter John Butler Yeats (1839–1922), on 27 July 1901. A fragment of this letter is included in *J. B. Yeats: Letters to His Son W. B. Yeats and Others, 1869–1922*, edited by Joseph Hone (New York: Dutton, 1946), 67 (misdated 27 October 1901); and the letter is also quoted from in CL3 86n1. *Underwoods* (1640) is a collection of poems by the English writer Ben Jonson (1572–1637); Yeats presumably means to refer to his *Timber: or, Discoveries* (1640), a commonplace book. Although Jonson does not directly quote Shakespeare, he does describe his "gentle expressions: wherein he flow'd with that facility, that sometime it was necessary he should be stop'd. . . ." There are several apocryphal accounts of Shakespeare's conversation, most notably in *The History of the Worthies of England* (1662) by the English writer Thomas Fuller (1608–61), which describes but does not actually quote conversations between Shakespeare and Jonson. "Eliza" is Elizabeth I (1533–1603), queen of England from 1558.

13. *A Daughter of Erin,* a comedy in four acts by Miss Le Fanu Robertson, produced at the Theatre Royal, Dublin, on 19 August 1901, and the subject of a long and favorable review in the *Irish Times* for 20 August 1901.

14. The portrait (of "Miss B. Robertson") was published in *The Figaro and Irish Gentlewoman* for 24 August 1901, the journal noting the "signal success" of *A Daughter of Erin* (575).

15. The Fenians was an Irish nationalist society, formed in 1858 and responsible for the uprising of 1865. Although the movement had all but disappeared by 1885, its principles were adopted by the *Sinn Féin* party at the turn of the century.

16. Jeremiah J. Callanan (1795–1829), Irish poet and translator.

17. By the 1870s, there was a growing protest that the reforms of Alexander II (1818–81) had not sufficiently improved the conditions of the common people of Russia.

18. In the Bible, Moses kills an Egyptian who had murdered a Hebrew.

19. A cromlech is a prehistoric stone structure consisting of a large flat stone resting on three or more horizontal stones; in many parts of Ireland cromlechs are knows as "beds" of Diarmaid and Gráinne, where they are supposed to have spent a night while in flight from Fionn. This issue of *Samhain* included "The Legend of Diarmuid and Grania," a summary of the story by Lady Gregory (16–19).

20. Tara, a hill in County Meath, is the ancient seat of the High Kings of Ireland; Ben Bulben is a mountain in County Sligo.

21. Yeats refers to attacks on his *The Countess Cathleen* ("heresy") and George Moore's *The Bending of the Bough* ("sedition").

Samhain: 1902

1. Yeats refers to "The Lay of Diarmaid" in J. F. Campbell, *Superstitions of the West Highlands & Islands of Scotland* (Glasgow: James MacLehose, 1900); and Kuno Meyer's "Finn and Grainne," *Zeitschrift für Keltische Philologie* 1.3 (1897): 458–61. Most versions of the story treat Gráinne rather more favorably that did Yeats and Moore. In particular, only one of the forty-one extant manuscripts of the story has the ending adopted in the play, with Gráinne willingly returning to Fionn. Both the oldest and the second oldest manuscripts have Gráinne exhorting her children to wreak vengeance on Fionn.

2. Yeats has overlooked the production earlier in 1901 of *Eilis agus an Bhean Déirce* (*Lizzie and the Beggarwoman*) by Peter MacGinley.

3. Founded in 1900, the *Cumann na nGaedheal* (Society of the Gaels) was a radical political and cultural organization and the precursor of the *Sinn Féin* party.

4. George W. Russell (AE, 1867–1935), Irish writer and social reformer; James H. Cousins (1873–1956), Irish writer; and Frederick Ryan (1876–1913), Irish journalist and playwright.

5. The French actor and manager André Antoine (1858–1943) founded the Théâtre Libre in Paris in 1887.

6. The Daughters of Erin sponsored the first public performance of AE's *Deirdre* and the first performance of Yeats's *Cathleen ni Houlihan* on 2 April 1902 by W. G. Fay's Irish National Dramatic Society in St. Teresa's Hall in Dublin.

7. Maud Gonne played the title role in the 2 April 1902 production of *The Countess Cathleen.*

8. Yeats saw the production of Racine's *Phèdre* with the French actress Sarah Bernhardt (1844–1923) and the French actor Édouard De Max (1869–1925) in London on 20 June 1902.

9. Apparently derived from Goethe's "the Arts also produce much out of themselves, and . . . add much where Nature fails in perfection, in that they possess beauty in themselves," in *Maxims and Reflections of Goethe,* translated by Bailey Saunders (New York and London: Macmillan, 1893), 173.

10. In Shakespeare's *Macbeth* (performed 1606, printed 1623), Banquo refers to the "procreant cradle" (I.6.8) of a martlet.

11. Yeats was to lecture in London on "The Future of Irish Drama" on 7 February 1903 (*CL*3 xxi).

12. Yeats is quoting from the "Notes and Comments" by the Irish writer and historian Standish O'Grady (1846–1928) in the *All Ireland Review* for 12 April 1902: 84 (correctly "leave the heroic cycles alone and don't bring them down to the crowd . . .").

13. "The Dramatic Treatment of Heroic Literature" by AE was published in *The United Irishman* for 3 May 1902. AE argued that "it is pos-

sible we may yet hear on the stage, not merely the mimicry of human speech, but the old forgotten music which was heard in the duns of kings, which made the revellers grow silent and great warriors to bow low their faces in their hands" (3). A portion of AE's essay with an added footnote by Yeats was reprinted in this issue of *Samhain* (11–13) as well as in the *All Ireland Review* for 1 November 1902 (576–77).

14. Late in 1900, Yeats began a series of recitals in which poetry was chanted by the English actress Florence Farr (1860–1917) to the accompaniment of musical notes. In 1901 the English musician Arnold Dolmetsch (1858–1940) constructed for the experiments a psaltery, a lyre-shaped instrument of twenty-six strings; this was first used in public at Yeats's lecture on "Speaking to Musical Notes" in London on 10 June 1902.

15. Douglas Hyde's *An Pósadh* (*The Marriage*) was first produced at the Connacht Feis, Galway, on 20–21 August 1902.

16. Hyde's *An Tincéir agus an tSidheóg* (*The Tinker and the Fairy*) was privately performed for delegates to the Oireachtas (the annual festival sponsored by the Gaelic League) in George Moore's garden on 19 May 1902.

17. From the "Proverbs of Hell" in Blake's *The Marriage of Heaven and Hell* (ca. 1790–93): "Improvement makes strait roads, but the crooked roads without Improvement, are roads of Genius."

18. In *The Tinker and the Fairy*, the first kiss saves the fairy from death; the second (and third) looks forward to their anticipated marriage. When at the end of the play the fairy returns to her realm, the tinker turns to his bottle for consolation.

19. Not exactly. In *Tribulat Bonhomet* (1887) by the French writer Villiers de l'Isle-Adam (1838–89), the title character enjoys killing swans so that he can hear their dying song. Villiers invented other anecdotes about Bonhomet which were never published; some of these were collected by his future biographer (a distant cousin). Yeats's source was most likely Lady Mary Loyd's *Villiers de l'Isle Adam: His Life and Works from the French of Vicomte Robert du Pontavice de Heussey* (London: William Heinemann, 1894), in which the following anecdote is recounted: "Then, as a pendant to Bonhomet the slayer of swans, there was Bonhomet the ermine-hunter, who, having read that one of these immaculate creatures dies as soon as a stain marks its snowy whiteness, hides himself with a wonderful silent gun, charged with ink, and thus exterminates several dozen!" (230). Yeats recalls his hybrid version in "Coole and Ballylee, 1931," describing a "mounting swan" as "So arrogantly pure, a child might think / It can be murdered with a spot of ink" (P 248). Whether Yeats was confused or simply decided to substitute the symbolic swan for the ermine is an open question.

20. *An Tobar Draoidheachta* (*The Enchanted Well*) by Father Patrick S. Dinneen was performed at the Oireachtas in Dublin, 20–22 May 1901. Yeats had discussed Father Dinneen's *Creideamh agus Gorta* (*Faith and Famine*) in the 1901 *Samhain*.

21. Fionn mac Cumhaill is the hero of the Fionn or Ossianic cycle of heroic tales. In "The Coming of Finn" in *Gods and Fighting Men* (London: John Murray, 1904), Lady Gregory describes one part of Fionn's early training: "they would leave him in a field, and hares along with him, and would bid him not to let the hares quit the field, but to keep before them whichever way they would go . . ." (160).

22. The unpublished play by Father Peter O'Leary is untraced. His *La an Amadán* (*Fool's Day*) was also apparently not published.

23. As noted in "'Hugh Roe O'Donnell' at Sheestown" in *The Kilkenny Journal* for 20 August 1902, "Close on two thousand persons were present at the production of Mr Standish O'Grady's Irish Historical play, 'Hugh Roe O'Donnell,' at Sheestown, on the demesne attached to the residence of Capt the Hon Otway Cuffe, Vice-President of the Kilkenny Branch of the Gaelic League, on Friday night [15 August 1902]." See also "'Hugh Roe O'Donnell': An Irish Historical Masque," *Ulster Journal of Archaeology*, 8.4 (October 1902) by Francis Joseph Bigger (who took part in the production). Bigger notes that the play was "printed in Belfast for private circulation" (172). The play climaxes with the installation of Hugh Roe O'Donnell (ca. 1571–1602) as chief of the O'Donnells in May 1592.

24. Douglas Hyde's play was *An Naomh ar Iarraidh;* also included was a translation by Lady Gregory, as *The Lost Saint* (14–23).

25. In a note to his poem "Baile and Aillinn" in *The Monthly Review* for July 1902, Yeats described Lady Gregory's *Cuchulain of Muirthemne* (London: John Murray, 1902), to which he had contributed a Preface, as "the most important book that has come out of Ireland in my time."

26. Yeats refers to Jedediah Cleishbotham, the supposed author of framing sections in several novels by Sir Walter Scott.

27. Hyde's *Love Songs of Connacht* was published by T. Fisher Unwin (London) in 1893.

28. Hyde's *Dráma Breite Críosta,* translated by Lady Gregory as *The Nativity,* was performed at the Ursuline Convent in Sligo on 8 December 1903. *The Sligo Champion* noted on 19 December 1903 that "if the presentation of the play was good, the staging of it by those responsible for that department was perfect" (1). The play was not produced at the Abbey Theatre until 5 January 1911.

29. Frédéric Mistral (1830–1914), Provençal poet.

30. Hyde's *Beside the Fire: a Collection of Irish Gaelic Folk Stories* was published by D. Nutt (London) in 1890.

31. Yeats refers to the so-called "Genesis Manuscript" (ca. 1826–27),

an incomplete illustrated manuscript of eleven leaves, now in the Huntington Library.

32. The standard Bible in Irish was the so-called "Bedell Bible," named after William Bedell (1571–1642), a Church of Ireland Bishop who in 1634 called for the completion of the project to produce an Irish Bible, which had been authorized by Elizabeth I. The work was completed in 1640 but not published until 1685. The entire Bible was issued for the first time in 1690 as *An Bíobla Naomhtha* (*The Holy Bible*).

33. Although Yeats attributed this thought to the French writer and literary critic Charles Augustin Sainte-Beuve (1804–69) at least four other times, in fact it is found in *Dreamthorp: A Book of Essays Written in the Country* (London: Strahan, 1863) by the Scottish writer Alexander Smith (1829–67): "And style, after all, rather than thought, is the immortal thing in literature." Style itself is defined as "the amalgam and issue of all the mental and moral qualities in a man's possession, and which bears the same relation to these that light bears to the mingled elements that make up the orb of the sun" (43). Smith's remarks come in a discussion of the French essayist Montaigne (1533–92), which perhaps explains Yeats's ascription to another French writer.

34. In the chapter on "Personal Expression" in "The Novel," included in *The Experimental Novel and Other Essays* (1894), the French novelist Émile Zola (1840–1902) suggests that many novelists "who write very correctly, and who have finally obtained very great literary renown," nevertheless have the "misfortune to be without any individual expression, and that is enough to make them forever commonplace." Zola argues that "Personal expression does not necessarily include a perfect form. You can write badly, incorrectly, like the devil, and yet, with it all, retain a true originality of expression." He notes that like Stendhal, Balzac "has been accused of writing badly" but concludes that "Whatever may be his faults, his is a grand style."

35. In "The Dramatic Treatment of Irish Literature," published in *The United Irishman* for 3 May 1902, AE noted that "Men too often forget in this age of printed books, that literature is, after all, only an ineffectual record of speech. The literary man has gone into strange byways through long contemplation of books, and he writes with elaboration what could never be spoken, and he loses that power of the bards on whom tongues of fire had descended, who were masters of the magic of utterance, whose thoughts were not meant to be silently absorbed from the lifeless page" (3).

36. A letter from Edward Martyn about the 2 April 1902 productions of AE's *Deirdre* and Yeats's *Cathleen ni Houlihan* had been published in *The United Irishman* for 19 April 1902. Martyn regretted the lack of "more competent acting and stage management" and was partic-

ularly critical of W. G. Fay's performance as Peter Gillane in Yeats's play; he ended by hoping that "with practice, Mr. Fay's company will improve and be able to grapple with the more advanced forms of modern drama" (1). Yeats responded with a letter in *The United Irishman* for 26 April 1902, accusing Martyn of preferring "a form of drama that is essentially modern, that needs for its production actors of what is called the 'natural school,' the dominant school of the modern stage" (*CL3* 178).

37. By the 1870s, there was a growing protest that the reforms of Alexander II (1818–81) had not sufficiently improved the conditions of the common people of Russia.

Samhain: 1903

1. The first series of plays were offered on 12–14 February 1903. Hyde played the part of Raftery in his *An Pósadh* (*The Marriage*). Also performed was *Aodh Ó Néill* (*Hugh O'Neill*, 1902), by the Irish writer Pádraig Ó Séaghdha (1855–1928). (Hugh O'Neill [1550–1616], inaugurated as the O'Neill in 1595, was one of the leaders of the Irish forces at the Battle of Kinsale in 1601.) *Tobar Draoidheachta* (*The Enchanted Well*) by Father Patrick S. Dinneen was presented at the Rotunda on 14 May 1902, as part of the Oireachtas, the annual festival sponsored by the Gaelic League; it was accompanied by Hyde's *An Pósadh*, offered by the Ballaghadereen Branch of the Gaelic League.

2. *Meadhbh* (*Maeve*) by Father Peter O'Leary (1839–1920) was apparently never published.

3. Douglas Hyde's *An Cleamhnas* (*The Matchmaking*) was performed at the Galway Feis on 20 August 1903. Yeats had missed the production on 19 August 1903 of *The Rent-Day* by E. L. O'Toole, described by the *Galway Observer* for 22 August 1903 as "an admirable performance, which would deserve special praise" (3). The play was apparently never published.

4. Douglas Hyde's *An Naomh ar Iarraidh* (*The Lost Saint*) was performed by children of classes of the Daughters of Erin on 29–30 January 1903. *The Saxon Shillin'* by the Irish writer Padraic Colum (1881–1972) was revived by the Daughters of Erin at the Banba Hall in Dublin on 15 May 1903. The play about the Royal Visit of Edward VII in July 1903 was Joseph Ryan's *A Twinkle in Ireland's Eye*.

5. That is, *The Laying of the Foundations*.

6. Arthur Bingham Walkley (1855–1926) was the drama critic for *The Times* (London). Yeats reprinted his commentary on the productions, "The Irish National Theatre" (*The Times*, 8 May 1903), in this issue of *Samhain*.

7. The acting area of the Abbey stage was ca. 20 feet by 15 feet.

8. Yeats had met the Irish playwright John Millington Synge (1871–1909) in Paris in 1896, and urged him to concentrate his attention on Irish materials.

9. The play is based on the early Irish tale *The Great Visitation to Guaire,* in which Guaire, King of Connacht, is visited by 150 poets, headed by Seanchan the Chief Poet. Guaire is a market town in County Galway.

10. The play by the Irish playwright George Bernard Shaw (1856–1950) was *John Bull's Other Island* (1904). The character of Broadbent would have required a trained English actor.

11. Hyde's "The Oireachtas Ode" was published in *The United Irishman* for 14 June 1902: 3.

12. Hanrahan is the main character in Hyde's *Casadh an tSúgáin (The Twisting of the Rope).* The other play referred to is *An Naomh ar Iarraidh.*

13. This issue of *Samhain* included Hyde's *Teach na mBocht,* translated by Lady Gregory as *The Poorhouse,* and Synge's *Riders to the Sea.*

Samhain: 1903—The Reform of the Theatre

1. An earlier version of this essay was published under the same title in *The United Irishman* for 4 April 1903.

2. In "The Best Men of the Fianna" in Lady Gregory's *Gods and Fighting Men* (London: John Murray, 1904), Finn offers advice to the Son of Lugaidh: "If you have a mind to be a good champion, be quiet in a great man's house . . ." (184).

3. Although Yeats attributed this thought to the French writer and literary critic Charles Augustin Sainte-Beuve (1804–69) at least four other times, in fact it is found in *Dreamthorp: A Book of Essays Written in the Country* (London: Strahan, 1863) by the Scottish writer Alexander Smith (1829–67): "And style, after all, rather than thought, is the immortal thing in literature." Style itself is defined as "the amalgam and issue of all the mental and moral qualities in a man's possession, and which bears the same relation to these that light bears to the mingled elements that make up the orb of the sun" (43). Smith's remarks come in a discussion of the French essayist Montaigne (1533–92), which perhaps explains Yeats's ascription to another French writer.

4. Falstaff is a character in several plays by Shakespeare.

Samhain: 1903—Moral and Immoral Plays

1. In "Mr. Yeats and Theatre Reform," published in *The Leader* 6.5 (28 March 1903), "Chanel" (Arthur Clery) argued that when Yeats "began his lecture on dramatic reform by saying he did not care

whether a play were moral or immoral, provided it were not vulgar, and preached the doctrine of Art for Art's Sake, one might fairly say that he straightway put himself out of court as a writer of 'morality' plays, unless that word is to be wrenched out of its proper meaning"(72).

In the 1903 *Samhain*, this essay (untitled) was the second section of "The Reform of the Theatre"; it was first published in this format in the 1908 *Collected Works*.

2. Quotation untraced. Yeats had met the Belgian poet Émile Verhaeren (1855–1916) in late 1898 or early 1899 in London. Yeats's main source of knowledge of Verhaeren was the English teacher, critic, and translator Osman Edwards (1864–1936), whose "Émile Verhaeren" had appeared in the November 1896 issue of *The Savoy* (65–76), preceding Yeats's "The Tables of the Law."

3. *Mice and Men: A Romantic Comedy in Four Acts* by the American playwright Madeleine Lucette Ryley (1868–1934) was performed by the Forbes-Roberston Company at the Gaiety Theatre in Dublin on 1–6 June 1903. The play had first been produced at the Lyric Theatre in London, 27 January 1902–4 February 1903. The reviewer for *The Times* (London) objected to the improbability of the plot but nevertheless described the work as "a very wholesome entertainment" and "as pretty a picture of girlhood as the stage can show" (28 January 1902: 8). Likewise, the critic of *The Athenaeum* concluded that although the play was "slight to fragility," it was "pleasing and idyllic" (1 February 1902: 156).

4. *Parzival* is a German Grail romance by Wolfram von Eschenbach (1170–1220). Yeats owned the translation by Jessie L. Weston, *Parzival: A Knightly Epic* (London: D. Nutt, 1894). Thuringia is a region in central Germany. According to legend, when St. Elizabeth of Thuringia (1207–31) was surprised by her husband as she was on a secret errand of mercy, the bread she was trying to conceal was turned to roses.

5. Untraced. Connacht is a province in the west of Ireland.

Samhain: 1903—An Irish National Theatre

1. This essay was first published in *The United Irishman* for 10 October 1903. It was revised and added to the 1903 *Samhain* in the *Collected Works* (1908). The newspaper version is reprinted at *CL3* 439–41 but with the title omitted.

Synge's *The Shadow of the Glen* was produced by the Irish National Theatre Society at the Molesworth Hall in Dublin on 8 October 1903. The play was attacked by various newspapers for presenting an unflattering picture of Irish womanhood. *The United Irishman* for 8 November 1903, for instance, claimed that "To take the Widow of Ephesus and rechristen her Mrs. Burke, and relabel Ephesus Wicklow, is not a brilliant thing." Moreover, Synge is "as utterly a stranger to the Irish character as any Englishman who has yet dissected us for the enlightenment of his countrymen" (1).

2. In 1892 Yeats was involved in a dispute with the Irish nationalist Sir Charles Gavan Duffy (1816–1903) over control of a series of books to be called the "New Irish Library." Duffy eventually prevailed.

3. *The Spirit of the Nation* was a collection of mainly patriotic poems and ballads collected from *The Nation,* first published in 1843; a second part was issued in 1844 and an enlarged edition in 1845. By 1870 the collection was in its fiftieth printing.

4. Michael Doheny (1805–63), Irish poet and nationalist. Yeats refers to "A Cuisle Gael Mo Chroidhe" ("Bright Pulse of My Heart"), written in the mountains after the collapse of the 1848 Rebellion. "On his keeping" is an Irish expression for someone being hunted as a fugitive, in this instance by the English.

5. John 3:8.

6. I Cor. 13:13.

Samhain: 1903—The Theatre, the Pulpit,
and the Newspapers

1. "An Irish National Theatre," published in *The Irish Daily Independent and Nation* for 8 October 1903. The editorial writer objected to "the perversion of the Society's avowed aims" and "these unwholesome productions" (4).

   Yeats's essay was first published in *The United Irishman* for 17 October 1903. It was revised and added to the 1903 *Samhain* in the *Collected Works* (1908). The newspaper version is reprinted at *CL*3 445–49 but with the title omitted.

2. Falstaff is a character in several plays by Shakespeare, whose *Antony and Cleopatra* follows closely the account by the Greek historian Plutarch (A.D. ?46–120), in the version by Sir Thomas North (?1535–?1601), published in 1595. In Greek mythology, Pandora had been warned by the gods not to open a box they gave her; when she disobeyed and opened it, the world was subjected to numerous evils. *The Golden Treasury of Best Songs and Lyrical Poems in the English Language* (1861) by Francis Turner Palgrave (1824–97) was a very popular anthology.

3. In *The Tripartite Life of Patrick,* written in Irish probably in the eleventh century, St. Patrick becomes enraged when he learns that his sister, Lupait, was unchaste and had become pregnant. He kills her by driving his chariot over her three times.

4. In *Reveries Over Childhood and Youth* (1916), Yeats recalled a remark by the Irish patriot John O'Leary (1830–1907): "'Never has

there been a cause so bad', he would say, 'that it has not been defended by good men for good reasons'" (*Au* 100).

5. In Yeats's *The King's Threshold*, Seanchan asks "When did the poets promise safety, King?" (*Pl* 147).

6. Untraced.

7. In the 1903 *Samhain* (see p. 25).

8. Prince Pyotr Alexeievitch Kropotkin (1842–1921) and Sergius Stepniak (1852–95), Russian revolutionaries. Both fled Russia and settled in London. Yeats recalled meeting Kropotkin at the home of William Morris (*Au* 131); he probably also knew Stepniak, as his portrait was painted by his father, John Butler Yeats (1839–1922).

Samhain: 1904—The Dramatic Movement

1. After Yeats's curtain speech at the performance of John Millington Synge's *In the Shadow of the Glen* on 20 October 1903, Annie E. F. Horniman (1860–1937), an Englishwoman of some wealth and a considerable interest in the theatre (and in Yeats), promised Yeats "I will find you a theatre" (*Au* 415). By January 1904, negotiations had begun to acquire leases on the Hall of the Mechanics' Institute in Abbey Street and on the old City Morgue, adjoining in Marlborough Street. The formal offer was made in a letter of 4 April 1904, which was reprinted in this issue of *Samhain*. Although Horniman planned to spend £1,600 on the renovations, the final cost was almost £3,000, plus annual leasing costs of £170.

2. Sarah Henrietta Purser (1848–1943) was an Irish painter; in 1903 she founded an Irish stained-glass industry, *An Túr Gloine* (The Tower of Glass). Youghal is a town in County Cork. John Butler Yeats produced portraits of Annie Horniman, W. G. Fay, Frank Fay, Douglas Hyde, AE, and the Irish actress Mary Walker ("Máire Nic Shiúbhlaigh," d. 1958). Yeats's portrait, however, was by a French artist, Madame Troncy (he disliked it, and it was removed in 1906).

3. Robert Gregory (1881–1918), Lady Gregory's son, had studied at the Slade School of Art in London. "Honor Lavelle" was the stage name of the Irish actress Helen S. Laird (1874–1957).

4. Probably the English artist Charles de Sousy Ricketts (1866–1931).

5. Biblical drama was popular in England from the thirteenth to the sixteenth centuries. Yeats is distinguishing between plays which deal with Gospel events (Mystery Plays) and those which concern the lives of the saints (Miracle Plays). Racine's plays performed by the girls at the convent school of Saint-Cyr were *Esther* (1689) and *Athalie* (1691).

6. From "St. Luke the Painter," part of the sonnet sequence "The House of Life" by the English artist and poet Dante Gabriel Rossetti (1828–82).

7. Standish James O'Grady was quoting from the Preface to *The Raven*

and Other Poems (1845) by the American writer Edgar Allan Poe (1809–49).

8. The objections to the granting of a patent to the Abbey Theatre were heard on 4 August 1904. Nevertheless, the patent was granted on 20 August, with the restrictions mentioned as well as others (e.g., the theatre could not be enlarged beyond its present capacity). Yeats had seen the production of *Everyman,* a morality play of ca. 1509–19, by the Elizabethan Stage Society in London on 17 March 1902; the Dublin production, on 24–29 October 1902, took place in the large Round Room of the Rotunda.

9. The Abbey had a total of 562 seats: 186 in the pit, 178 in the stalls, and 198 in the balcony.

10. The Independent Theatre Society had been formed in London in 1890; it came to an end in December 1898 (Yeats was never very adept at mathematics). *L'Intruse* (*The Intruder*), a one-act play about death by the Belgian writer Maurice Maeterlinck (1862–1949), was first performed in Paris at the Théâtre d'Art on 21 May 1891 and in London at the Haymarket Theatre on 27 January 1892.

11. Sophocles' *Oedipus Tyrannus* dates from ca. 430–425 B.C.

12. After the political satire in *Pasquin* (1736) and *The Historical Register for 1736* (1737) by the English writer Henry Fielding (1707–54), the Prime Minister, Sir Robert Walpole (1676–1745), introduced the Licensing Act of 1737. The Lord Chamberlain became licenser of theatres in London and Westminster and in other places of residence of the sovereign: penalties were to be imposed on the performance for hire anywhere in Great Britain of plays not licensed by him, and it was required that a copy of every new play proposed to be performed should be sent to him for approval.

13. *The Sign of the Cross* by the English actor and writer Wilson Barrett (1846–1904) was performed in London from 4 January 1896 to 30 January 1897.

14. Douglas Hyde's *Dráma Breite Críosta,* translated by Lady Gregory as *The Nativity,* was performed at the Ursuline Convent in Sligo on 8 December 1903. *The Sligo Champion* noted on 19 December 1903 that "if the presentation of the play was good, the staging of it by those responsible for that department was perfect" (1). The play was not produced at the Abbey Theatre until 5 January 1911.

15. Fionn mac Cumhaill is the hero of the Ossianic cycle of Irish heroic tales and the father of Oisín; Patrick is St. Patrick.

16. John Milton's *Samson Agonistes* was published in 1671. In Greek mythology Heracles (Hercules in Roman mythology) is renowned for his strength.

17. The English poet is untraced. Jack and the Beanstalk is an English folktale.

18. *Gírle Guairle* (*Hurly Burly,* 1904) by Father Patrick S. Dinneen.

19. The play is untraced and apparently unpublished.

20. *Seaghán na Scuab* (*Sean of the Brushes*) by the Irish writer Tomás O hAodha (1866–1935) was performed at the Oireachtas on 1 and 6 August 1904. *The United Irishman* for 20 August 1904 claimed that "On all sides it is conceded that 'Seaghan na Sguab' is the best Irish drama we have had yet . . ." (1), explaining in its issue for 6 August 1904 that the play was "founded upon the old story of the broommaker from Cork who became unexpectedly Mayor of Limerick" (1).

21. *An Doctúir* (*The Doctor*) by Seamus O'Beirne was performed at the Oireachtas on 1 and 6 August 1904.

22. The Connacht Feis was held in Galway on 17–19 August 1904. The play performed was *An Deoraidhe* (*The Exile*, 1905) by E. L. O'Toole. The *Galway Observer* for 20 August 1904 noted that the "Irish play, 'The Exile,' by the Galway Gaelic Leaguers, evoked much enthusiasm, the evils of emigration being most effectively presented in the piece" (3).

23. Slightly misquoted from the version in Lady Gregory's *Poets and Dreamers: Studies and Translations from the Irish by Lady Gregory Including Nine Plays by Douglas Hyde* (Dublin: Hodges Figgis; London: John Murray, 1903), 240–41. A less accurate text had also been included in the 1903 *Samhain*.

24. In the *Táin Bó Cuailgne*, Mebd (Maeve), Queen of Connacht, steals a bull from the Ulstermen in order to have a bull to rival that of her husband, Ailill. Cruachan was the ancient capital of Connacht.

25. Yeats found Goethe's remark in *Maxims and Reflections of Goethe*, translated by Bailey Saunders (New York and London: Macmillan, 1893), 59. Philippus Aureolus Paracelsus (Theophrastus Bombastus von Hohenheim, ?1493–1541) was a Swiss alchemist and physician. Although Yeats quoted this sentence in several contexts, it remains untraced.

26. The plays produced on 26 March 1904 at the Royalty in London were Synge's *Riders to the Sea* and *The Shadow of the Glen,* Padraic Colum's *Broken Soil,* and Yeats's *The King's Threshold* and *The Pot of Broth.* Although the reviews were generally favorable, Yeats noted in a letter of 31 March [1904] that "A good many of the critics complain that my King's Threshold lacks action . . ." (*CL*3 561).

27. Lady Gregory's plays were *Kincora* and *Hyacinth Halvey.*

28. *Sigrid* by the Irish barrister and writer W. Kingsley Tarpey (1858–1911) had been approved for performance on 12 March 1904 while Yeats was returning from his American lecture tour; in the event, it was never produced at the Abbey Theatre. His *Windmills* had been performed by the Stage Society in London on 16–17 June 1901. The play by the Irish playwright William Boyle (1853–1922) was *The Building Fund.*

29. The St. Louis World's Fair, billed as "The Greatest of Exhibitions,"

was held from 30 April to 1 December 1904. Augustus Thomas
(1857–1934), a playwright and former St. Louis journalist, had suggested to Yeats that any performances by the Irish National Theatre
Society would be overshadowed by the more popular attractions of
the fair (*CL3* 499n1).

30. Margaret Wycherley (1884–1956) was an American actress.

31. *The Duchess of Malfi* by the English dramatist John Webster (ca.
1578–ca. 1632) was written 1612/1613 and published in 1623.

32. Sir Walter Ralegh (?1554–1618), English courtier, explorer, and
writer; and Sir Philip Sidney (1554–86), English courtier, soldier, and
poet.

Samhain: 1904—First Principles

1. Yeats presumably refers to the controversy about the bigotry of the
press between AE and David Patrick Moran (1871–1936), editor of
The Leader, which began with an article by AE in the September 1904
issue of *Dana* and continued in *The Leader* until 15 October 1904.
In the Bible, Martha and Mary are sisters of Lazarus; Martha is at first
uncertain about the nature of Christ's divinity.

2. Yeats refers to "Ethics and Economics" by "Ċ," published in *The
Leader* for 8 October 1904 (104–6). The slight misquotation is from
p. 105.

3. The Irish orator and barrister John Francis Taylor (1850–1902) was
described by Yeats in *Reveries Over Childhood and Youth* as "an
obscure great orator" (*Au* 101), noting in a later draft of his *Autobiographies* that Talyor "knew nothing of poetry or of painting, though
he seemed to know by heart whole plays of Shakespeare and all the
more famous passages in Milton, and was deeply read in eighteenth-
century literature. He understood alone eloquence, an impassioned
pleading. He sometimes gave me an impression of insanity" (*Mem* 53).
Taylor's speech comparing the Irish to the Jews and the English to the
Egyptians is discussed at some length in James Joyce's *Ulysses* (1922).
    On 11 May 1899, T. P. Gill (1858–1931), the editor of the Dublin
Daily Express, gave a dinner in honor of the Irish Literary Theatre.
In *Dramatis Personae,* Yeats recalled that in his speech Taylor suggested
that William O'Brien had made "the sacrifice of Mr. Yeats' *Countess
Cathleen,* damning his soul for his country" (*Au* 314).

4. Although Yeats told the American lawyer and patron of the arts John
Quinn (1870–1924) on 15 April 1904 that Lady Gregory's *The Rising of the Moon* "goes into rehearsal almost at once" and again on
25 April 1904 that it would be produced "next month" (*CL3* 580,
586), in fact it was not performed until 9 March 1907. The untraced
criticism must have been based on the text published in *The Gael* (New
York) in November 1903.

5. In "Il conte di Carmagnola. Tragedia di Alessandro Mazoni. Milano," first published in *Über Kunst und Altertum* (September 1820), Goethe stated that "for the poet no person is historical, it is his pleasure to create his moral world and for this purpose he renders to certain persons in history the honour of lending their names to his creations."

6. Shakespeare's Falstaff is based on Sir John Oldcastle (d. 1417), a leader of the Lollards, an heretical sect that adopted the ideas of John Wycliffe (ca. 1320–84).

7. The *Chronicles* by Raphael Holinshed (d. ?1580) and others was a major source for Shakespeare's History Plays. Bolingbroke became King Henry IV after deposing Richard II. The quotation is untraced. Yeats also described Richard II as " 'too friendly' to his friends" in "At Stratford-on-Avon," first published in *The Speaker* (11 and 18 May 1901) and included in a shortened form in *Ideas of Good and Evil* (London: A. H. Bullen, 1903).

8. See *Four Old Irish Songs of Summer & Winter,* edited by Kuno Meyer (London: David Nutt, 1903); the poems are sometimes ascribed to Fionn. Although Chaucer is not especially known for his references to trees, Yeats is perhaps thinking of the short catalogue of trees in *The Knight's Tale.*

9. The "old cabalistic writer" has not been traced. In his Journal for 9 February 1909, Yeats referred to "that fall into the circumference the mystics talk of" (*Au* 355); and in "Art and Ideas," first published in *The New Weekly* (20 and 27 June 1914) and included in *Essays* (London: Macmillan, 1924), he cited "the fall of man into his own circumference." It is a common idea in mystical tradition that man's loss of unity with God moves him from the center to the circumference, God being a circle whose center is everywhere but whose circumference is nowhere. The Blake quotation is from his *Public Address* (1809–10): "Princes appear to me to be Fools Houses of Commons & Houses of Lords appear to me to be fools they seem to me to be something Else beside Human Life."

10. In Shakespeare's *King Richard III* (performed 1591, printed 1597), Richmond defeats Richard III at the Battle of Bosworth and becomes King Henry VII. Cervantes's *Don Quixote* was published in parts in 1605 and 1615.

11. Prophecies offered in Virgil's *Fourth Eclogue* (40 B.C.). Jason and the Argonauts sailed in search of the Golden Fleece; Troy was sacked by the Greeks at the end of the Trojan War.

12. Ludovico Arisoto (1474–1533) was an Italian poet, best known for his *Orlando Furioso* (1516; revised 1532). In 1522 he was commissioned to suppress an insurrection in the mountain district of Garfagnana; he succeeded and remained as governor of the province for three years.

13. References to Shakespeare's *Macbeth* (performed 1606; published 1623), *Antony and Cleopatra* (1623), and *Coriolanus* (1623).

14. *"ego absolve te"* ("I absolve thee"), said by the priest in the Roman Catholic Church rite of penance, signifying and enacting the forgiveness of sins by God.

15. In *Antony and Cleopatra,* the dying Antony is brought to the monument in which Cleopatra has taken refuge and dies in her arms. *Explorations* (1962) replaces Yeats's "tower" with "monument." At the end of *Coriolanus,* the title character is publicly killed by Aufidius. In the Old Testament, the Ten Commandments were given to Moses by God on Mount Sinai.

16. Although Dante Gabriel Rossetti was born in London, his father was the Italian patriot Gabriele Rossetti (1783–1854). Swift (1667–1745) was born in Ireland but spent considerable time in England, and only a relatively small portion of his work is directly connected with Irish matters.

17. St. Columbanus (?543–615) was born in Leinster but left Ireland ca. 590. His *Sermon V* begins "Oh human life, feeble and mortal, how many have you deceived, beguiled, and blinded! While you fly, you are nothing, while you are seen, you are a shadow, while you arise, you are but smoke. . . . You are the roadway of mortals, not their life, beginning from sin, enduring up till death . . . you have allotted all your travelers to death."

18. *Vathek, an Arabian Tale* by the English writer William Beckford (1759–1844) was written in French but translated with the author's assistance by Samuel Henley and published in English in 1786.

19. The Irish scholar Edward Dowden (1843–1913) held the Chair of English Literature at Trinity College Dublin from 1867 until his death. On 5 September 1871, Dowden sent Whitman a letter telling him that he "will name some of your friends on this side of the water whom I know myself." A letter from Whitman to Dowden on 18 January 1872 refers to a group of letters from these people, apparently sent by Dowden. There were ten admirers, including Dowden; in addition to him and to Yeats's father, at least two others were Irish.

20. James Russell Lowell (1819–91), American poet and essayist.

21. "Highland Mary" by Robert Burns was first published in 1799, "The Cotter's Saturday Night" (often considered by others one of his best poems) in 1786.

22. Chaucer was described as the "father of English poetry" in the Preface to *Fables Ancient and Modern* (1700) by John Dryden and as the "well of English undefyled" in Book IV of *The Faerie Queene* (1596) by Edmund Spenser.

23. In 1892 Yeats was involved in a dispute with the Irish nationalist Sir Charles Gavan Duffy (1816–1903) over control of a series of books to be called the "New Irish Library." Duffy eventually prevailed. Fred-

erick York Powell (1850–1904), Regius Professor of History at Oxford University, lived near the Yeatses in Bedford Park in London.

24. The English poet Thomas Campbell (1777–1844), immensely popular in his own time.

25. Oliver Goldsmith, Richard Brinsley Sheridan, and Edmund Burke were all born in Ireland but spent most of their lives in England.

26. In 1898 Yeats engaged in a debate with the Irish essayist "John Eglinton" (William Kirkpatrick Magee, 1868–1961), initiated by Eglinton's "What Should be the Subjects of a National Drama?", published in the Dublin *Daily Express* for 18 September 1898. Eglinton rejected Irish myth and saga as proper subjects for a national school of drama.

27. Possibly "The Development of the French Drama," *International Quarterly* 7 (March–June 1903): 14–31, by the American writer and critic Brander Matthews (1852–1929). Although Matthews does not comment on *Phèdre,* he discusses *Andromaque* and quotes the French critic Hippolyte Taine (1828–93) on the emergence of drama under Louis XIV: "French tragedy appeared, as Taine has told us, 'when a noble and well-regulated monarchy, under Louis XIV., established the empire of decorum, the life of the court, the pomp and circumstance of society, and the elegant domestic phases of aristocracy'; and French tragedy could not but disappear 'when the social rule of nobles and the manners of the antechamber were abolished by the Revolution'" (25–26).

28. *Salammbô* (1862) by the French novelist Gustave Flaubert (1821–80) is set after the first Punic War and deals with the revolt against Carthage by its unpaid mercenary army. The title character, as a priestess, is the daughter of the leader of Carthage. In a letter to Charles Augustin Sainte-Beuve on 23–24 December 1892, Flaubert argued that no one could say whether Salammbô was portrayed realistically because it is impossible to get to know an Oriental woman since one cannot spend time in her company.

29. Along with the Ibsen, the Norwegian political leader and writer Bjørnstjerne Bjørnson (1832–1910) was primarily responsible for the rise of Norwegian drama.

30. Keats's "Ode on a Grecian Urn" was published in 1820. In Virgil's *Aeneid,* Aeneas plucks the Golden Bough before beginning his journey to the Underworld; the scene is depicted in a famous painting by the English artist J. M. W. Turner (1775–1851).

31. In Book I of Milton's *Paradise Lost* (1667), Lucifer (Satan) rouses the spirits of the other defeated rebellious angels. The "Ballade des dames du temps jadis" by the French poet François Villon (?1431–?1463) is included in *Le grand testament* (1461). In Shakespeare's *Timon of Athens* (1623), Timon's epitaph expresses his hatred of mankind.

1. See pp. 173–75.
2. In his curtain speech after the first production of *The King's Threshold* on 8 October 1903, Yeats outlined his plans for the Irish National Theatre Society and argued that it should produce foreign masterpieces as well as Irish plays. Annie E. F. Horniman was sufficiently impressed so as to make her offer of a theatre. Horniman had designed the costumes for the production.
3. Racine's *Phèdre* and *Andromaque* were both first performed in 1677.
4. *Les Trente-six situations dramatiques* (Paris: Mercure de France, 1895) by Georges Polti (1868–?).
5. *A Doll's House* (1879) was first produced in London by the Player's Club on 22 June 1903.
6. The English writer Sir Max Beerbohm (1872–1956) was the drama critic for the *Saturday Review* from 1898–1910. Arthur Bingham Walkley was the drama critic for *The Times* (London). The English drama critic and playwright William Archer (1856–1924) was largely responsible for introducing Ibsen's plays in England.
7. Not a quotation from *A Doll's House* but apparently Yeats's parody of Ibsen's style as translated by William Archer.
8. Yeats is most likely referring to Beerbohm's "Mr. Pinero's Literary Style," published in *The Saturday Review* for 24 October 1903. Beerbohm argued that in realistic drama "the words must be far easier, more colloquial and familiar, than the words of the ordinary writer. . . . The first essential is that the persons must speak in the manner of human beings." Thus, "whereas in ordinary writing style is the perfect expression of the writer's self, in plays it is the perfect expression of various selves." In "Mr Street, Playwright," published in the *Saturday Review* for 4 February 1905, Beerbohm replied to Yeats's remark: "The other day, in an essay about the Irish Literary Theatre, Mr. W. B. Yeats quoted me as saying that no modern play could have style. . . . But, as I was careful to suggest, aptness of phrase and beauty can be smuggled in."
9. In his *Public Address* (1809–10), Blake argues that "Nor can an Original Invention Exist without Execution Organized & minutely Delineated & Articulated Either by God or Man."
10. Falstaff is a character in several plays by Shakespeare.
11. Untraced.
12. Yeats is recalling another passage from Blake's *Public Address:* "Princes appear to me to be Fools Houses of Commons & Houses of Lords appear to me to be fools they seem to me to be something Else beside Human Life."
13. Ibsen's *Ghosts* (published 1881, performed 1882) was first pro-

duced by the Independent Theatre Society at the Royalty in London on 13 March 1891.

14. Yeats is quoting from Blake's *Jerusalem* (1804–20): "They enquire after Jerusalem, in the regions of the dead / With the voices of dead men, low, scarcely articulate, / And with tears cold on their cheeks they weary repose." Maeterlinck's *Aglavaine and Sélysette* (1896) was produced in London at the Court Theatre on 15, 17–18, 22, and 24–25 November 1904. Yeats had reviewed Alfred Sutro's 1897 translation of the play in *The Bookman* (London) for September 1897 (*UP2* 51–54).

15. Yeats left for an extended lecture tour in America on 4 November 1903, returning on 16 March 1904.

16. As in Shakespeare's *Coriolanus* (1623).

17. From Blake's *Auguries of Innocence* (ca. 1804–10), correctly "should doubt."

18. David Garrick (1717–79) was an English actor and playwright. The first Dublin playhouse constructed after the Restoration of Charles II in 1660 was the Smock Alley Theatre in 1662. Yeats refers to its co-founder, John Ogilby (1600–1676), Master of Revels in Ireland.

19. *The Way of the World* by William Congreve was produced in London on 17–19 April 1904 at the Court Theatre and again on 7–12 November 1904 at the Royalty. Lady Wishfort was played by the American actress Mrs. Theodore Wright (Alice Austin, d. 1922). She had played Mrs. Alving in the first performance of Ibsen's *Ghosts* mentioned earlier in this essay.

20. Yeats is quoting from the second speech by Lady Wishfort in act 5, scene 1 of *The Way of the World*.

21. Sir Thomas Urquhart (1611–60) translated the first three books of the French writer François Rabelais (ca. 1494–ca. 1553).

22. The most popular plays by Richard Brinsley Sheridan (1751–1816) were *The Rivals* (1775) and *The School for Scandal* (1777).

23. Gargantua is the giant hero of a series of popular burlesque romances featuring well-known characters from the Arthurian legends. Rabelais offers his version of the birth, education, and military prowess of the figure in *Gargantua* (1534–35).

24. In "Stage Management in the Irish National Theatre," published in *Dana* for September 1904, George Moore (writing under the pseudonym "Paul Ruttledge," the main character in Yeats's *Where There is Nothing*) criticized the stage management of W. G. Fay in comparison with the "miraculous" stage management of the French actor and manager André Antoine (1858–1943), the founder of the Théâtre Libre in Paris in 1887. The German religious reformer Martin Luther (1483–1546) was highly critical of the Catholic Church.

25. This quotation from Antoine is untraced. Yeats perhaps learned of

it from Frank J. Fay, who had studied Antoine's career, or from George Moore, who had been in contact with Antoine in Paris.

26. E. D. A. Morshead's abridged translation of Aeschylus's Orestian Trilogy was produced by the Benson Company at the Stratford-upon-Avon Festival in late April–early May 1904; Yeats probably attended the matinée performance on 30 April 1904.

27. "Twinkle, twinkle, little star" is the opening of "The Star" in *Rhymes for the Nursery* (1806) by the English writers Jane Taylor (1783–1824) and Ann Taylor (1782–1866).

28. Late in 1900, Yeats began a series of recitals in which poetry was chanted by the English actress Florence Farr (1869–1917) to the accompaniment of musical notes. In 1901 the English musician Arnold Dolmetsch (1858–1940) constructed for the experiments a psaltery, a lyre-shaped instrument of twenty-six strings; this was first used in public at Yeats's lecture on "Speaking to Musical Notes" in London on 10 June 1902.

29. Gilbert Murray's translation of *Hippolytus* (428 B.C.) by Euripides, with Florence Farr leading the chorus, was first produced at the Lyric Theatre in London on 26 May 1904.

30. Edward Gordon Craig (1872–1966) was an English actor, producer, author, editor, and stage designer. Yeats had been interested in working with Craig for some years; eventually Craig provided a set of screens for the Abbey Theatre, first used in January 1911.

31. Adolphe Appia (1862–1928) was a Swiss scene designer and theatrical producer. In 1902–1903 he was working on a production of scenes from Wagner's *Tristan and Isolde* to be performed at the private theatre of the Countess René de Béarn in Paris; this proved too difficult, however, and thus the production on 25 March 1903 consisted of scenes from Robert Schumann's *Manfred* and Georges Bizet's *Carmen*. For a time he collaborated with the Spanish painter Mariano Fortuny y Madrazo (1871–1949), who was experimenting with a new form of stage lighting. Yeats mentions the work of Fortuny in "The Theatre of Beauty," first published in *Harper's Weekly* for 11 November 1911 (*LAR* 129–33).

Samhain: 1905

1. The site of the productions of the Irish National Theatre Society in 1903.

2. Philip Carr (1874–1957), English drama critic and producer, attempted to revive Elizabethan and Jacobean plays in authentic productions.

3. In his essay "On Beauty" the English writer Francis Bacon (1561–1626) observed that "There is no excellent beauty that hath not some strangeness in the proportion." Yeats had referred to this pas-

sage in an 1892 review, ascribing it to "the Elizabethan," and had cited
it without ascription in a 1901 essay. He finally cited the correct author
in a speech to the Poetry Society of Chicago on 1 March 1914 (*UP2*
412). It has been argued that Yeats took the reference from Poe's
"Ligeia" (*CL2* 448n6), but this assertion overlooks the 1892 quotation. Yeats's first published allusion to Poe is not found until 1898.

4. Lady Gregory's play was *Hyacinth Halvey,* William Boyle's, *The
Eloquent Dempsy.* Padraic Colum revised *Broken Soil* as *The Fiddler's
House,* but this was not performed at the Abbey Theatre (it was first
produced by the Theatre of Ireland at the Rotunda on 21 March
1907). John Millington Synge's play was *The Playboy of the Western World.*

5. A translation of *The Well of the Saints* by the German critic and translator Dr. Max Meyerfeld (1875–1952) was produced at the
Deutsches Theater in Berlin on 12 January 1906. A translation of *The
Shadow of the Glen* by the Czech actor and stage manager Karel
Mušek (1867–1924) was produced at the Bohemian National Theatre in Prague on 7 February 1906. A translation of *Cathleen ni Houlihan* by the Irish playwright Tomás Ó Ceallaigh (Father Thomas
O'Kelly, 1879–1924) was performed in the Rotunda at the Oireachtas in Dublin on 14 August 1905. The text had been published in five
consecutive issues of *The United Irishman* (11 February–11 March
1905) and in book form in the same year by M. H. Gill & Son, Dublin.

6. This particular maxim is untraced. However, in a volume which
Yeats owned, Hjalmar Boyesen's *A History of Norway from the Earliest Times with a New Chapter on the Recent History of Norway by
C. F. Keary* (London: T. Fisher Unwin; New York: G. P. Putnam's Sons,
1904), the discussion of the attempt "to build the intellectual life of
the people upon a strictly national basis" notes that "The national literature, under the lead of men like Björnstjerne Björnson and Henrik Ibsen, is moving in the same direction, its language being
continually enriched from the dialects, and its themes largely drawn
from the ancient sagas and the life of the people" (535–36). In *Bjørnstjerne Bjørnson: A Study in Norwegian Nationalism* (New York:
King's Crown Press, 1944), Harold Larson quotes Bjørnson's recol-
lection in 1880 of the early days in the establishment of the modern
Norwegian theatre: "I began within the ring of the saga and the *bonde*
[freehold farmers], in that I let the one illustrate the other, which at
that time was new" (32).

7. The National Schools educated primarily the lower and working
classes.

8. Yeats refers to Mrs. Grogan in *The Building Fund.*

9. From "St. Luke the Painter," part of the sonnet sequence "The
House of Life" by Dante Gabriel Rossetti (1828–82).

10. Killaloe, a village in County Clare, was the site of the stronghold of

Brian Bóroime (Brian Boru, 941–1014), King of Ireland, the main character in Lady Gregory's *Kincora,* first produced at the Abbey Theatre on 25 March 1905.

11. Cuchulain kills his son in *On Baile's Strand.*

12. In the "G" version of the Prologue (1394) to *The Legend of Good Women,* the God of Love complains of Chaucer's treatment of women in both *Troilus and Crisyede* (ca. 1385–88) and *The Romaunt of the Rose* (ca. 1370–75), a translation of part of the thirteenth-century *Roman de la Rose* by Chaucer and others (typically attributed entirely to Chaucer prior to the work of the scholar W. W. Skeat in the late 1890s).

13. Johann Christoph Friedrich von Schiller (1759–1805), German historian, poet, and dramatist.

14. Gerald Griffin (1803–40), Irish playwright, novelist, and poet; Charles Joseph Kickham (1828–82), Irish novelist, poet, and political activist.

15. James Clarke Hook (1819–1907), English genre painter and etcher, best known for his seafaring pictures.

16. *Caste* by the English playwright Thomas William Robertson (1829–71) was first produced in 1867. Yeats refers to the production at the Gaiety Theatre in Dublin on 19–21 October 1905. The leading actor, the English comedian and manager Sir John Hare (1844–1921), was absent in order to attend the funeral of the English actor Sir Henry Irving (1838–1905).

17. Martin Cosgar is a character in Padraic Colum's *The Land,* Shan Grogan in William Boyle's *The Building Fund,* Nora Burke in John Millington Synge's *The Shadow of a Glen,* Gormleith in Lady Gregory's *Kincora.*

18. Yeats refers to the French writer Jean Adrien Antoine Jules Jusserand (1855–1932). He is perhaps drawing on a passage in *The Literary History the English People,* trans. Elizabeth Lee (London: T. Fisher Unwin, 1895): "The French who were now living in England in large numbers, introduced there the taste for merry tales of trickery and funny adventures, stories of curious mishaps of all kinds; of jealous husbands, duped, beaten, and withal perfectly content, and of fit wives for such husbands. It already pleased their teasing, mocking minds, fond of generalisations, to make themselves out a vicious race, without faith, truth, or honour: it ever was a *gab* of theirs. The more one protests, the more they insist; they adduce proofs and instances; they are convinced and finally convince others" (1: 155).

19. In the "Discours de la tragédie et des moyens de la traiter selon le vraisemblable ou le nécessaire," included in *Trois discours sur le Poème dramatique* (1660), the French dramatist Pierre Corneille (1606–84) discusses why terrible crimes—particularly incest—are required for successful tragedies.

20. From "To Althea: From Prison" by the English poet Richard Lovelace (1618–58).

21. The American ethnologist and folklorist Jeremiah Curtin (1836–1906) published *Myths and Folklore of Ireland* in 1890. The "Story of the Red-haired Man's Wife" is included in Douglas Hyde's *Songs Ascribed to Raftery* (Dublin: Gill, 1903), 206–19; Hyde explains that "everybody knows the old song of the Red-haired Man's Wife. It is more than a hundred, or perhaps two hundred years old" (204–5). *Cúirt an Mheán-Oíche* (*The Midnight Court*) is a long poem written ca. 1780 by the Irish poet Brian Mac Giolla Meidhre (Brian Merriman, ?1745–1805). The *Aislinge meic Conglinne* (*The Vision of Mac Conglinne*) was composed in the twelfth century. In the *Fled Bricrenn* (*Feast of Briciu*), a tale of the Ulster cycle from the eighth century, the mischief-maker Bricriu Nemthenga (Poison-Tongue), creates dissension between three Ulster heroes, Cú Chulainn, Lóegaire Buadach, and Conall Cernach; Yeats's play *The Green Helmet* (first published in 1908 as *The Golden Helmet*) is based on this tale.

22. Yeats had studied at the Metropolitan School of Art in Dublin from May 1884 to April 1886. Yeats described John Hughes (1865–1941), later a well-known Irish sculptor, as one of "certain elder students who had authority among us" (*Au* 90).

23. The Holy Family consists of Christ, the Virgin Mary, and her husband, Joseph.

24. Stefan Lochner (?1410–51), a German painter; Yeats refers to his *Madonna of the Rose Bower* (1450).

25. Yeats refers to the penultimate paragraph of "Notes" from the 1902 *Samhain* (see p. 19).

26. In the opening paragraph of the *Satyricon* (ca. A.D. 63–65) by the Roman writer Petronius Arbiter (A.D. ?66–), Encolpius complains that "our hapless youngsters are turned into total idiots in the schools of rhetoric, because their eyes and ears are trained not on everyday issues, but on pirates in chains on the sea-shore, or on tyrants signing edicts bidding sons to decapitate their fathers, or on ocular responses in time of plague urging the sacrifice of three or more maidens. These are nothing but verbal gob-stoppers coated in honey, every word and deed sprinkled with poppy seed and sesame!"

27. The art collector and critic Sir Hugh Percy Lane (1875–1915) was a nephew of Lady Gregory. His Loan Exhibition of Modern Art opened at the Royal Hibernian Academy on 21 November 1904. Giovanni Segantini (1858–99) was an Italian painter. His technique, known as divisionism, consisted of applying strokes of unmixed pigment to the canvas, allowing the viewer at a sufficient distance to combine the colors optically.

28. Heroes of Homer's *Odyssey*, Cervantes's *Don Quixote*, and Shakespeare's *Hamlet*.

29. Yeats alludes to Keats's "Ode on a Grecian Urn" (1820) and a character in several plays by Shakespeare.

30. *The Spirit of the Nation* was a collection of mainly patriotic poems and ballads collected from *The Nation*, first published in 1843; a second part was issued in 1844 and an enlarged edition in 1845. By 1870 the collection was in its fiftieth printing.

31. Moore had been born and raised a Catholic but declared himself a Protestant in 1903.

32. In *Conservations of Goethe* (1836–48), the German writer Johann Peter Eckermann (1792–1854) recalls him saying "Schiller's *Wallenstein* is so great that there is nothing else like it of the same sort; yet you will find that even these two powerful helpers—history and philosophy—have injured parts of the work, and hinder a purely poetical success" (23 July 1827); and "I have always kept myself free from philosophy" (4 February 1829).

33. In the essay "Peace in Life and Art," first published in *Merry England* for September 1892, the English poet Coventry Patmore (1832–96) argued that "peace . . . is the common character of all true art." The essay was collected in *Religio Poetae Etc.* (London: George Bell and Sons, 1893). Yeats may have had his attention drawn to the passage by his friend the English poet and critic Arthur Symons (1865–1945), who in his "Coventry Patmore" in the *New Review* for 30 January 1897 explained that for Patmore, "peace . . . was the sign of great art" (75).

34. The quotation is untraced. In a draft of his autobiography, Yeats recalled that the English writer Lionel Pigot Johnson (1867–1902) "said, quoting I know not what Catholic saint, 'God asks nothing from even the highest soul but attention'"; and in an October 1909 entry in his journal, Yeats asked "Can one reach God by toil? He gives himself to the pure in heart. He asks nothing but attention" (*Mem* 36, 234).

35. Thomas à Kempis (?1380–1471), a German monk and writer, is traditionally credited with the authorship of the *Imitation of Christ*. Yeats has elevated him to sainthood. The quotation is untraced.

36. Tara, a hill in County Meath, is the ancient seat of the High Kings of Ireland.

37. The review in *The United Irishman* for 17 January 1905 noted that "We are glad to find that Mr. Yeats has come to recognize two truths which we pointed out—that the arts lose something of their sap when cut off from the people as a whole, and that if his theatre is to live, it must be moulded by the influences which are moulding the National life at present." Moreover, Yeats "has come to agree that what we insisted as the essential of the theatre—that it should be moulded by the influences which mould the national life—was wise and right. We trust he will come to agree with us that only by turning their backs

on London can Irishmen of letters serve as reasonably, Ireland and their own souls" (5).

38. Yeats's edition of *A Book of Irish Verse* was first published in 1895 and in a revised version in 1900, both by Methuen & Co. in London. In the Introduction to the 1895 text, Yeats noted that "Except these mystics [Charles Alexandre Weekes and AE] and Prof. Dowden at an odd moment, no Irishman living in Ireland has sung excellently of any but a theme from Irish experience, Irish history, or Irish tradition" (xxv). In 1892 Yeats was involved in a dispute with Sir Charles Gavan Duffy over control of a series of books to be called the "New Irish Library." Duffy eventually prevailed.

39. *Ideas of Good and Evil,* which includes essays dating from 1895 to 1902, was published in 1903. *The Celtic Twilight: Men and Women, Dhouls and Faeries* was published in 1893 and in an expanded edition (without the subtitle) in 1902.

40. Not exactly. Among Lady Gregory's papers in the Berg Collection at the New York Public Library is a one-page typescript fragment of this essay, numbered 13 and corresponding to the conclusion. It shows various holograph corrections and revisions. For instance, the penultimate paragraph of the typescript ended up in revised form as the second paragraph of the essay. Moreover, the last sentence of the published version is a holograph addition, and it is followed by another sentence which Yeats did not publish: "After all dictating gives one a certain vitality as of vehement speech."

 As so little pre-publication material for *Samhain* has survived, one has to wonder if Lady Gregory deliberately saved this single page of typescript so that Yeats's exaggeration could eventually be documented. . . .

Samhain: 1906—
Literature and the Living Voice

1. Unless the essay was later revised, the reference to the Dublin production of Beerbohm Tree's version of Shakespeare's *The Tempest* establishes the date of composition as no earlier than ca. 15 May 1905, nearly five months after the opening of the Abbey Theatre.

2. Yeats attended a ceremony on 26 August 1900 to unveil a memorial to Antony Raftery. As noted in the *Tuam News* for 31 August 1900, as part of the festivities Yeats "delivered a masterly ovation in support of the spread of the Irish language, and, alluding to the poet they were honouring, said that when kings and rulers would be forgotten, the memory of the poor poet would ever be alive, enshrined in the hearts of the people."

3. Yeats's text essentially follows that in Lady Gregory's *Poets and Dreamers* (Dublin: Hodges, Figgis; London: John Murray, 1903), 37.

A somewhat different version is included in Douglas Hyde's *Songs Ascribed to Raftery* (Dublin: Gill, 1903), 41.

4. Alexander Dumas *père* (1802–70), French novelist and playwright, and Sir Walter Scott (1771–1832), Scottish novelist. Both are best known for their historical fiction.

5. In occult tradition, the Smaragdine or Emerald Tablet was found on the dead body of Hermes Trismegistus (a clumsy translation of "Thoth the very great," the Egyptian god of the moon, wisdom, and learning).

6. Fiach MacHugh O'Byrne (ca. 1544–97), chief of the O'Byrnes of Wicklow, fought against the English. An O'Loughlin as his companion is untraced. The O'Loughlins (*Ó Lochainn*) were an important clan in the ancient district of Thomond (*Tuathmhumhan*), now most of County Clare and parts of County Limerick and County Tipperary. In his essay "Away," first published in the *Fortnightly Review* for April 1902, Yeats discusses "one O'Loughlin" of County Clare who was taken by the fairies every night "for seven years" (*LAR* 70). Cú Chulainn is the hero of the Ulster cycle of heroic tales. Fionn, hero of the Ossianic cycle, is described as "golden salmon of the sea, clean hawk of the air" in "Oisin's Laments" in Lady Gregory's *Gods and Fighting Men* (London: John Murray, 1904), 457.

7. The legendary English outlaw is variously placed from the twelfth to the fourteenth centuries.

8. Possibly a local saying, as it is not listed in the standard compilations of proverbs.

9. A coin worth ten shillings (50 percent of a pound).

10. The reason for the revision is unclear. Although described elsewhere in Arthurian legends, the death of Gawain is not narrated in Wolfram of Eschenbach's *Parzival*, which Yeats had cited earlier in *Samhain* as well as below in this essay. Additionally, perhaps Yeats had been reminded that although Gawain is the hero of the earliest Arthurian tales, in later versions he is treated less favorably and is eclipsed by Launcelot. The "Table" in Yeats's comment is the legendary Round Table of King Arthur.

11. In *The Nine Worthies of London* (1592), the English writer Richard Johnson (1573–?1659) chronicles the lives of nine important figures.

12. The musical *The Girl from Kay's* by the Irish born "Owen Hall" (James Davis, 1853–1907) and others, first produced in London from 11 November 1902 to 23 January 1904, was performed in Dublin on 24–29 April 1905 at the Gaiety Theatre, opposite an Abbey Theatre production of William Boyle's *The Building Fund* and the revised version of Yeats's *The King's Threshold*. Sir Herbert Beerbohm Tree (1853–1917) was an English actor and manager. His elaborate production of Shakespeare's *The Tempest,* mockingly retitled by Yeats *The Girl from Prospero's Island,* was offered at the Theatre Royal in Dublin

on 15–20 May 1905—"The entire production, with all the scenic effects, direct from His Majesty's Theatre, London," where it had been produced from 14 September 1904 to 19 January 1905.

13. The friend was Annie Horniman, the theatre the Abbey.

14. The English writer Thomas Percy (1729–1811) published a three-volume collection of *Reliques of Ancient English Poetry* in 1876.

15. In biblical tradition, the fruit of the Forbidden Tree of Knowledge in the Garden of Eden was an apple.

16. "The Dream of Eugene Aram, the Murderer" by the English poet Thomas Hood (1799–1845) was first published in *The Gem* for 1829.

17. In her essay on "Raftery" in *Poets and Dreamers,* a revised version of "The Poet Raftery" from the *Argosy* (January 1901), Lady Gregory refers to "The truths of God that he strove in his last years, as he says, 'to have written in the book of the people'" (21–22). She also recalls the tale that having performed at a wedding, Raftery "went to bed after, without them giving him a drop to drink; but he didn't mind that when they haven't got it to give" (35). However, according to the account of "The Wedding at Shlahaun Mor" in Douglas Hyde's *Songs Ascribed to Raftery,* Raftery was not in fact present at the wedding. Moreover, in the poem Raftery depicts himself as less than content: "They left Raftery the poet go to sleep without a drop" (257).

18. Yeats apparently refers to an Egyptian love song from Harris Papyrus 500 in the British Museum, later translated as "The Love-lorn Sister" by Terence Gray in *'And in the Tomb were Found . . .'* (1923):

> I am come to prepare my snare with my hands,
> My cage, and my hiding place, for all the birds of Puanit.
> They swoop upon the Black Land, laden with incense.
> The first which cometh, he shall seize my worm-bait,
> Bearing from Puanit the fragrance which he exhales,
> His claws full of sweet-smelling resins.
> My heart desires that we take them together,
> I with thee alone.

Yeats directly alluded to the poem in "The Child and the State" (1925): "I am thinking of an Egyptian poem, where there are birds flying from Arabia with spice in their claws" (*LAR* 197).

19. In "Dreams that have no Moral," first published in the expanded edition of *The Celtic Twilight* in 1902, Yeats recounts a story told by an "old man" at the end of which Bill and Jack, raised as brothers although they had different mothers, "lived happily after, and they had children by the basketful, and threw them out by the shovelful. I was passing one time myself, and they called me in and gave me a cup of tea" (*Myth* 125, 137).

20. A particularly maleficent Faery, described by Yeats as "a fool of the

forth" in "The Queen and the Fool," an essay first published as "The Fool of Faery" in *The Kensington* for June 1901 and included in the 1902 expanded edition of *Celtic Twilight* (*Myth* 112).

21. The translation by Dante Gabriel Rossetti of Villon's "Ballade des dames du temps jadis" was first published as "The Ballad of Dead Ladies," one of "Three Translations from François Villon, 1450," in his *Poems* (1870).

22. "Words and Music," *Musical News* (11 February 1905): 129. The anonymous writer was less than impressed by Yeats's experiments in speaking verse to the accompaniment of the psaltery: "Mr. Yeats is evidently an enthusiast on the results attained by Miss Farr's methods, although we gather that the critics found the effect very monotonous, which, indeed, is not surprising to learn" (130).

23. *Aucassin and Nicolette* is a thirteenth-century French courtly story, composed in alternating prose and songs. Gilbert Murray's translation of *Hippolytus* (428 B.C.) by Euripides, with Florence Farr leading the chorus, was first produced at the Lyric Theatre in London on 26 May 1904; his translation of Euripides' *The Trojan Women* (415 B.C.) was first produced at the Court Theatre in London on 11 April 1905.

24. *The Earthly Paradise* by the English writer, designer, and socialist William Morris (1834–96) was published in 1868–70. It is composed in Chaucerian meters.

The Arrow: 20 October 1906—The Season's Work

1. There were five numbers of *The Arrow,* from 20 October 1906 to 25 August 1909.

2. In Dublin, London, and Paris, respectively.

3. Adapted from "The Shepheards Wives Song" (1590) by the English writer Robert Greene (1558–92): "Ah what is love? It is a pretty thing, / As sweet unto a shepheard as a king. . . ."

The Arrow: 23 February 1907— The Controversy Over *The Playboy of the Western World*

1. Ben Jonson's *The Alchemist* was performed in 1610 and printed in 1612; his *Volpone* was performed in 1605–6 and printed in 1607.

2. John Millington Synge's *The Playboy of the Western World* opened at the Abbey Theatre on 26 January 1907 and ran until 2 February 1907. Only about eighty people were present for the second performance on 28 January 1907. The debate about the play was held at the Abbey Theatre on Monday, 4 February 1907. Even at the first performance, Christy Mahon's reference to "drifts of chosen females standing in their shifts [underclothes]" provoked considerable hiss-

ing. Many of the reviewers attacked the play as a libel upon the Irish character.

3. On 3 February 1907, the *Sunday Independent* (Dublin) noted that "After a stormy week 'The Playboy of the Western World' finished up his career for the present in the Abbey Theatre last night. He left the stage amidst quite a thunder of applause from a crowded house" (1).

4. Total receipts for the week were £55.10s.

The Arrow: 1 June 1907—On Taking *The Playboy* to London

1. During the Abbey Theatre tour of Glasgow, Birmingham, Cambridge, Oxford, and London, 11 May–15 June 1907, *The Playboy* was produced only in the latter three cities (10, 12, 14 June).

2. Young Ireland was a nationalist group established in October 1842.

3. The most prominent Young Ireland writer was the poet Thomas Osborne Davis (1814–55). In an essay in *The Bookman* for July 1895, Yeats commented that "countless ballad-writers, who combined a little of Gaelic manner with a deal of borrowed rhetoric, . . . created that interesting, unsatisfying, pathetic movement which we call in Ireland 'the poetry of Young Ireland'" (*UP1* 362).

Samhain: 1908—First Principles

1. The Abbey Theatre performed in Galway at the Galway Great Exhibition of Irish Manufactures on 16–19 September 1908. Yeats offered a lecture in connection with the performance on 18 September 1908, summarized in the *Connacht Champion* for 26 September 1908 under the headline "Hypnotised. / W. B. Yeats on Commercial Conquest. / National Theatre's Aim" (13). The paper noted that "The production of the Irish plays was a great success, and at each performance hundreds had to be turned away."

2. Count Florimond de Basterot (1836–1904); his house was at Duras, a promontory in County Clare. Quotation not traced.

3. In Balzac's *Un grand homme de province à Paris* (*A Distinguished Provincial at Paris,* 1839), Étienne Lousteau tells Lucien de Rubempré that "Actresses will pay you likewise for praise, but the wiser among them pay for criticism. To be passed over in silence is what they dread the most; and the very best thing of all, from their point of view, is criticism which draws down a reply; it is far more effectual than bald praise, forgotten as soon as read, and it costs more in consequence. Celebrity, my dear fellow, is based upon controversy."

4. Utilitarianism, developed primarily by the English theologian William Paley (1743–1805) and the English philosopher Jeremy Bentham (1748–1832), argued that any act should produce the greatest happiness for the greatest number of people.

5. Thomas Babington Macaulay (1800–1859), English historian and poet.

6. Yeats had offered the motion to establish a National Literary Society at a public meeting on 9 June 1892. Katharine Tynan (1861–1931) was an Irish poet and novelist. The essay by Lionel Johnson was included in *Poetry and Ireland: Essays by W. B. Yeats and Lionel Johnson* (Churchtown, Dundrum: Cuala Press, 1908).

7. James Clarence Mangan (1803–49), Irish poet.

8. The most prominent Young Ireland writer was Thomas Osborne Davis. In an essay in *The Bookman* for July 1895, Yeats commented that "countless ballad-writers, who combined a little of Gaelic manner with a deal of borrowed rhetoric, . . . created that interesting, unsatisfying, pathetic movement which we call in Ireland 'the poetry of Young Ireland'" (*UP*1 362). The Irish novelist Maria Edgeworth (1767–1849) published *Castle Rackrent* in 1800.

9. John Millington Synge's *The Playboy of the Western World*; Charles Joseph Kickham (1828–82), Irish novelist; Michael Banim (1796–1874), Irish novelist; John Banim (1798–1842), Irish novelist and playwright; Anne Radcliffe (1764–1823), English novelist; Gerald Griffin (1803–40), Irish novelist and playwright; William Carleton (1794–1869), Irish novelist.

10. Charles Lever (1806–72), Irish novelist. The Greek philosopher Socrates (?470–?399 B.C.) stressed the importance of self-knowledge.

11. With the assistance of Lady Gregory, Yeats began collecting folklore in the summer of 1897.

12. The aphorism is untraced. Both the Scottish writer Thomas Carlyle (1795–1881) and the American writer Ralph Waldo Emerson (1803–82) argued that history is essentially biography. The French sense of *posé* suggests seriousness and gravity.

13. From the second entry in *The Maxims and Reflections of Goethe,* translated by Bailey Saunders (New York and London: Macmillan, 1893): "How can a man come to know himself? Never by thinking, but by doing" (59).

14. The Flemish painters Hubert van Eyck (?1370–1426) and Jan van Eyck (?1390–1441).

15. In "Il conte di Carmagnola. Tragedia di Alessandro Mazoni. Milano," first published in *Über Kunst und Altertum* (September 1820), Goethe stated that "for the poet no person is historical, it is his pleasure to create his moral world and for this purpose he renders to certain persons in history the honour of lending their names to his creations."

16. The German theosophist and mystic Jacob Boehme (1575–1624) experienced a religious epiphany in 1600 when a ray of sunlight reflected into a pewter dish produced an ecstatic vision of Godhead penetrating all existence.

17. The Italian artist Antonio Mancini (1852–1930) had painted Yeats's portrait in 1907. Yeats had been photographed by the Dublin photographer James Lafayette (James Stack Lauder, 1853–1923) in 1894 and ca. 1899 (and would be again in 1924).

18. Presumably *Das moderne Drama* (1852) by the German literary historian Herman Hettner (1821–82), a short book which was an important influence on Ibsen.

19. In Balzac's *Les Comédiens sans le savoir* (*The Unconscious Mummers*, 1846), the artist Dubourdieu has been "driven crazy" by the ideas of the French philosopher and socialist Charles Fourier (1772–1837); he describes his painting (not a statue) of an "allegorical figure of Harmony" with six breasts and, at her feet, "an enormous Savoy cabbage, the Master's symbol of Concord" (Savoy is a region in France). Bixiou suggests that "When every one is converted to our doctrine, you will be the foremost man in your art, for the ideas which you put into your work will be comprehensible to all—when they are common property. In fifty years' time you will be for the world at large what you are now for us—a great man. It is only a question of holding out till then." However, Léon de Lora objects that "while opinions cannot give talent, they inevitably spoil it. . . . An artist's opinion ought to be a faith in works; and his one way to success is to work while Nature gives him the sacred fire."

20. Presumably the Irish actor J. Dudley Digges (1874–1947), who played the Wise Man in the first production of *The Hour-Glass* on 14 March 1903, although he and several others resigned from the Irish National Theatre Society in protest over the production of John Millington Synge's *In the Shadow of a Glen* on 8 October 1903.

21. Two-thirds of Rome burned in July 64 while the Emperor Nero (37–68) was in Antium, according to legend playing on his violin.

22. Yeats refers to his *Cathleen ni Houlihan* and two plays by Lady Gregory.

23. The potential donor's confusion is understandable, as the National Literary Society had agreed to sponsor the Irish Literary Theatre at a meeting on 16 January 1899. The Irish Literary Theatre was superseded by the Irish National Theatre Society on 1 February 1903.

24. *La Comédie humaine* (*The Human Comedy*) was the title given by Balzac to his collected stories and novels, published from 1842 to 1846 with a supplementary volume in 1847. In the Preface (1842), Balzac argued that since he was attempting to portray all of society, it was inevitable that "some part of the fresco represented a guilty couple."

25. At the end of Yeats's *Cathleen ni Houlihan*, Michael Gillane leaves to join the 1798 Rising against the British. In Lady Gregory's *Dervorgilla*, the title character's love for Diarmuid results in the Norman invasion of Ireland. Patrick Sarsfield (d. 1693), who fought against the English, is a major character in Lady Gregory's *The White Cockade*.

In "L'Épicier" ("The Grocer"), which Yeats could have read in *Pictures of the French: A Series of Literary and Graphic Delineations of French Character by Jules Janin, Balzac, Cormenin, and Other Celebrated French Authors* (London: W. S. Orr, 1840), Balzac explained that ". . . the Grocer's wife is virtuous. Rarely does conjugal unfaithfulness afflict him. His lady has neither will to betray him, nor occasion . . ."; and that ". . . true it is, that the Grocer's lady is faithful, and that nowhere is Hymen more honoured than by those of her class" (13). "L'Épicier," first published in *La Silhouette* for 22 April 1830, was significantly revised and expanded for *Les Français peints par eux-mêmes* (1840) and eventually collected in Balzac's *La Femme de soixante ans* (1846–47).

26. The Abbey Theatre presented a special matinée performance on 4 September 1908 for the British Association for the Advancement of Science, which was meeting in Dublin. Yeats's speech was published in a special Program on 8 September 1908; the final two paragraphs are included here.

27. In the Bible, Adam, the first man, numbers and names the creatures in the Garden of Eden.

28. In Lady Gregory's *Gods and Fighting Men* (London: John Murray, 1904), Oscar declares that "The best music is the striking of swords in a battle" (312).

A People's Theatre: A Letter to Lady Gregory

1. *Le Théâtre du peuple* (1903) by the French writer Romain Rolland (1866–1944) was translated by Barrett H. Clark as *The People's Theatre* (London: G. Allen Unwin, 1919). "A People's Theatre" was first published in *The Irish Statesman* for 29 November 1919 (1.23: 547–49) and 6 December 1919 (1.24: 572–73).

2. *The Daily Mirror* was a London newspaper. The "Red Terror" refers to the series of mass executions by the Russian government which began in the summer of 1918.

3. Emanuel Swedenborg (1688–1772) was a Swedish scientist, mystic, and religious writer. See especially *The Delights of Wisdom Pertaining to Conjugal Love; After which follow the Pleasures of insanity relating to Scortatory Love* (1768), translated A. H. Searle (1876), revised by R. L. Tafel (1891) (London: Swedenborg Society, 1891) 73–75, 320–21. A year earlier, in *Per Amica Silentia Lunae* (1918), Yeats noted that the dead "make love in that union which Swedenborg has said is of the whole body and seems from far off an incandescence" (*LE* 25).

4. Untraced.

5. Rosencrantz and Guildenstern are characters in Shakespeare's *Hamlet* (performed 1602, printed 1603 and later).

6. The German philosopher Friedrich Wilhelm Nietzsche (1844–1900) formulated the concept of *ewige Wiederkehr* ("eternal recurrence"), in which all life is understood as a continual pattern of birth and decay.

7. From "St. Luke the Painter," part of the sonnet sequence "The House of Life" by Dante Gabriel Rossetti.

8. The National Schools educated primarily the lower and working classes.

9. John Galsworthy (1867–1933), English writer.

10. Untraced. Possibly the Irish writer and critic St. John Ervine (1883–1971) who had considerable conflicts with the Company during his brief tenure as Manager of the Abbey Theatre in 1915–16.

11. The role of Maurya in the first production of John Millington Synge's *Riders to the Sea* on 25 February 1904 was played by the Irish actress "Honor Lavelle" (Helen S. Laird, 1874–1957); she left the Abbey Theatre late in 1905. The play is set on the Aran Islands.

12. Yeats refers to Book I, chapter three, of Dante's *Il Convito* (*The Banquet*), an unfinished philosophical work written 1304–8. The *Confessions* of St. Augustine of Hippo (354–430) date from ca. 400.

13. Although Yeats often referred to Dante's description of a "perfectly proportioned human body," the precise phrase has not been traced. Several passages in *Il Convito,* however, suggest the concept (see *LE* 382n22).

14. In chapter VI of *Smoke* (1867) by the Russian novelist Ivan Sergeevich Turgenev (1818–83), Litvinov "was struck by a strong, very agreeable, and familiar fragrance, and saw in the window a great bunch of fresh heliotrope in a glass of water. Litvinov bent over them not without amazement, touched them, and smelt them. . . . Something seemed to stir in his memory, something very remote . . . but what, precisely, he could not discover" (ellipses in text). The flowers had been sent by his former beloved, Irina, to whom he had given a bouquet of heliotrope during their courtship some years earlier.

   In Greek mythology, Paris is married to Helen, Peleus to Thetis.

15. In *The Poetry of Robert Burns,* edited by the English writer and critic Ernest William Henley (1849–1903) and Thomas F. Henderson (Edinburgh: T. C. and E. C. Jack, 1897), it is argued that Burns "was the last of a school. It culminated in him, because he had more genius, and genius of a finer, a rarer, and a more generous quality, than all his immediate ancestors put together. But he cannot be fairly said to have contributed anything to it except himself." Burns is contrasted with Keats, Shelley, and Byron, "new men all, and founders of dynasties" (4: 271). Henry Wadsworth Longfellow (1807–82) was an American poet.

16. Yeats refers to the Prologue to the anonymous psuedo-Chaucerian *Tale of Beryn* (15th/16th century), in which the Pardoner and the Miller,

"countirfeting gentlimen," comment on the stained glass windows in a church.

17. Plutarch (?46–120), Greek biographer and essayist, best known for his *Parallel Lives.*

18. Spiddal is a village in northwestern Galway. Yeats noted in an 1898 essay that there "the most talk nothing but Gaelic" (*UP2* 74).

19. "The Grief of a Girl's Heart" is included in "West Irish Ballads" in Lady Gregory's *Poets and Dreamers* (Dublin: Hodges Figgis; London: John Murray, 1903), 64–65.

20. Yeats seems to have invented this particular genre of Elizabethan poetry, perhaps working backwards from John Taylor (?1578–1653), "the water poet," who had been a Thames waterman. *All the Workes of John Taylor, the Water Poet,* was published in 1630.

21. Yeats refers to Dante's canzone entitled "Donne, ch'avete intelletto d'amore" ("Women, you who have an understanding of love"), which describes the principle of the "cor gentile" ("noble heart"). Yeats probably read the poem in the form in Dante's *Vita Nuova* (ca. 1292).

22. Yeats refers to the attacks upon John Millington Synge's *The Playboy of the Western World* at its first production at the Abbey Theatre, 26 January–2 February 1907.

23. Yeats was now experimenting with plays based on the Japanese Noh drama. Noh means "Accomplishment." Yeats wrote the introduction to *Certain Noble Plays of Japan: From the Manuscripts of Ernest Fenollosa, Chosen and Finished by Ezra Pound* (Churchtown, Dundrum: Cuala Press, 1916). The essay was also published in *Drama* for November 1916 and was included in the expanded edition of *The Cutting of an Agate* (London: Macmillan, 1919).

24. Edmund Dulac (1882–1953) was an English artist and musician; Walter Morse Rummel (1887–1953) was an American musician.

25. William Blake's *The Book of Thel* dates from 1789.

26. Yeats refers to Molière's *Le Misanthrope* (1666), 1.1, in which the courtier Alceste complains to his friend Philinte "I have seen and suffered too much. Court and city alive provoke me to fury. It fills me with depression—reduces me to utter despair to see men living as they do. I meet with nothing but base flattery, injustice, selfishness, treachery, villainy everywhere."

27. Fedor Ivanovich Chaliapin (1873–1938), Russian bass singer.

28. *At the Hawk's Well* was produced privately in Lady Cunard's drawing room in London on 2 April 1916; the Young Man was played by the English actor Henry Hinchliffe Ainley (1879–1945). The rehearsal at which the American writer Ezra Pound (1885–1972) substituted has not been traced.

29. Sir Henry Irving (1838–1905), English actor; Tommaso Salvini (1830–1915), Italian actor. Both were renowned for their performances in Shakespeare's plays.

30. After the Treaty of Limerick in 1691, many of the leaders (and soldiers) who had fought against the English left for the Continent, especially France, Spain, and Austria.

31. Gabriele D'Annunzio (1863–1938), Italian writer.

32. Henry Fielding (1707–54), English novelist and dramatist; Daniel
Defoe (1660–1731), English writer; Count Lev Nikolaevich Tolstoy
(1828–1910), Russian writer; Fyodor Mikhailovich Dostoevsky
(1821–81), Russian writer.

33. Blake did not say this. Yeats is most likely extrapolating from the
doctrines of contraries expressed in *The Marriage of Heaven and
Hell* (1790–93): "Without contraries is no progression. Attraction
and Repulsion, Reason and Energy, Love and Hate, are necessary to
Human existence."

34. Yeats refers to his "The Phases of the Moon" and "The Double
Vision of Michael Robartes," both first published in the expanded edition of *The Wild Swans at Coole* (London: Macmillan, 1919). In the
Introduction to *A Vision* (London: privately printed by T. Werner Laurie, 1925; issued to subscribers 15 January 1926), Owen Aherne and
Michael Robartes, two characters from Yeats's early fiction, discuss
the discovery by Robartes of many of the doctrines expounded in the
book. Aherne notes that on a "walking tour in Connaught" with
Robartes, "words were spoken between us slightly resembling those
in the 'The Phases of the Moon' . . ." (xx–xxi).

35. In *A Vision,* Yeats uses the figure of the gyres, a set of two interlock-
ing cones, to symbolize the inherent tension between opposites on
which reality is based.

36. "The Double Vision of Michael Robartes," ll. 9–16 (*P* 172).

[Preface] in *The Collected Works in Verse and Prose* (1908)

1. Printed without title and in italics (except for "1908") opposite the
first page of *Samhain: 1901,* in volume IV of *The Collected Works
in Verse and Prose* (Stratford-on-Avon: Shakespeare Head Press,
1908).

2. Although the revisions were minor in comparison to Yeats's usual
practice, there were significant changes, including the omission of various sections as well as the inclusion of two essays from *The United
Irishman* and several footnotes. Yeats also does not mention that some
of the material was taken from *The Arrow.* In addition, there were
some verbal changes (see pp. 213–14).

3. *Samhain* was published each year from 1901 to 1906. The final regular *Samhain,* published in November 1908, appeared too late for
inclusion in *The Collected Works in Verse and Prose.*

Preface to *Plays and Controversies* (1923)

1. The Preface was printed before the Contents of the volume. The plays were *The Countess Cathleen,* first published in *The Countess Kathleen and Various Legends and Lyrics* (London: T. Fisher Unwin, 1892), though since much revised; *The Land of Heart's Desire,* first published in *The Land of Heart's Desire* (London: T. Fisher Unwin, 1894); *At the Hawk's Well,* first published in *Harper's Bazaar* (March 1917); *The Only Jealousy of Emer* and *The Dreaming of the Bones,* first published in *Two Plays for Dancers* (Dundrum: Cuala Press, 1919); and *Calvary,* first published in *Four Plays for Dancers* (London: Macmillan, 1921).

2. Dáil Éireann, the representative assembly of Ireland. The campaign by the Abbey Theatre for government support eventually resulted in an endowment of £850, announced by Yeats from the stage on 8 August 1925.

3. Lady Gregory, *Our Irish Theatre: A Chapter of Autobiography* (New York and London, G. P. Putnam's Sons, 1913).

Note in *Mythologies* (Edition de Luxe proofs, 1931–32)

1. The 1931 Edition de Luxe page proofs of *Mythologies* end with two "Notes." The first, extracted from the "Notes" in *Early Poems and Stories* (London: Macmillan, 1925), concerns the prose fiction with which the volume began: *The Celtic Twilight,* first published as *The Celtic Twilight: Men and Women, Dhouls and Faeries* (London: Lawrence and Bullen, 1893), and revised and expanded as *The Celtic Twilight* (London: A. H. Bullen, 1902); *The Secret Rose* (London: Lawrence and Bullen, 1897); *The Tables of the Law* [and] *The Adoration of the Magi* (London: privately printed, 1897); and *Stories of Red Hanrahan,* included in *The Secret Rose* but substantially revised with Lady Gregory's assistance as *Stories of Red Hanrahan* (Dundrum: Dun Emer Press, 1904). After some white space, Yeats supplied this commentary on *The Irish Dramatic Movement.* Yeats is incorrect in stating that any material from *Beltaine* (1899–1900) is included. He also does not mention the inclusion in this version of *The Irish Dramatic Movement* of either the two letters from *The United Irishman* (done for the 1908 *Collected Works*) or "A People's Theatre: A Letter to Lady Gregory," first published in *The Irish Statesman,* 29 November and 6 December 1920, and included in *Plays and Controversies* (London: Macmillan, 1923).

In *Explorations* (London: Macmillan, 1962), Yeats's remarks were printed as a "Note" opposite the first page of *Samhain: 1901.* However, the reference to "this volume" was incorrectly glossed as *Plays and Controversies.*

2. The "irascible friend" was perhaps the American writer Ezra Pound (1885–1972); Yeats had recently referred to Pound's "irascible mind" in *A Packet for Ezra Pound* (Dublin: Cuala Press, 1929).

Beltaine: May 1899—Plans and Methods

1. This issue of *Beltaine* included C. H. Herford's "The Scandinavian Dramatists" (14–19), reprinted from the Dublin *Daily Express*. Herford argued that "Norway has led the way among the nations in acquiring possession of a living drama of classical rank as literature, for which the barriers of language and race have ceased to exist" (14).
    The first two paragraphs of "Plans and Methods" are revised from the beginning of "The Irish Literary Theatre," published in the Dublin *Daily Express* for 14 January 1899.
2. In addition to Ibsen and Maeterlinck, Yeats refers to the German playwright Gerhart Hauptmann (1862–1946), and the Spanish playwright José Echegaray y Eizaguirre (1832–1916).
3. The Théâtre Libre, founded in Paris in 1877 by André Antoine, was the model for the Independent Theatre, founded in London in 1891 by J. T. Grein (1862–1935).
4. Edward Walsh (1805–50) was the editor of *Reliques of Irish Jacobite Poetry* (1844) and *Irish Popular Songs* (1850).
5. The translation from Calderón (1600–1681) by the Irish journalist and writer Denis Florence MacCarthy (1817–82) was not produced by the Irish Literary Theatre.
6. Fiona Macleod was the pseudonym of the Scottish writer William Sharp (1856–1905); none of his plays was produced by the Irish Literary Theatre. Nor was *Hugh Roe O'Donnell* by Standish James O'Grady.
7. Yeats refers to Martyn's *The Heather Field*.
8. Yeats's play was *The Countess Cathleen*.
9. Yeats included in this issue of *Beltaine* two lyrics from *The Countess Cathleen*, "Impetuous heart, be still, be still" and "Who will go drive with Fergus now" (13). The first had been published as "The Lover to his Heart" in the special Christmas number of *The Social Review* (Dublin) for 7 December 1894. The latter was eventually published as a separate poem, "Who goes with Fergus?", beginning in the 1912 edition of *Poems* (*P* 543, 39).
10. This issue of *Beltaine* included "The Countess Cathleen" (10–11) by Lionel Johnson. Johnson noted that "the date of its story is the later part of the sixteenth century" (10), which is in accord with the stage direction in the 1892 text: *"The Scene is laid in Ireland in the Sixteenth Century."* However, in a note to the 1895 edition Yeats explained that he had mistakenly believed that the story on which the play was based "was indigenous Irish folklore; he has since heard that it is of recent

origin." The stage direction was thus revised to *"The Scene is laid in Ireland and in old times"* (*VPl* 3, 4, 178).

11. Calderón wrote a substantial number of *autos sacramentales*, sacred allegorical dramas on the Eucharist.

12. "The Abdication of Fergus Mac Roy," in *Lays of the Western Gael and Other Poems* (London: Bell and Daldy, 1864) by the Irish writer Sir Samuel Ferguson (1810–86).

13. Most of these identifications follow those in the "Glossary" in *Poems* (1895), which included *The Countess Cathleen*. Lilith is a demon in Jewish tradition.

Beltaine: May 1899—The Theatre

1. This essay was reprinted with slight revisions from *The Dome* for April 1899. With some further revision, it became part I of "The Theatre" in *Ideas of Good and Evil* (London: A. H. Bullen, 1903).

2. The Irish physician, writer, and scholar John Todhunter (1839–1916) was a neighbor of the Yeats family when they lived in Bedford Park in London. Todhunter's *A Sicilian Idyll* was first produced at the Bedford Park Social Club on 5 May 1890. Yeats favorably reviewed the play in several publications. *A Sicilian Idyll* was then produced at St. George's Hall in London on 1 July 1890 and, along with Todhunter's *The Poison Flower,* at the Vaudeville Theatre in the Strand in London on 15 July 1890. Yeats reviewed the later production favorably as well. In a letter to *The Fortnightly Review* for July 1923, Mrs. Todhunter denied that Yeats had any role in the production of *A Sicilian Idyll:* "There is no truth in Mr. Yeats's statement that he caused Dr. Todhunter to produce the latter's *Sicilian Idyll;* the play was written and produced without any intervention on his part, though he no doubt took an interest in the production, as several of the players were personally known to him" (163).

3. In addition to Dante Gabriel Rossetti and Ibsen, Yeats refers to the French sculptor Auguste Rodin (1840–1917).

4. "Mr. Bridges' 'Prometheus' and Poetic Drama" by the English poet and art critic Laurence Binyon (1869–1943), published in *The Dome* for March 1899: "the manager who bars" should be "the managers who bar" (203).

5. The poems are mentioned by Lady Gregory in *Poets and Dreamers* (Dublin: Hodges Figgis; London: John Murray, 1903), 48–49: "Another song I have heard was a lament over a boy and girl who had run away to America, and on the way the ship went down. And when they were going down, they began to be sorry they were not married; and to say that if the priest had been at home when they went away, they would have been married; but they hoped that when they were drowned, it would be the same with them as if they were married. And

I heard another lament that had been made for three boys that had lately been drowned in Galway Bay. It is the mother who is making it; and she tells how she lost her husband the father of her three boys. And then she married again, and they went to sea and were drowned; and she wouldn't mind about the others so much, but it is the eldest boy, Peter, she is grieving for. And I have heard one song that had a great many verses, and was about 'a poet that is dying, and he confessing his sins.'"

Oisín, the poet-hero of the Fionn cycle of Irish tales, is lured by Niamh to Tír na nÓg (Land of Youth) and stays there for several hundred years.

6. *The Return of Ulysses* by the English poet Robert Bridges (1844–1930) was published in 1890. Yeats wrote about it at length in "Mr. Robert Bridges," published in *The Bookman* for June 1897 and reprinted as *"The Return of Ulysses"* in *Ideas of Good and Evil.*

7. From William Blake's *A Vision of the Last Judgment* (1810): "The Nature of my Work is Visionary or Imaginative it is an Endeavour to Restore what the Ancients called the Golden Age."

8. *Locrine* (1887) by the English poet Charles Algernon Swinburne (1837–1909) was first produced by the Elizabethan Stage Society at St. George's Hall in London on 20 March 1899.

9. Yeats refers to part of a chorus in Sophocles' *Oedipus at Colonus* ("Come praise Colonus's horses, and come praise / The wine-dark of the wood's intricacies" in his 1934 translation) and to Shakespeare's *Macbeth* (performed 1606, printed 1623), 1.6.8, although the speaker is not Duncan but Banquo (speaking to Duncan) and "the pendent" should be "his pendent."

10. Ford Madox Brown (1821–93), English painter.

11. In footnotes added to this essay when *Ideas of Good and Evil* was reprinted in *Essays* (London: Macmillan, 1924), Yeats noted that "I had Charles Ricketts in mind" as the painter and identified the orator as John Francis Taylor.

Beltaine: February 1900—Plans and Methods

1. Blake did not say this directly, but he discusses the concept of "States" often in his work, as in *Milton* (ca. 1809–1810): "Distinguish therefore States from Individuals in those States. / States Change: but Individual Identities never change nor cease . . . ."

2. Both the Irish historian W. E. H. Lecky (1838–1903) and the agricultural leader Sir Horace Plunkett (1854–1932) were Unionists.

3. This passage from the Irish poet William Allingham (1824–89) is untraced. In "Popular Ballad Poetry of Ireland," first published in the *Leisure Hour* for November 1889, Yeats introduced the same quotation by claiming that "An Irish poet was to write on his title-page

later on [after 1845]: . . ." (*UP*1 152). In *A Descriptive Catalog of Yeats's Library* (New York and London: Garland, 1985), Edward O'Shea notes that the inside front cover of Yeats's copy of Thomas D'Arcy McGee's *A Memoir of the Life and Conquests of Art Mac-Murrogh,* 2nd edition (Dublin: James Duffy, [1886]), has the same passage inscribed, assigned to "Allingham" and "followed by a brief entry deleted" (160; item 1187). There are other inscriptions relating to Irish materials on the back flyleaf and the inside back cover. O'Shea speculates that all the inscriptions are "possibly early WBY." If so, then Yeats may have copied the passage from an inscription in one of Allingham's personal copies of his work. I have been unable to verify O'Shea's speculation about the handwriting.

4. Debates between the hero Oisín and St. Patrick about Christianity are common in the Fionn cycle of Irish tales.

5. Yeats refers to *The Last Feast of the Fianna* by the Irish writer Alice Milligan (1866–1953).

6. Yeats refers to *Maeve* by Edward Martyn and to *The Bending of the Bough,* a revision by George Moore, with some assistance by Yeats, of Martyn's *The Tale of the Town.* Alfred T. Nutt (1856–1910) was an English publisher, folklorist, and Celtic scholar.

7. Ernest Renan (1823–92) was a French philosopher and historian. Yeats discussed his views on the Celtic race in "The Celtic Element in Literature," first published in *Cosmopolis* for June 1898 and included in *Ideas of Good and Evil* (London: A. H. Bullen, 1903).

8. Presumably a reference to the plays projected for 1900 in the May 1899 *Beltaine,* none of which were produced.

9. No further plays by Martyn were produced by the Irish Literary Theatre; his next work to be performed was *An Enchanted Sea* (1902), produced by the Players Club on 18 April 1904. George Bernard Shaw eventually wrote *John Bull's Other Island* in 1904, but it was not accepted for production at the Abbey Theatre. It was produced at the Royal Court Theatre in London on 1 November 1904. The collaboration between Yeats and George Moore on *Diarmuid and Grania* (produced 21 October 1901; published 1951) was not without contention.

10. Yeats had finished a revised version of *The Shadowy Waters* in early January 1900; it was published in the *North American Review* for May 1900 but not produced by the Irish National Theatre Society until 14 January 1904.

11. This issue of *Beltaine* included "Is the Theatre a Place of Amusement?"(7–10) by Moore and "A Comparison between Irish and English Theatrical Audiences" (11–13) by Martyn. Moore argued that "Artistic intelligence has dwindled in the last twenty years in England . . ." and that the English theatre has "declined to the level of a mere amusement" (8–9). Martyn claimed that "the great drama of

England has given place to brutish and imbecile parade . . ." and that England was a "rank garden" (12).

12. From Shelley's *The Defence of Poetry* (written 1821, published 1840).
13. In addition to John Ruskin, William Morris, and Matthew Arnold, Yeats refers to the Scottish writer Thomas Carlyle (1795–1881).
14. At the conclusion of his speech to the Irish Parliament on 14 February 1788 urging the commutation of tithes, the Irish politician Henry Grattan (1746–1820) praised the Irish people, noting "those principles not only of justice, but of fire, which I have observed to exist in your composition" and "those warm susceptible properties which abound in your mind, and qualify you for legislation." *The Speeches of the Rt. Hon Henry Grattan,* ed. D. O. Madden (Dublin, 1845), 141.

Beltaine: February 1900—*Maeve,* and certain Irish Beliefs

1. In Martyn's *Maeve,* Peg Inerny is an incarnation of Medb (Maeve), a legendary queen of Connacht.
2. Yeats describes Biddy Early (1798–1874) at length in "Ireland Bewitched," published in *The Contemporary Review* for September 1899 (*UP1* 167–83).
3. Yeats offered a revised version of this anecdote in his essay "Away," published in *The Fortnightly Review* for April 1902 (*LAR* 67–68). The friend is Lady Gregory; Cruachmaa is a hill in County Galway; Isabella Wood is in Coole Park.
4. The "old Gaelic poet" is untraced.
5. A somewhat different translation of this poem is included in the "Midhir and Etain" chapter in Lady Gregory's *Gods and Fighting Men* (London: John Murray, 1904), 96.
6. A character in Shakespeare's *A Midsummer Night's Dream* (printed 1600 and 1619).
7. Yeats refers to "The Literary Movement in Ireland," first published in the *North American Review* for February 1899 and in revised form in *Ideals in Ireland,* edited by Lady Gregory (London: at the Unicorn, 1901). The rest of the *Beltaine* essay follows the 1899 text closely, although the closing allusion to Blake is new. The episode is also recounted in "'And Fair Fierce Women,'" a story added to the revised edition of *The Celtic Twilight* (London: A. H. Bullen, 1902). In *The Trembling of the Veil* (London: privately printed by T. Werner Laurie, 1922), Yeats ascribes this vision to Mary Battle (d. ca. 1907), a servant of his uncle George Pollexfen (1839–1910).
8. *Maeve* opens with Finola *"reading from an old book"*:

> Every hill which is at this Oneach
> Hath under it heroes and queens,

> And poets and distributors,
> And fair fierce women.

The quotation is from a poem on the death of Dathi in *The Book of the Dun Cow,* an eleventh-century manuscript collection. Martyn would have found a translation by John O'Donovan in George Petrie's "The Ecclesiastical Architecture of Ireland, Anterior to the Norman Invasion, Comprising an Essay on the Origin and Uses of the Round Towers of Ireland," *Transactions of the Royal Irish Academy* 20 (1845): 104–5. Yeats entitled one of the stories added to the 1902 *The Celtic Twilight* "'And Fair, Fierce Women.'"

9. The "present queen" is Victoria (1819–1901), queen of England since 1837.

10. In his *Descriptive Catalogue* (1809), William Blake argued that "The face and limbs that deviates or alters least, from infancy to old age, is the face and limbs of greatest Beauty and perfection."

Beltaine: February 1900—
[Note] to Alice Milligan's "The Last Feast of the Fianna"

1. In her essay "The Last Feast of the Fianna" in *Beltaine* (18–21), Alice Milligan noted that "I understand that Mr. W. B. Yeats has explained my little play as having some spiritual and mystical meaning, but to tell the truth I simply wrote it on thinking out this problem. How did Oisin endure to live in the house with Grania as a stepmother after all that had happened?" (20–21). Milligan is probably referring to Yeats's comment on *The Last Feast of the Fianna* in "The Irish Literary Theatre, 1900," published in *The Dome* for January 1900 and reprinted slightly revised in this issue of *Beltaine*—that the play "would make one remember the mortality and indignity of all that lives" (24). Yeats placed an asterisk after "mystical meaning" and added his commentary at the foot of the page.

Beltaine: February 1900—The Irish Literary Theatre, 1900

1. This essay was reprinted with slight revisions from *The Dome* for January 1900. The first paragraph from "Dionysius the Areopagite" to the end later became part II of "The Theatre" in *Ideas of Good and Evil* (London: A. H. Bullen, 1903). Part I of the 1903 essay had first been published as "The Theatre" in *The Dome* for April 1899 and had been reprinted in the May 1899 issue of *Beltaine* (20–23).

In "Is the Theatre a Place of Amusement?" printed in this issue of *Beltaine,* George Moore had argued that "The essence of the whole matter lies in the fact that the humour of the London theatrical public is an avid desire of amusement; and as the theatre relies on the

humour of the London public, it has necessarily declined to the level
of a mere amusement; to the level of a circus, a fair, a racecourse,"
thus providing the opportunity to make "Dublin an intellectual centre" (9). Moore had also criticized the current state of the English theatre in his Preface to *The Bending of the Bough*.

2. In biblical tradition, after their exile from Egypt the Jewish people wander for several months in the wilderness before arriving at the sacred
mountain of Sinai, on which Moses receives the Ten Commandments from God.

3. Dionysus the Areopagite was supposedly an Athenian converted to
Christianity at Athens by St. Paul. The works ascribed to him,
including *The Celestial Hierarchy*, the source of Yeats's quotation,
almost surely date from the early sixth century A.D. Yeats first
learned of this phrase from Charles Johnston (1867–1931), a fellow
student at the Erasmus Smith High School in Dublin, although in *A
Vision* (1937) he claims that Lionel Johnson "was fond of quoting from
Dionysius the Areopagite, 'He has set the borders of his nations
according to his angels. . . .'"

4. Yeats is perhaps recalling an anecdote about the Greek playwright
Euripides (ca. 485–406 B. C.) by the Roman writer Lucius Annaeus
Seneca (ca. 4 B.C.–A.D. 65) in his *Letter to Lucilius:* "When these
last verses had been uttered in a tragedy of Euripides, the whole people arose with one accord to throw out both the actor and the play
until Euripides himself leapt into the middle of the stage begging
them to wait and see what kind of end the admirer of money would
come to."

5. From Blake's *Milton* (ca. 1809–10): "Every Time less than a pulsation
of the artery / Is equal in its period & value to Six Thousand Years. /
For in this Period the Poets Work is Done: and all the Great / Events
of Time start forth & are conceived in such a Period / Within a
Moment: a Pulsation of the Artery."

6. In Shakespeare's *The Winter's Tale* (performed 1611, published 1623),
the infant Perdita is abandoned on the sea coast of Bohemia.

*Beltaine: April 1900—The Last Feast of the Fianna, Maeve, and The
Bending of the Bough, in Dublin*

1. Untraced.

2. The play by Alice Milligan was *The Last Feast of the Fianna. The
Bending of the Bough* was a revision by George Moore, with some
assistance by Yeats, of Martyn's *The Tale of the Town*.

3. Slight misquotations of speeches by Jaspar Dean in act 4, Arabella
in act 5, and again Jaspar Dean in act 4.

4. In "The Irish Literary Theatre" in the *Irish Times* for 21 February
1900, the reviewer complained of Moore's play that "story there is

none, plot there is none. Of dull, dry, insipid, unnatural, wretchedly commonplace conversation there is an immensity . . . (6).

5. The *Irish Daily Independent* reviewed the play in "Irish Literary Theatre: George Moore's Brilliant Play," in the issue for 21 February 1900. Yeats's quotation is accurate (5). In the issue for 22 February 1900, the *Irish Daily Independent* published a general account of the Irish Literary Theatre, entitled "The Literary Theatre" (4). Yeats's quotation is not present. Although the article offered a very favorable assessment of the movement, it was not quite as optimistic as Yeats suggests: ". . . though no Shakespeare has yet arisen to give Ireland drama which takes admiration captive, there is hope that out of the new literary movement there may come dramatic seed which, like the small grain in the parable, shall grow until it spring into the greatest tree in the forest of pure literature" (4).

6. *The Times* (London) review of *The Last Feast of the Fianna* and *Maeve* noted that "There was a crowded house, and the plays were enthusiastically received" (20 February 1900: 7). Yeats is quoting from "Mr. George Moore's New Play," *The Observer* (London), 25 February 1900: 6. It is possible that both notices were by the same individual. *The Times* noted that "It is doubtful, however, whether the play will appeal to an audience which is unfamiliar with the sources of its inspiration," and *The Observer* commented that ". . . I rather question whether it would be appreciated in London. . . ."

Samhain: 1901—*from* Windlestraws

1. Yeats refers to the ellipses in the preceding section (see p. 9).
2. Both the text of Douglas Hyde's *Casadh an tSúgáin* (*The Twisting of the Rope*) and an English translation by Lady Gregory were included in this issue of *Samhain*. This section was the penultimate paragraph of "Windlestraws."
3. The bound volume of *Beltaine* was probably available sometime in the third week of May 1900. In a letter apparently misdated [2 June 1900] in the *Collected Letters,* Yeats told Lady Gregory that "I send you the bound 'Be[l]taines'. They look well, & should sooth our guarantors if at any time we think it worth sending them" (*CL2* 532). However, this dating (based on a postmark) does not accord with some contemporaneous references to Lady Gregory's scissors. Lady Gregory had dinner with Yeats at Woburn Buildings in London on 3 May 1900 (*CL2* 520). On 13 May 1900 she wrote Yeats that she had left behind her "little folding scissors" and asked that they be sent to her at Coole Park (*CL2* 526n1). Yeats's "[2 June 1900]" letter begins "I have not been able to find the scissors anywhere. Are you certain you left them here? (*CL2* 532; n1 reads "See p. 497," but there is no reference there to the scissors). On [20 May 1900], however,

Yeats had begun his letter to Lady Gregory by telling her "I send the scissors . . ." (*CL2* 526). The letter enclosing the bound *Beltaine* must therefore date from between 14 or 15 May, when Yeats would have received Lady Gregory's request for the missing implement, and its return on 20 May. Apparently the April issue of *Beltaine* was not available until ca. [12 May 1900], as on that day Yeats sent copies to Lady Gregory (*CL2* 525). Thus the production of the separate issue and the bound volume was simultaneous, with the bound volume available about a week later.

Samhain: 1901—[Note] to George Moore's "The Irish Literary Theatre"

1. Moore had argued in "The Irish Literary Theatre" that the production of *The Countess Cathleen* "met with every disadvantage. Here is a list which must not, however, be considered exhaustive:—First, the author's theory that verse should be chanted and not spoken . . ." (12). Yeats placed an asterisk after "chanted" and added his commentary at the foot of the page.

Samhain: 1902—*from* Notes

1. "St. Mark's Lane" is an error for St. Martin's Lane, as Yeats noted in a letter of 2 November 1902 (*CL3* 259n1 is incorrect).

Samhain: 1902—[Note] to AE's "The Dramatic Treatment of Heroic Literature"

1. Standish James O'Grady published his *History of Ireland: The Heroic Period* in 1878. AE had noted that "Mr. O'Grady in his youth had the epic imagination, and I think few people realise how great and heroic that inspiration was . . ." (12). Yeats placed an asterisk after "O'Grady" and added his commentary at the foot of the page. AE's essay was first published in *The United Irishman* for 3 May 1902. Yeats's note was attached when the essay was excerpted both in *Samhain* and in the *All Ireland Review* for 1 November 1902. Sir Edward Coley Burne-Jones (1833–98) was an English painter and designer. Neither his comment nor that by William Morris has been traced.

Samhain: 1903—*from* Notes

1. Yeats refers to the following item in this issue of *Samhain,* "The Reform of the Theatre," a revision of an essay first published in *The United Irishman* for 4 April 1903. Yeats gave the lecture between

the productions of his *The Hour-Glass* and Lady Gregory's *Twenty-five* by the Irish Literary Theatre on 14 March 1903. This and the next section are the conclusion to "Notes."

2. Blake did not make such a statement. Yeats is perhaps vaguely recalling his remark in the "Annotations to *The Works of Sir Joshua Reynolds*" (ca. 1798–1809) that "The difference between a bad Artist & a Good One Is the Bad Artist Seems to Copy a Great Deal: The Good one Really Does Copy a Great Deal"; and Palamabron's prayer in *Milton* (ca. 1809–10) "O God, protect me from my friends, that they have not power over me. . . ."

3. The frontispiece to this issue of *Samhain* was a portrait of William G. Fay by John Butler Yeats. Fay's brother and collaborator was Frank J. Fay.

Samhain: 1904—[Interpolations]

1. This interpolation comes at the end of "First Principles" and precedes "The Play, the Player, and the Scene."

2. This interpolation comes at the end of "The Play, the Player, and the Scene" and precedes the date of "December, 1904." The text of *In the Shadow of the Glen* begins on the next page.

Samhain: 1904—Miss Horniman's Offer
of Theatre and the Society's Acceptance

1. Yeats sent a version of this letter to AE on 8 April 1904, warning him "You need do nothing about it except hold your tongue absolutely. We must not let the slightest rumour get out until we have secured our patent" (*CL3* 572).

2. On 29 July 1904 Annie Horniman wrote to George Roberts to thank him for forwarding the letter of acceptance, commenting "I am rather amused at the Irish lettering of some of the names & am much obliged to you for your translations" (*CL3* 596n1). Like his wife, Mary Walker (Máire Nic Siúbhlaigh), Frank Walker acted under his Irish name (Proinsias Mac Siúbhlaigh). The other signators not mentioned elsewhere in *The Irish Dramatic Movement* are James Sullivan Starkey ("Seumas O'Sullivan," 1879–1958), poet, editor, and sometime actor (as in the 1904 production of Yeats's *The Shadowy Waters*, as the Helmsman); Udolphus ("Dossie") Wright (1887–1942), an electrician, stage manager, and sometime actor; the actress Mary Garvey (Márget Ní Ghárbhaigh, d. 1946); the actress Vera Esposito ("Emma Vernon"); Dora L. Ainnesley, a Dublin music teacher who was associated with the Irish National Theatre Society but never played in a production; George Roberts (1873–1953), a Dublin publisher active in the Irish National Theatre Society;

Thomas Goodwin Keohler (after 1914, Keller), a solicitor, poet, and theosophist who had worked with the Fays since 1901; Harry F. Norman (1868–1947), a theosophist and a founder-member of the Irish National Theatre Society; and the Irish writer Stephen Gwynn (1864–1950), who in 1904 was Secretary of the Irish Literary Society. *An Craoibhín Aoibhín,* the pseudonym of Douglas Hyde, is usually translated "The Pleasant Little Branch." Patrick Colm (*Pádraig MacCuilim*) eventually settled on Padraic Colum as his usual name.

The small capitals in the text have not been reproduced. The periods (or in one instance, a comma) after many of the signatures have also been deleted. Other corrections, including "Augusta" for "Agusta," are listed in the "Corrections and Regularizations" section of "Textual Emendations and Corrections" (pp. 229–31).

Samhain: 1904—*from* An Opinion

1. Yeats's remarks follow the reprinting of a favorable commentary on the Irish National Theatre Society by A. B. Walkley in his "Chronique Théatrale/L'Année Théatrale en Angleterre," published in *Le Temps* (Paris) for 25 July 1904 (1–2). In the September 1903 issue of *Samhain,* Yeats had reprinted Walkey's "The Irish National Theatre," another favorable assessment, from *The Times* (London) of 8 May 1903. An editorial in *The United Irishman* for 17 October 1903 argued that "Irishmen as Irishmen should take no criticism from the enemy, Briton or West-Briton. And with scorn they should reject praise from either source. . . . With regret . . . we observe that Mr. W. B. Yeats includes in *Samhain* a flattering notice of the Irish National Theatre Society from the London *Times . . .*" (1).

2. The Irish journalist and politician Frank Hugh O'Donnell (1848–1916) had harshly attacked *The Countess Cathleen* in a letter to the *Freeman's Journal* (Dublin) on 1 April 1899. This and another rejected letter were published in a pamphlet entitled *Souls for Gold!: A Pseudo-Celtic Drama in Dublin* (London: Nassau Press, 1899) shortly before the first production of the play on 8 May 1899. O'Donnell further attacked Yeats and his work in *The Stage Irishman of the Pseudo-Celtic Drama* (London: John Long, 1904). Although true to the spirit of O'Donnell's diatribes, the quotation is not found in either publication and has not been traced. Foster incorrectly quotes the passage as a description of Yeats (209).

3. Described by Yeats as a "Hebrew saying" in "Verlaine in 1894," published in *The Savoy* for April 1896 (*UP1* 399); presumably derived from Exodus 33.20: "thou canst not see my face, for there shall no man see and live."

The Arrow: 20 October 1906—*from* The Season's Work

1. Yeats omitted the opening of this essay from the text in *The Irish Dramatic Movement*. The cover of *The Arrow* showed a design by the Irish artist Elinor Monsell (1878–1954) of Queen Maeve, armed with a bow and arrows, and an Irish wolfhound. The design had been used on the cover of the program for the opening of the Abbey Theatre and became its crest.

2. The list consisted of *The Canavans,* The *Gaol Gate, Hyacinth Halvey, The Rising of the Moon, Spreading the News,* and *The White Cockade* by Lady Gregory; *The Playboy of the Western World, Riders to the Sea,* and *The Shadow of the Glen* by John Millington Synge; *The Building Fund, The Eloquent Dempsy,* and *The Mineral Workers* by William Boyle; *Teach na mBocht* by Douglas Hyde, translated by Lady Gregory as *The Poorhouse* and first produced by the National Players at the Samhain Festival in Molesworth Hall, 31 October 1905; *Cathleen ni Houlihan, Deirdre,* and *On Baile's Strand* by Yeats; Molière's *Le Médecin malgré lui,* translated by Lady Gregory as *The Doctor in Spite of Himself;* Racine's *Les Plaideurs,* "translated from the French" as *The Pleaders; Fand* by the English writer Wilfrid Scawen Blunt; and Sophocles' *Antigone,* translated by Robert Gregory. It was noted that the "list includes seven Plays to be produced for the first time on any stage" ([6]). Neither *Antigone* nor *The Pleaders* was produced at this time by the Abbey Theatre.

3. The revised version of *The Shadowy Waters* was produced at the Abbey Theatre on 8 December 1906; Robert Gregory designed the set and supervised the lighting. *The Jackdaw* by Lady Gregory was produced at the Abbey Theatre on 23 February 1907; the revised version of her *Kincora* (1905) was produced at the Abbey Theatre on 11 February 1909. Neither Sophocles' *Oedipus Rex* nor Racine's *Phèdre* was produced by the Abbey Theatre at this time.

The Arrow: 20 October 1906—
A Note on *The Mineral Workers*

1. Presumably Standish James O'Grady; quotation untraced.

The Arrow: 20 October 1906—
The Irish Peasant on *Hyacinth Halvey*

1. *The Irish Peasant* (Dublin), a weekly newspaper, carried a short review of the first production of Lady Gregory's *Hyacinth Halvey* on 19 February 1906 in its issue for 24 February 1906. Unfortunately, the issue for 3 March 1906, which presumably included the article

which Yeats quotes by "Pat" (a regular contributor), is missing from the microfilm copy in the National Library of Ireland and the British Library newspaper collection at Colindale.

The Arrow: 20 October 1906—[Notes]

1. The listing of the revival by the Abbey Theatre on 10 November 1906 of *The Doctor in Spite of Himself,* a translation by Lady Gregory of Molière's *Le Médecin malgré lui,* indicated that the play would now be "rehearsed from the directions of M. Jules Truffier, Sociétaire of the Comédie Française." Truffier (1856–?), a French actor and dramatist, had supplied a prompt copy of the play (*Theatre Business: The Correspondence of the first Abbey Theatre Directors: William Butler Yeats, Lady Gregory and J. M. Synge,* edited by Ann Saddlemyer [University Park & London: Pennsylvania State University Press, 1982], 142n2).

2. In "The Deserted Abbey," published in *The Leader* (Dublin) for 28 April 1906, "Chanel" (Arthur Clery) commented that "How far the 'low comedy,' or broad farce of the play as presented, was due to Molière, how far to Lady Gregory, and how far to the actors I cannot say, as I do not happen to have read the original. But if it be due to Molière, it is the first failure of his I have come across. Unless Lady Gregory desired to show the superiority of her own plays—and Hyacinth Halvey is a hundred times a better play—there was no special reason for producing in the Abbey Theatre a performance fit only for a pantomime or a music-hall 'sketch'" (151).

3. Yeats refers to William Boyle's *The Eloquent Dempsy.*

4. Yeats refers to John Millington Synge's *Riders to the Sea,* Lady Gregory's *The Gaol Gate,* and his own *Cathleen ni Houlihan.* The music was composed by the Irish musician Arthur Darley (1873–1929).

5. The italicized paragraphs were most likely written not by Yeats but by Frederick J. Ryan, the Secretary of the National Theatre Society, Ltd. The lack of 6d. seats had been a matter of considerable controversy from the opening of the Abbey Theatre. This italicized material is reprinted at the end of the notes in next issue of *The Arrow* (24 November 1906) as well.

The Arrow: 24 November 1906—[Notes]

1. Yeats is perhaps referring to the controversy over the reorganization of the Irish National Theatre Society into the Irish National Theatre Society Limited on 22 September 1905, which resulted in the departure of several of the leading actors by the end of the year. An editorial in *The United Irishman* for 10 March 1906, for example, complained that "The National Theatre Society, Limited, is a body

run in the interest of one person, Mr. W. B. Yeats, who has proved himself capable of absorbing for his own personal ends the disinterested work of a large number of people given on the understanding that they were aiding in a work which was devoted primarily to the development of the highest interests of nationality in this country. . . . Everybody will be sorry for the conversion of our best lyric poet into a limited liability company" (1).

2. In German theatre programs a guest of the Company is usually listed with "a. G." attached to the name, for *als Gast,* "as a Guest."

3. "Miss Darragh" was the stage name of the actress Florence Laetitia Marion Dallas (d. 1917). She had played Salomé opposite Florence Farr as Herodias in a single performance of *Salomé* by Oscar Wilde, produced by the Literary Theatre Society in London on 10 June 1906. She had played Lady Althea in a production of *The Walls of Jericho* by the English dramatist Alfred Sutro (1863–1933) at the Shaftesbury Theatre in London, 2 October–25 November 1905.

4. When the revised version of *The Shadowy Waters* was first produced at the Abbey Theatre on 8 December 1906, it was accompanied not by William Boyle's *The Building Fund* but by the first production of *The Canavans* by Lady Gregory (when this issue of *The Arrow* was printed, *The Canavans* was scheduled to be produced along with *Deirdre* on 24 November 1906). *The Playboy of the Western World* by John Millington Synge was not produced until 26 January 1907, after the production of Lady Gregory's *The White Cockade* on 9 December 1906.

5. In 1876 the German composer Richard Wagner (1813–83) founded a theatre in Bayreuth for the production of his operas. *The Arrow* used a quotation from Wagner as the epigraph to each issue.

The Arrow: 24 November 1906—*Deirdre*

1. Lady Gregory's *Cuchulain of Muirthemne* was published by John Murray (London) in 1902.

2. In Greek mythology, the abduction by Paris of Helen from her husband, Menelaus, results in the Trojan War.

3. Armagh is a town and district in Ulster.

4. Arthur Darley (1873–1929) was an Irish musician. Robert Gregory (1881–1918), Lady Gregory's son, had studied at the Slade School of Art in London.

The Arrow: 24 November 1906—*The Shadowy Waters*

1. *The Shadowy Waters* was first published in *The North American Review* for May 1900. A revised version was published in 1906 and an acting version in 1907.

2. The play was first produced by the Irish National Theatre Society on 14 January 1904. Yeats was in America at the time, though he was quite aware of the planned production. The reviews were not positive.

Samhain: 1906—Notes

1. The following essay in this issue of *Samhain,* "Literature and the Living Voice," had been published in *The Contemporary Review* for October 1906. By "opening of the Theatre" Yeats presumably refers to the opening of the Abbey Theatre on 27 December 1904.
2. Yeats refers to "Dates and Places of the First Performances of Plays produced by the National Theatre Society and its Predecessors" ([36]). The version from the 1908 *Samhain* is reprinted below (pp. 203–6).
3. Yeats refers to Sir Frank Robert Benson.

The Arrow: 23 February 1907— from The Controversy Over *The Playboy*

1. Yeats omitted the opening sentences of "The Controversy Over *The Playboy*" from the revised version of the essay in *The Irish Dramatic Movement.* In *The Arrow,* "The Controversy Over *The Playboy*" was followed by "Previous Attacks on Irish Writers of Comedy and Satire," in which Yeats reprinted negative comments on John Millington Synge from *The United Irishman* for 11 February 1905; on William Boyle from *The United Irishman* for 6 May 1905; on Padraic Colum by "Pittite" from *The United Irishman* for 31 October 1905; and on Boyle and Synge by J. Bull from *The Leader* for 15 December 1906. This section was followed by "Answers to Some of the Criticisms from the 'Samhain' of 1905," in which Yeats included two slightly revised sections from the 1905 *Samhain.*
2. William Boyle withdrew his plays from the Abbey Theatre on 31 January 1907 in protest over the production of John Millington Synge's *The Playboy of the Western World,* although he had other complaints against the Directors of the Abbey as well.

The Arrow: 23 February 1907— *from* Mr. Yeats' Opening Speech at the Debate of February 4th, at the Abbey Theatre

1. Yeats omitted the first two, part of the third, and the final paragraph of his speech from the excerpt included in the version of "The Controversy Over *The Playboy*" in *The Irish Dramatic Movement.* A

series of disturbances occurred during the production of John Millington Synge's *The Playboy of the Western World* from 26 January to 2 February 1907. An open discussion of the play was held in the Abbey Theatre on 4 February 1907.

2. In a letter published in the *Freeman's Journal* (Dublin) on 4 February 1907, William Boyle, quoting from William Archer, complained that "Because there is no censor in Ireland, this 'decent-minded public' proceeding to do what Mr. Archer calls 'its duty,' results in several people being denounced to the police and fined by a reluctant magistrate" (4).

3. *Sinn Féin* was the nationalist party.

4. The production of Yeats's *The Countess Cathleen* by the Irish Literary Theatre on 8 May 1899 aroused some relatively minor protests (at least in comparison to those of 1907); some police were present in the theatre.

5. Various groups were involved in celebrations to commemorate the 1798 Rebellion. Yeats was President of the '98 Centennial Association of Great Britain and France, established by the London Young Ireland Society.

6. Presumably a group different from the thirty students at the National University of Ireland (not including James Joyce) who had published a letter attacking the play in the *Freeman's Journal* for 10 May 1899.

The Arrow: 1 June 1907—from [Notes]

1. All but the opening sentence of the first paragraph of "[Notes]" was included in *The Irish Dramatic Movement* as "On Taking *The Playboy* to London"; the second paragraph was not reprinted. Yeats refers to his speech published in *The Arrow* for 23 February 1907.

2. Yeats wrote this essay while in Italy in early May 1907. In the event, the Abbey Theatre tour of 11 May–15 June 1907 included not only *The Shadowy Waters* but also *Cathleen ni Houlihan, The Hour-Glass,* and *On Baile's Strand.*

   Cú Chulainn is the hero of the Ulster cycle of tales and the central figure in the *Táin Bó Cuailgne* (*Cattle Raid of Cooley*).

3. Although Yeats also attributed this thought to the French writer and literary critic Charles Augustin Sainte-Beuve (1804–69) at least four other times, in fact it is found in *Dreamthorp: A Book of Essays Written in the Country* (London: Strahan, 1863) by the Scottish writer Alexander Smith (1829–67): "And style, after all, rather than thought, is the immortal thing in literature." Style itself is defined as "the amalgam and issue of all the mental and moral qualities in a man's possession, and which bears the same relation to these that light

bears to the mingled elements that make up the orb of the sun" (43). Smith's remarks come in a discussion of Montaigne, which perhaps explains Yeats's ascription to another French writer.

Samhain: 1908—Events

1. *Samhain* had last been published in December 1906. *The Arrow* had begun publication on 20 October 1906.
2. The English actress Mrs. Patrick Campbell (1865–1940) was honored with a special matinée performance by the Abbey Theatre on 25 October 1907, after which she announced that she would return in a year to play in Yeats's *Deirdre*. She fulfilled her promise by performing in a production of *Deirdre* at the Abbey Theatre on 9 November 1908.
3. Yeats had seen Mrs. Campbell perform in London on 1 July 1904 opposite Sarah Bernhardt in a special matinée production (in French) of *Pelléas et Mélisande* by Maurice Maeterlinck.
4. "Ballade of Dead Actors" by William Ernest Henley, included in his *A Book of Verses* (London: David Nutt, 1888).
5. Yeats's first book (aside from an offprint of *Mosada* in 1886) was *The Wanderings of Oisin and Other Poems* (London: Kegan Paul, Trench & Co.), published in January 1899. Holborn Viaduct is in London. Yeats retold this anecdote about William Morris in *The Trembling of the Veil* (1922), where he has Morris saying "You write my sort of poetry" (*Au* 135). An earlier version read "it is my kind of poetry" (*Mem* 21).
6. Yeats refers to "Matters Theatrical" in the *Freeman's Journal* (Dublin) for 18 September 1908. The first quotation is inaccurate: the paper rather noted that "the Abbey seems destined to be the only stand-by left to us." In the second quotation, which is accurate, the passage which Yeats omitted reads "... to lose, if warring actors and authors are to be brought together again, under a judicious management, to make the little theatre the permanent home of an intellectual Irish drama. Should these hopes not be fulfilled, would it ..." (6).
7. Yeats refers to *The Piper* by the Irish writer "Norreys Connell," the pen name of Conal Holmes O'Connell O'Riordan (1874–1948), and to John Millington's Synge's *The Shadow of the Glen, The Well of the Saints,* and *The Playboy of the Western World*. The attack on *The Shadow of the Glen* was led by *The United Irishman*.
8. After their departure from the Abbey Theatre, William G. Fay, the Irish actress Brigit O'Dempsey (Fay's wife), and Frank J. Fay undertook an American tour, under the sponsorship of Charles Frohman (1860–1915), an American manager and producer. They had permission to perform Lady Gregory's *The Rising of the Moon,* Yeats's *The Pot of Broth,* and AE's *Deirdre*. Frohman was responsible for the false

billing of the Company as the "Irish National Theatre Company," although the Fays did not protest.

9. The play by William Boyle was *The Building Fund*.

10. The Fays resigned from the Abbey Theatre on 13 January 1908. Yeats's letter was published in *The Dublin Evening Mail* for 14 January 1908 and in various newspapers on 15 January 1908, including the *Irish Times* (8).

11. The English actor and director William Poel (1852–1934) was the founder of the Elizabethan Stage Society. He recruited the Irish actress Sara Allgood (1883–1950) to appear in a production of Shakespeare's *Measure for Measure* by Annie Horniman's Company. This was produced at the Gaiety Theatre, Manchester, on 11–18 April 1908, and at Stratford-on-Avon on 21–22 April 1908. Allgood had joined the Company in 1903. She performed in the first production of Lady Gregory's *Dervorgilla* on 31 October 1907 and, among other roles, in revivals of Yeats's *Cathleen ni Houlihan,* such as that on 19 February 1906.

   An errata slip in later issues of the 1908 *Samhain* indicated that "*Measure for Measure* was not produced by the Elizabethan Stage Society, as stated in mistake on page 4, but by Miss Horniman's company, in the Elizabethan fashion, with Mr. Poel as producer."

12. On 30 March 1907, the Ulster Literary Theatre had performed at the Abbey Theatre *The Pagan* by "Lewis Purcell" (David Parkhill) and *The Turn of the Road* by the Irish actor and playwright "Rutherford Mayne" (Samuel Waddell, 1878–1967). Yeats was in London when the Ulster Literary Theatre again performed at the Abbey Theatre, on 24 April 1908.

13. The play was perhaps *The Passing of the Third Floor Back* by the English playwright and novelist Jerome Klapka Jerome (1859–1927), which had opened at the St. James's Theatre in London on 1 September 1908 and ran until 13 February 1909. As noted by the reviewer in *The Times* (London) for 2 September 1908, the play takes place in "an ugly, squalid household" in a "vulgar London boarding-house" (11). Yeats may have decided to attend because of the presence in the cast of the English actor and manager Sir Johnston Forbes-Robertson (1853–1937). A *Mannequin d'Osier* is a wicker mannequin.

14. *The Corsican Brothers* (1848) was adapted from the French of the novelist and playwright Alexandre Dumas *père* (1802–70), by the Irish actor and writer Dion Boucicault (1820–90). Yeats may be referring to the production at the Adelphi Theatre in London, 9 September–3 October 1908.

15. Though many writers had made this argument, Yeats may be thinking of Shelley's comment in *The Defence of Poetry* (1821; published 1840) that "it was as wise to cast a violet into a crucible that you

might discover the formal principle of its colour and odour, as seek to transfuse from one language into another the creations of a poet."

16. Molière's *Le Médecin malgré lui* was translated by Lady Gregory as *The Doctor in Spite of Himself*. Kiltartan is a barony near Coole Park; "Kiltartanese" refers to the style of speech in most of Lady Gregory's plays.

17. The Independent Dramatic Company was founded in 1908 by a Polish artist, Casimir Dunin, Count de Markiewicz (1874–1932), who in 1900 had married the Irish artist and politician Constance Gore-Booth (1868–1927). On 9 March 1908 the Company had performed Count Markiewicz's *Seymour's Redemption* at the Abbey Theatre. The Theatre of Ireland was established on 13 June 1906, largely by individuals who had left the Abbey Theatre. On 22–23 May 1908 the Theatre of Ireland had performed at the Abbey Theatre *The Miracle of the Corn* by Padraic Colum, *Maeve* by Edward Martyn, and *The Enthusiast* by Lewis Purcell.

18. The 22–23 May 1908 performances by the Theatre of Ireland were on a Friday and Saturday. The Independent Dramatic Company was scheduled to perform at the Abbey Theatre on Thursday to Saturday, 3–5 December 1908.

19. *Robert Emmet* by the Irish writer Henry Connell Mangan was first performed by the National Players Society at the Molesworth Hall, Dublin, on 31 October 1903; *The United Irishman* for 7 November 1903 described it as "the best Irish historical play staged" (1). The revival which Yeats attended has not been traced. St. Cecilia's Hall is apparently an error for St. Teresa's Hall, the site of numerous dramatic productions.

20. In addition to Thomas Davis, Yeats refers to John Mitchel (1815–75), Irish writer and patriot.

Samhain: 1908—Alterations in *Deirdre*

1. After this introductory paragraph, Yeats supplied revised texts for *Deirdre*, lines 149ff. and 289ff., with instructions for their placement. An almost identical text, with one additional change, appeared in *Alterations in Deirdre*, also published in November 1908 and inserted in the published copies of the play. Both passages were later subject to further revision.

Samhain: 1908—Dates and Places of the First Performance of Plays produced by the National Theatre Society and its Predecessors

1. This list is expanded from that first published in the 1906 *Samhain* and then updated as Appendix IV in volume IV of *The Collected*

Works in Verse & Prose (Stratford-on-Avon: Shakespeare Head Press, 1908). That Yeats compiled these lists is uncertain but not likely. What is almost surely the first state of the cover of the 1906 *Samhain* described the issue as "An Occasional Review, Edited by W. B. Yeats, containing Hyacinth Halvey by Lady Gregory, and Thoughts upon the Work of the Abbey Theatre, with list of plays produced by the National Theatre Society and its forerunners, by the Editor. Published in December, 1906, by Maunsel & Co., Ltd., Dublin; and sold for sixpence net." What is presumably the second state reads ". . . Abbey Theatre, by the Editor, with list of plays produced by the National Theatre Society and its forerunners. The Sixth Number. Published by Maunsel & Co., Ltd., Dublin; and sold for sixpence." It thus seems that Yeats was correcting the ascription of the list to himself. In any case, though, Yeats was responsible for the note to the 1908 *Samhain* version as well as the two paragraphs at the end of the *Collected Works* text: "In addition to these plays, many of which are constantly revived, translations of foreign masterpieces are given occasionally"; and "It was not until the opening of the Abbey Theatre that Lady Gregory, Mr. J. M. Synge, and Mr. W. B. Yeats became entirely responsible for the selection of plays, though they had been mainly so from 1903."

The number and variety of textual problems in this list has called for rather extensive regularization. For example, most of the authors' names end with a period, but some end with a comma or have no punctuation; all have been revised to end with a period. The 1900 publications have been listed in chronological order. Abbreviated names of the months have been expanded, and "By/by" has been resolved in favor of "by." Although changes of such nature have not been recorded, corrections such as "Yeats" rather than "Yeates" are included in the "Corrections and Regularizations" section of "Textual Emendations and Corrections" (pp. 229–31). Three errors in dating and one other revision have been treated as specific emendations.

2. Incorrect. The production of Peter T. MacGinley's *Eilis agus an Bhean Déirce* (*Lizzie and the Beggarwoman*) by the Daughters of Erin at the Antient Concert Rooms on 27 August 1901 has been overlooked (possibly the second production, but the first in Dublin).

3. Frederick Ryan was the Secretary of the Irish National Theatre Society.

The Arrow: 25 August 1909—
The Shewing-Up of Blanco Posnet: Statement by the Directors

1. *The Shewing-Up of Blanco Posnet* by George Bernard Shaw had been refused a license for production in England by the Lord Chamberlain, Charles Robert Spencer, Viscount Althorp (1857–1922), in

his capacity as ex officio President of the Advisory Board for Censorship of Plays. It was then accepted by the Abbey Theatre and first produced there on 25 August 1909. Several Dublin newspapers had printed a statement by Yeats and Lady Gregory about the controversy on Saturday, 21 August 1909.

2. George Alexander Redford (d. 1916) was the Lord Chamberlain's Reader of Plays. The Lord Lieutenant was John Campbell Hamilton Gordon, Earl of Aberdeen (1847–1934). William James Walsh (1841–1921) had been Archbishop of Dublin since 1885. The Dublin Horse Show, held each August, was a major social event. The English monarch was Edward VII (1841–1910).

3. The paper was *The Nation* (London), which had published on 29 May 1909 an essay supporting Shaw and attacking the censorship, reprinted in this issue of *The Arrow*.

4. The question of the censorship of plays was currently under discussion in the English Parliament.

The Arrow: 25 August 1909—*from* [Note]

1. After this sentence, Yeats printed an except from a letter by Shaw of 22 August 1909, followed by an essay supporting Shaw and attacking the censorship from *The Nation* (London) for 29 May 1909.

The Arrow: 25 August 1909—The Religion of Blanco Posnet

1. Shaw's play was *The Shewing-Up of Blanco Posnet.*

History of the Text

1. Indeed, the 20 October 1906 *Arrow* begins "I have been so busy finishing *Deirdre,* a play in verse, that I have put off *Samhain* for a month or so. . . ."

2. Except for pages 121, 123, 125, and 127, which use as running head "THE UNITED IRISHMAN: 1903."

3. Yeats was never quite content with this passage. When he reprinted part of the 1905 *Samhain* in *The Arrow* for 23 February 1907, he tried "weighed down by the conventional idealism."

4. The compositor of *Plays and Controversies* would of course have had no way of knowing which page breaks coincided with a paragraph space and which did not, and apparently Yeats did not concern himself with the issue when reading proofs.

5. *SR* xxviii. As printed in the second edition, the last sentence makes no sense, and it was not corrected in the inserted Corrigenda. The material provided in brackets is taken from *The Secret Rose, Stories by W. B. Yeats: A Variorum Edition,* ed. Phillip L. Marcus, Warwick

Gould, and Michael J. Sidnell (Ithaca and London: Cornell University Press, 1981), xxix. The second edition corrects some errors, adds some information, and revises the order of the editors.

6. The red ink correction is cited in "Textual Emendations and Corrections."

7. See *SR* xlii n46: "Mrs. Thomas Mark very kindly examined the pencilled notes, but could not say conclusively that any of them had been made by her husband." Nevertheless, there are two or three queries in pencil that, to judge from the size of the hand, may be by Mark. But the crucial point is that Yeats did not respond to those queries; thus the possibility that they were present on the proofs when he reviewed them is altogether unlikely.

8. Although the proofs may have arrived later on 6 July 1932, Mark had not received them (sent under separate cover) when he acknowledged receipt of Yeats's letter of the previous day (BL 55730/301); and the revised set of proofs was printed in Edinburgh on 8 July 1932 (*SR* xxxviii n44). As one does not imagine the printers of R. & R. Clark anxiously awaiting the arrival of *The Flying Scotsman* at Waverley Station on the morning of 8 July 1932, the proofs must have been on their way from London to Edinburgh no later than early on 7 July 1932.

9. Mrs. Yeats apparently did not return the 1931–32 proofs of *Mythologies* to Macmillan after she had received them in late June 1939, so Sutherland's comments could not have been made thereafter.

10. These proofs have the same problem with the running heads as in *Plays and Controversies* and make further errors in the spacing between sections.

11. Mark would surely have reviewed and corrected the proofs of *Essays* before sending them to Mrs. Yeats on 26 June 1939. When a new proof of *The Irish Dramatic Movement* section was required because of the addition of the essay from the 1908 *Samhain*, Mark would simply have transferred his corrections to the new proof and also corrected the added essay, with the prospect of quickly sending this fourth proof to Mrs. Yeats.

12. Admittedly, one of the editors has argued elsewhere, especially in "Text and Interpretation in the Poems of W. B. Yeats," *Representing Modernist Texts,* ed. George Bornstein (Ann Arbor: University of Michigan Press, 1991), 17–47, against the theory of "delegation"— i.e., that Yeats relied on his wife and Thomas Mark to tidy up his texts and that therefore their posthumous editing of the canon should be accepted. But leaving aside Emerson on consistency, the question of "First Principles" seems a special case, for at least three reasons: 1) the near simultaneous publication of volume four of the *Collected Works* and the 1908 *Samhain;* 2) the strong possibility that Yeats used sheets from the *Collected Works* as copy for the next printing; and 3) the apparent fact that he did not retain a copy of the 1908

Samhain in his library (certainly none was present in 1939, as Mrs. Yeats indicated in her 9 July 1939 letter to Mark, nor did the later inventory of the library by Edward O'Shea disclose one). On balance, then, the omission of "First Principles" seems an oversight rather than a considered judgment.

13. Doubtless the first paragraph of "Events" would have been omitted. Yeats would presumably have also altered the title "First Principles," as a 1904 essay of that name was already included in *The Irish Dramatic Movement*.

Textual Emendations and Corrections

1. Although Mark retired in 1959 and was replaced by Lovat Dickson, he continued to consult on Yeats editions; the precise extent of his involvement with *Explorations* (London: Macmillan, 1962) is unknown. The errors in the 1962 edition begin opposite the first page of text, where Yeats's commentary on *The Irish Dramatic Movement* from the 1931–32 proofs is offered as a "Note": the reference to "this volume" is incorrectly glossed as "[*Plays and Controversies*]" (p. [72]). Various errors continue until the final item in *The Irish Dramatic Movement,* where the last name of Walter Morse Rummel is given correctly on page 256 but as "Rummell" a page earlier.

2. On the Edition de Luxe proofs, Mark had placed "italics?" in the margin after "SAMHAIN: 1901." Yeats at first canceled the notation and wrote "not italics unless I put the title on page," but he then canceled his comment and wrote "Italics" in the margin. Yeats also accepted Mark's suggested italics on *THE ARROW.*

INDEX